FROM LUMBER HOOKERS
TO THE HOOLIGAN FLEET

A Treasury of Chicago Maritime History

Chicago Maritime Society

Rita L. Frese and David M. Young, editors

First Edition

www.lakeclaremont.com

Chicago

From Lumber Hookers to the Hooligan Fleet: A Treasury of Chicago Maritime History

Published March 2008 by:

P.O. Box 711
Chicago, IL 60690-0711
lcp@lakeclaremont.com

Publisher's Cataloging-In-Publication Data
(Prepared by The Donohue Group, Inc.)

From lumber hookers to the hooligan fleet : a treasury of Chicago maritime history / The Chicago Maritime Society ; Rita L. Frese and David M. Young, editors.

p. : ill. ; cm.

Includes bibliographical references and index.
ISBN-13: 978-1-893121-30-0
ISBN-10: 1-893121-30-5

1. Navigation—Illinois—Chicago—History. 2. Navigation—Great Lakes (North America)—History. 3. Seamanship—Illinois—Chicago—History. 4. Seamanship—Great Lakes (North America)—History. 5. Great Lakes Region (North America)—History. I. Frese, Rita. II. Young, David, 1940 Sept. 22- III. Chicago Maritime Society.

VK23.7 .F76 2007
386.5/0977   2005931530

20 10 09 08   10 9 8 7 6 5 4 3 2 1

TABLE OF ██████

Preface

The impetus for this book was a visit by a Chicago Maritime Society member some years ago to do a little informal research on the city's waterways. The member, Deane Tank Sr., was surprised to learn that precious few such books had ever been written on the topic. There were plenty of general histories of Chicago that alluded to the city's maritime origins, but few books covered the city's maritime past. In fact, a casual observer consulting a bibliography on Windy City history would probably come away with the conclusion that railroads were responsible for the metropolis on the prairie, an entirely logical conclusion when you consider that the city is more than a thousand miles from the nearest ocean port. Yet the city sprung from the waterways, and where no such shipping avenues existed, it built them.

Tank's discovery led to a discussion by members of the society, which had only been founded at the rather late date of 1982, and a decision by that group that one of its goals would be to publish serious histories of the city's rich but largely forgotten maritime history. Society members Rita L. Frese, John Heinz, and John Holton, enthusiastically taking over Tank's idea that someone needed to write a general maritime survey of Chicago, produced this volume.

What references to the city that did exist in the historical literature were invariably passages contained in books on the Great Lakes maritime scene, such as J.B. Mansfield's epic but seriously out-of-date *History of the Great Lakes*. It has been reprinted but never updated since it was originally published in 1899.

The same general comments could be made of James Putnam's 1918 work *The Illinois and Michigan Canal*; Henry N. Barkhausen's 1947 album on Great Lakes sailing ships; and Milo Quaife's *Lake Michigan*, a study published in 1944. In fact, the most prolific authors in the last half of the twentieth century on the subject of the Great Lakes were the writers who ground out a succession of books on seagoing disasters that included such local calamities as the *Lady Elgin* and *Eastland*.

Fortunately, beginning in the final decade of the twentieth century, there has been something of a renewal of interest in the Chicago maritime scene. George Hilton's 1995 book *Eastland: Legacy of the Titanic* and David M. Young's 2001 *Chicago Maritime: An Illustrated History* both were published independently of the society. Hilton's book is the most comprehensive study of the *Eastland* disaster ever printed, and Young's book is more of a strategic look at how Chicago fit into the national maritime picture. Two books on the Chicago River and its history were also published independently: geographer David O. Solzman's *The Chicago River* in 1998 and Libby Hill's book with an identical title two years later.

The society was the impetus for Professor Theodore J. Karamanski's *Schooner Passage* in 2000 and his pictographic collaboration with Tank, *Maritime Chicago*, also published in 2000. The present work is an even greater collaboration begun in 1997 and involving more society members than the earlier books.

This work is also an anthology reprinting long-ago accounts of the events that shaped Chicago's waterfront, such as A.T. Andreas's description of the 1849 flood, as well as new material written by several CMS members. Besides pieces by Heinz, Karamanski, and Young, the work includes essays by members Tom and Chris Kastle, J.S. Wall, Philip R. Elmes, and Richard

Brady. Professor John Lamb assembled most of the material for the chapters on the Illinois and Michigan Canal. John Hadfield secured the chapter on fireboats and provided some photos from his personal collection. Justin Ruhge provided not only the article on the hooligan fleet but the photos as well. George Miller worked diligently on obtaining photos. Dave Metzger did the necessary legal work. The Seneca Public Library was generous in providing their photos and research collection on the LST shipyard there.

Rita Frese, John Holton, and John Heinz worked tirelessly behind the scenes to put the volume together. Dave Young did the final editing and assembly. Deane Tank was the guiding force behind the project from the beginning.

The purpose of this book is to impart to the reader a sense of the people and events that collectively are the stuff of Chicago's illustrious maritime history. These stories consist of accounts of and by people who lived when Chicago was the fourth busiest port in the world or by historians who have researched that period to describe maritime events such as they were. The book discusses operations on the Illinois and Michigan Canal that carried the harvest of the prairies to market, the hazards of life aboard the sailing schooners bringing lumber to build Chicago, and, somewhat surprisingly, the city's role in building the U.S. Navy in World War II. There are accounts of some of the great disasters, including the worst in Great Lakes history: it occurred not on the storm-tossed inland sea but the sluggish waters of the Chicago River. One piece explores the time when Checagou was nothing more than a canoe portage, and others examine the now forgotten flood of 1849, lighthouses, and ballads.

Hopefully, the book will provide a clear portrayal of the city's maritime origins to those generations born after the port of Chicago had declined almost to inconsequence and whose only knowledge of the Sanitary and Ship Canal until now came from a quick glimpse of it while speeding over it on an expressway. The waterways were the city's lifeline to the world before the appearance of railroads, automobiles, motor trucks, and airplanes.

Since the Chicago Maritime Society's founding in 1982, it has amassed a large collection of watercraft, models, photographs, displays, artifacts, photographs, art, books, and articles. Many of the chapters and illustrations in this book were culled from that collection.

—Chicago Maritime Society

Introduction

by David M. Young

The French-Canadian voyageur Louis Jolliet was the first to notice the potential utility of the place that was to become Chicago when in 1673 he paddled through the area on his way home to Montreal toward the end of his voyage of discovery with Jacques Marquette. The American Indian nations who had inhabited the area, the Illiniwek and Wea, as well as the Potawatomi, who were soon to live there, knew the place as a canoe portage between the Mississippi and St. Lawrence rivers' watersheds, but they considered Checagou too marshy for permanent settlements.

However, Jolliet had commerce on his mind; he wanted to establish a fur-trading business in the American interior and saw the utility of digging a canal "half a league" long to connect the Des Plaines River flowing to the Mississippi and the Chicago River flowing the other way via the Great Lakes to the St. Lawrence. Although he did not mention it in the accounts of his voyage, such a canal would inevitably result in some sort of settlement. He had no way of knowing that within two centuries, the sluggish Chicago River would become one of the busiest ports in the world and the city that arose on its banks would become one of the largest on the continent—the transportation center of the North American interior.

The enlightened disinterest of Louis xiv in colonizing the American interior, assorted Indian wars, and the eventual collapse of New France at the end of the Seven Years' War (French and

Indian War in America) in 1763 conspired to put an end to any Gallic plans for a canal or settlement at Chicago. The British, who won the war, had little interest in developing Chicago: Detroit was their western outpost. So it was up to the newly independent United States after 1783 to try to develop Chicago. The first task the new nation faced in the interior was to neutralize the sometimes hostile tribes, and with that in mind in 1803 it built Fort Dearborn at the mouth of the Chicago River, where it empties into Lake Michigan.

Still the place languished as a sleepy trading post for almost three decades, until the federal government and the newly created State of Illinois dusted off Jolliet's proposal for a canal and decided to do something about it. Two events that occurred far from Illinois's borders were to have an enormous influence on Chicago's eventual development. At the other end of the Great Lakes, New York State in 1825 completed DeWitt Clinton's Erie Canal to link the lakes at Buffalo with the Hudson River and the growing port of New York. That led to the settlement of the Great Lakes basin.

The other event was the application of the steam engine to power vessels in the early nineteenth century by a variety of inventors in Britain and America. That led to the development of steamboats that could plod upstream against the current on rivers that were navigable within a hundred miles of Chicago and, somewhat later, of ships (on the Great Lakes they are also called boats even though some of them dwarfed oceangoing craft) capable of quickly traversing those inland seas and into the Chicago River. The only problem that remained was connecting the rivers on which the steamboats operated and the lakes on which the ships sailed. Such a connection would extend New York's economic hegemony via the rivers inland across the Great Plains for another thousand miles to the foothills of the Rocky Mountains.

There wasn't much money available for digging a canal in a frontier state like Illinois in the early decades of the nineteenth century, and even a federal land grant for the project proved inadequate to finance it. But just the anticipation of such a project in the 1830s sparked a speculative land boom that resulted in the transformation of Chicago from a sleepy trading post to a bustling little city.

It might seem strange from our prospective in the twenty-first century, when airplanes span the continent in a matter of hours and automobiles are ubiquitous, that building a canal would generate that much excitement. But the first half of the nineteenth century was the Canal Age in America. People preferred the comfort of traveling by water. Stagecoaches were drafty, bumpy, dusty, hot in summer, and cold in winter, and at certain times of year when the rain fell, the roads became impassable. Freight wagons were slower and more expensive. So despite the fact that a new-fangled invention called the railroad had burst upon the scene, the states built canals as fast as they could to connect their natural waterways. Illinois' Internal Improvements Act, approved in 1837, provided the financial mechanism to build Chicago's canal as well as railroads covering much of the rest of the state.

When construction finally started on the canal, it had been decided that Jolliet's proposed ditch connecting the Chicago and Des Plaines rivers was inadequate, that a 97-mile canal was needed to connect Chicago with the head of navigation of the Illinois River at La Salle. By the time the canal was finished in 1848, after an interruption when the state almost went bankrupt, Chicago was already a bustling lake port and city approaching 30,000 inhabitants. The Illinois and Michigan Canal quickly turned the Chicago River into a traffic nightmare clogged with sailing ships and steamers off the Great Lakes, tugs, and canal boats.

As it turned out, 1848 was perhaps the most important year in Chicago's development. Not only did the canal open, but the steam elevator that permitted fast loading of ship holds, the telegraph, and the railroad all arrived. In fact, the Galena & Chicago Union Rail Road was built as an extension of the Great Lakes. Serving as a conveyance to meet the ships visiting Chicago, it hauled the manufactures and pioneers from the East out onto the prairie and the agricultural products of their labors to feed the populations of the Atlantic Seaboard and Europe. The Aurora Branch Railroad was built two years later with the same purpose in mind, and the Chicago & Rock Island Railroad in 1852 was intended as a competitor of the I & M Canal as well as an extension of the lakes.

By the time the Civil War began in 1861, Chicago was already the nation's largest railroad center, with ten lines fanning out across the Midwest and reaching various ports on the Atlantic Coast, and by the end of the decade it was linked by rail to California on the Pacific Coast. It was also possible for a person—or a bushel of wheat—to travel entirely by water from Chicago to New Orleans, New York, Montreal, and Europe.

Despite the growing presence of railroads, the defining characteristic of Chicago's skyline in the middle of the nineteenth century was the jungle of ships' masts looming above the Chicago River. For the most part, they were the tallest structures in town—at least before the Great Fire of 1871 caused the city to shift from wood frame to masonry construction.

The port, which was visited by thousands of ships annually, was a world unto itself. Lumber hookers—sailing schooners piled high with timber to build Chicago and the settlements across the treeless plains—crowded the river alongside canal boats, tugs, packets, side-wheelers, propellers, and assorted sailing vessels hauling the harvest east to market. In 1871 nearby a billion board feet of timber arrived in Chicago by ship, 32 million feet left by ship for points east after being processed into lumber, and another 37 million feet went west on the canal. More than 56.5 million bushels of grain left Chicago by ship for the East that year.

The city—and especially its port—was the place where sailors from small towns along the Great Lakes and immigrants bound for pioneer homesteads on the plains got their introduction to the Wild West. Hookers (the other kind) inhabited the sleazy dives along the banks of the river, where a teenage sailor from Ohio could lose his virginity, get drunk, and get mugged all in a night. Con men abounded to loot unsuspecting pigeons of their wealth without having to resort to violence. Some vessel captains insisted on being armed when they pulled into the Chicago River.

There were great disasters on the lakes that, as Herman Melville noted in *Moby Dick*, "have drowned many a midnight ship with all its shrieking crew." Besides storms there were collisions, fire, and explosions that claimed ships. Other ships simply disappeared, leaving anxious wives, shipowners, and consignment merchants on the docks wondering day after day what had happened. Finally they gave up, went home, and filed for probate. *Lady Elgin*, *Seabird*, *Phoenix*, and *Alpena* are the names of long-lost ships that are now largely forgotten. Sometimes even the sleepy Chicago River turned ugly, as it did in the flood of 1849 and when the *Eastland* capsized and went down a few feet from shore in the middle of downtown Chicago. The river last acted up in 1992, when a drilling crew poked a hole in an abandoned freight subway tunnel beneath it and flooded most of the basements in the Loop.

Even as the port of Chicago reached its zenith in the 1870s, maritime commerce was changing. The railroads had long before taken away from the lakes and canal the passenger and high-value merchandise freight business and quickly monopolized the growing meatpacking traffic for which the waterways were unable to compete. The refrigerated railcar was too fast and efficient. The forests of Michigan and Wisconsin that provided Chicago with its lumber trade by the end of the century had been expunged. Conservation was not a familiar topic in the nineteenth century. The last vestige of the lumber trade for all intents and purposes disappeared in 1912 when Herman Schuenemann's Christmas tree ship (*Rouse Simmons*) went down with all hands in a storm.

Advances in iron and steel construction and steam engines made possible the development of ever-larger vessels that rendered the sailing schooners obsolete. Thus ore boats and colliers capable of carrying thousands of tons of cargo came into existence to successfully compete with the inexpensive 200-ton schooners.

This coincided with the gradual shift of the city's port from the Chicago River downtown to the Calumet River on the Far South Side. As the city was rebuilding from the Great Fire of 1871, land downtown became too expensive for industrial use, so the growing steel industry moved its operations to the South Side, followed by assorted manufacturers. Steel needed huge quantities of iron ore and coal, which were most economically hauled by ship.

The Illinois and Michigan Canal could not compete forever against the rate-cutting railroads, so its primary role late in the nineteenth century became that of a sewage ditch. Chicago pumped its effluent into the canal and downriver to St. Louis and New Orleans to avoid polluting the lake from which it drew its drinking water. Eventually, when the canal proved inadequate as Chicago's sewer, the city dug new, bigger ones: the Sanitary and Ship Canal and the Cal Sag Channel.

As the twentieth century dawned, the nation's river and canal system was in dire straits, and Great Lakes traffic had begun what would be a long decline. The railroads had put most of the steamboats out of business, and the barges that replaced them were carrying little more than coal. The I & M Canal west of Joliet was rapidly obsolescing. The principal traffic on the new Sanitary and Ship Canal between Lockport and Chicago was sewage.

On the lakes, fewer ships called on Chicago, but they were made of steel and powered by steam engines and were larger than their predecessors. The declining cross-lake packet industry still carried some vacation passenger traffic and fruit and vegetables but was beginning to suffer from competition from motor trucks and automobiles. Ironically, the city built Municipal Pier (later Navy Pier) in 1916 to get the packets off the Chicago River docks just as that once bustling industry began its precipitous decline into oblivion, accelerated by the nation's hard-road building program after World War I.

The war had a positive effect on one segment of the maritime industry, however. The railroads became clogged with wartime traffic they couldn't handle and were federalized for the first and only time in their history. As a result, the federal government decided to resuscitate the moribund riverboat industry to provide some alternatives to railroads. The massive public works project included the creation of a nine-foot shipping channel from New Orleans to Chicago by building a series of locks and dams on the Mississippi, Illinois, and Des Plaines rivers between St. Louis and Chicago. The task was finished in 1933 with the completion of what is called the Illinois Waterway, connecting the Sanitary and Ship Canal with the Mississippi.

The improved waterway proved its utility during World War II, when assorted warships were built in Chicago (patrol craft), at Seneca on the Illinois River (LSTs), and at Manitowoc, Wisconsin (submarines), and floated down the rivers to the Gulf of Mexico. However, the decline in Chicago's maritime trade resumed despite another massive federal effort to revive it.

The United States and Canada combined to build the St. Lawrence Seaway to give oceangoing ships access to the Great Lakes. International traffic increased for a time, and the city reopened Navy Pier, which had been used as the Chicago campus of the University of Illinois, but the continuing development of ever-larger ships on the oceans limited the seaway's success. The new ships were too large for the seaway's new locks. So Navy Pier was redeveloped in the 1990s as a recreational facility catering to pleasure and excursion craft in belated recognition of the fact that the lakefront and Chicago River had become recreational waterways. The last big ship to regularly use the river was probably the tug barge E-63 on its trips between the lake and Sanitary and Ship Canal at the end of the twentieth century. By then the Calumet River and lake had become the city's principal port.

But the new port, too, was constrained by events beyond the city's control. One by one the big but obsolescing steel mills on the city's South Side closed, as did a number of industries serving them, like the coal trans-loading facilities. The container revolution in freight was another culprit.

The city and state built an intermodal (container) transfer port near 95th Street to serve the growing market, but it was closed and converted into a park after the railroads took away the container business. Once standard rail-marine shipping containers were developed in the early 1960s, it became cheaper to off-load (at ocean ports) containers bound between Europe and Asia and ship them across the North American continent (through Chicago) by rail than it was to use the Panama Canal or St. Lawrence Seaway.

As the twenty-first century dawned, a few lake freighters still called on Chicago as did some oceangoing tramp steamers. The two canals still had a healthy traffic in barges, but nowhere near their capacity. An occasional oceanic tour ship visited the city carrying Europeans across the Atlantic to see the fall colors along the Great Lakes, but the passengers flew home from O'Hare International Airport. The only appreciable cross-lake traffic was aboard the Badger, a rebuilt car ferry that plodded between Ludington, Michigan, and Manitowoc, Wisconsin, far north of Howard Street. The huge grain elevators that stood along the city's two rivers were silent.

Yet the Chicago River bustled with recreational boats, water taxis, and tour boats. Navy Pier's dock was crowded with tour boats during the summer season. The most exciting maritime events in Chicago by then were the Venetian Night festival, when the city was visited by surviving square riggers from around the globe, and the annual yacht race to Mackinac Island.

PART I

Early Times

Photography didn't exist when Jolliet and Marquette made their canoe voyage of exploration in 1673, but there are plenty of photos of the reenactment of that voyage 300 years later. The tricentennial expedition used two canoes, just like the original, and followed the same route. (Ralph Frese)

Chapter One

Opening of the Northwest
A Maritime Perspective

More than a century before the United States was founded and a century and a half before the City of Chicago came into existence, French explorers discovered the potential utility of a canoe portage at the southwestern tip of Lake Michigan that connected the St. Lawrence River watershed (which included the Great Lakes) with the great Mississippi River system of the American interior. With a few notable exceptions, the French were not particularly interested in colonizing the American wilderness, so far from Versailles, especially a marshland the local Indians called Checagou, and neither were the British who followed them. But the United States, after it gained its independence in 1783 (by means of a treaty signed in Paris, no less), was obsessed with western expansion, and it was not long before the new nation discovered the strategic importance of the Checagou portage.

Philip R. Elmes, a writer and founder and former president of the Chicago Maritime Society, wrote this heretofore unpublished essay in 1988.

by Philip R. Elmes

It was August on the Niagara River above the falls, and after months of preparation, the Dutch shipwrights had completed their work: *Le Griffon* was ready to launch on its epoch voyage across the largely unknown expanse of the Upper Great Lakes. Under the command of the young adventurer Robert Cavelier, Sieur de La Salle, the small 40-ton vessel set off across Lake Erie under fair winds only to encounter contrary winds and currents at

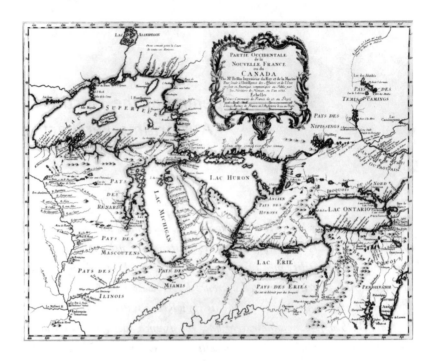

There is some evidence that the French for a few years operated a trading post or warehouse at the Chicago portage between 1683 and about 1700. This reproduction of a 1755 map shows "Port de Checagou" at the future site of Chicago, although the outpost had been abandoned years earlier. (Historic Urban Plans, Ithaca, New York)

the mouth of the Detroit River and a terrifying storm off Lake Huron's Thunder Bay. Under license granted by the French provincial governor Frontenac, La Salle was determined to explore and claim, on behalf of France, the territories west and south of what came to be known as Lake Michigan.

The headwaters of the Great Lakes had been known to the French for decades. French Recollet missionaries, closely followed by the Jesuits, had established mission outposts on Lake Huron as early as 1615. In 1634 Jean Nicolet discovered Lake Michigan, and the Jesuit priest Father Claude-Jean Allouez circumnavigated Lake Superior in a single bark canoe in 1667, twelve years before La Salle anchored just off the shore of Green Bay in September 1679.

The first European-style vessel to ply the Great Lakes, *The Griffin* [*Le Griffon* in French] had a short-lived career. Setting sail on its return voyage on September 17 from Washington Island under fair skies, the boat was never to be seen again—the first "ghost ship" of the Great Lakes. Unaware of the fate of his flagship, La Salle's expedition continued south along the western and southern shores of Lake Michigan to the St. Joseph River (later, Fort Miami). After a portage to the Kankakee River, which flows into the Illinois, the party descended to Lake Peoria, deep in the Illinois country. By late February, the first Fort Crevecoeur was completed, the first permanent establishment built by Europeans in the upper Mississippi River Valley. Two years later, on April 9, 1682, La Salle planted the flag of France on the shores of the Gulf of Mexico, claiming for his sovereign the entire Mississippi Valley, the province of Louisiana.

As is suggested in the exploits of the Frenchman La Salle, the European settlement and development of the North American interior from the earliest days was largely defined by the modes of transportation available at the time. It was not by accident that explorers and colonists, carried to the Americas by ship and dependent upon shipping for all contact with home, sought out coastal harbors for both refuge and settlement. As the imperial powers of Europe struggled for possession of the New World, control of major harbors and strategic waterways was to assure the ultimate success of England in its imperial ambitions. Not unlike an elegant demonstration of swordsmanship, as England seized control of the Atlantic coastal harbors (thrust), France claimed first the St. Lawrence River Valley and then the Mississippi River Valley (parry), only to be countered by English control of Hudson Bay.

As these efforts to control strategic harbors and waterways proved decisive to Great Britain's eventual supremacy, further development of inland waterways during the nineteenth century sped settlement and exploitation of the transmontane Northwest Territory. While the colonies and, later, the federal government

The development of the future city of Chicago began in 1803 when the federal government erected Fort Dearborn to protect the canoe portage there and subsequently established a trading post to deal with the Native Americans. (A.T. Andreas, History of Chicago*)*

struggled with development of a network of highways and canals to enhance communication and trade, the continent's natural waterways provided ready access to the interior. Until the advent of rail transportation in the mid-nineteenth century, it was largely waterborne—or maritime—transportation that determined the advance of settlement and development of the North American continent.

The early history of the Northwest Territory and the Upper Great Lakes is that of French exploration and largely failed attempts at colonization. Beginning with the seventeenth-century explorations of Samuel de Champlain, Jean Nicolet, and the Jesuit missionaries intent upon Christianizing the local tribes, the French pursued an almost random strategy of Indian alliance, intermittent settlement, and commercial exploitation of the fur trade. Trade routes followed waterways deep into the interior, anchored by trading outposts selected for their proximity to traditional Indian trade centers. Seldom more than poorly fortified wilderness encampments, these outposts were populated on a seasonal basis by a colorful assortment of French traders and their voyageur boatmen, the ubiquitous missionaries, and Indians of many tribes, often numbering in the thousands, gathered for the purpose of trade.

There is little evidence of serious attempts by French colonists at agriculture, mining or lumbering, or manufactures beyond rudimentary employment of "useful" crafts. The French were aware of the copper deposits, and probably the vast iron ore ranges, of the Lake Superior region from the very earliest explorations and attempted a short-lived mining effort at Chequamegon Bay in the 1730s, but 125 years were to pass before substantial mining activity got under way with the opening of the ship canal at Sault Ste. Marie.

Where towns of a more permanent nature grew up, they tended to be situated along waterborne trade routes in locations selected for militarily strategic advantage. Early French posts at Sault Ste. Marie in 1668, Detroit in 1701, and Michilimackinac (Mackinaw City) in 1715 were located at straits connecting the several upper lakes and were maintained by the French and then the English through the War of 1812. Until the population boom of the mid-nineteenth century, however, these continuously occupied sites were little more than villages ancillary to forts, trading posts, and missions. The French

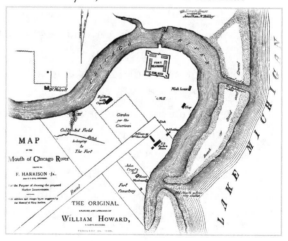

Fort Dearborn (on the bend in the river) and the adjacent government trading post (identified as the U.S. factor's house near the mouth of the river) had been abandoned by 1830 and the Chicago settlement was a backwater with only 40 to 50 residents when this map was drawn. (A.T. Andreas, History of Chicago*)*

frontiersman did not seek community in the wilderness; he could hardly be deemed a colonist.

Unlike the English agricultural settlements to the east, French frontier settlements were notably impermanent. Independent French fur traders (coureurs de bois) and trappers tended to settle in with the indigenous Indian tribes deep in the woods, venturing forth in the spring of each year to join with their countrymen in boisterous rendezvous for the purpose of trade and fellowship. With business completed, peltries graded, baled, and ready for shipment east, all that remained was to return again in the late summer to their Indian wives and half-breed children for another winter of trapping and trade.

In this way, France managed to spread its influence over 150 years across a vast area of the midcontinent on the dubious strength of a highly dispersed and, by every account, modest population of generally nomadic, uneducated, peasant voyageurs and coureurs de bois recruited from the villages and slums of France and the French-speaking New World. While cities on Lake Ontario and the lower St. Lawrence matured and acquired the trappings of civilization, the Upper Lakes passed the decades of the eighteenth and early nineteenth centuries nearly undisturbed by the presence of French colonial dominance. To the west and south, Prairie du Chien, Kaskaskia, Fort de Chartres, Prairie du Rocher, and Ste. Genevieve, on the banks of the Mississippi, and Vincennes, on the banks of the Wabash River, enjoyed the more sedentary pleasures of the pioneer village and looked to New Orleans downriver for government and commerce.

Failure to consolidate its holdings with permanent settlement was to prove France's downfall in America. In the 1750s, pressed by the British backed by a considerable population of English-speaking colonials, the French-Indian alliances collapsed and fortified trading centers surrendered, and in 1763 the French dominions in North America east of the Mississippi—including much of what became the Northwest Territory—passed to the control and sovereignty of Great Britain. French traders based deep in the north woods continued their annual rendezvous at the familiar places, trading their furs in turn with English agents of Hudson's Bay Company and then John Jacob Astor's American Fur Company. In most instances, notably nonmilitant French-speaking residents of nascent urban settlements such as Detroit, Vincennes, and Kaskaskia submitted peacefully first to the authority of the English and, later, to the new American government.

In the years just preceding the American Revolution, colonists were pressing the Crown for permission to move west across the Appalachians. Britain's American colonies had grown from a scattering of coastal harbor towns to a stable and growing population estimated at nearly 2.25 million. (This number was to double within 20 years and continue doubling every 24 years.) By the census of 1820, the U.S. population was counted at 9,638,000, with continued growth showing no signs of abatement.

Beginning in the mid-1760s, traders and explorers Benjamin Cutbird and Daniel Boone and others were prowling the Tennessee-Kentucky borderlands, sending back accounts of sweeping, fertile prairies and forests teeming with game. By the late 1760s, land speculators were securing, by treaty and purchase from the Indians, tens of millions of acres of land in the valley of the Ohio River, in Kentucky and West Virginia, and in eastern Tennessee. In April 1769 the land office in Pittsburgh was overrun by hordes of speculative western land purchasers anxious to get a piece of the action. Americans were glimpsing the possibilities of the frontier.

The American Revolution cast off the restrictive settlement policies of the British colonial office, and in the last decades of the eighteenth century, the new nation addressed the development of the Northwest Territory. The ordinances of 1784 and 1787 guaranteed representative government and the rule of law; a standard land survey was implemented that would delineate, record, and protect private land ownership; and ownership of unsettled lands was vested in the federal government, the proceeds from the sale of which would provide for national defense and internal improvements. Importantly, statehood on an equal footing with the original 13 states was assured; the developing western regions would be neither dependencies nor satrapies to the eastern states.

Freed of preoccupation with foreign entanglements and with governmental mechanisms in place, the young nation turned with enthusiasm to the development of its ever-expanding territories. With the settlement of the Ohio River Valley barely under way, the purchase in 1803 of France's interest in the Louisiana Territory effectively doubled the land area of the United States, extending the country's borders westward from the Mississippi to the Rocky Mountains. Importantly, the Louisiana Purchase finally guaranteed unrestricted access to the Gulf of Mexico — the entire Mississippi River Valley was thrown open to river navigation, settlement, and commercial exploitation.

Upriver from New Orleans, the relatively young river town of St. Louis was positioned to fulfill its destiny as a major entry point of the Upper Midwest. To the east, up the Ohio River, Louisville, Cincinnati, and Pittsburgh were, by the turn of the century, established urban centers serving the commercial needs of the interior. Indeed, well into the 1830s, Cincinnati was considered the economic center of the West and destined to reign supreme as the metropolis of the midcontinent. Each of these early centers of trade and commerce came into being, survived, and ultimately thrived due to water-related geographic peculiarities. St. Louis, Pittsburgh, and, to a slightly lesser extent, Cincinnati were located at or near the confluence of tributary rivers — intersections, one might say, of major thoroughfares. Louisville, on the other hand, grew up to serve the transshipment needs of those unable to pass through or around the Falls of the Ohio at Louisville, a two-mile stretch of particularly violent rapids.

As towns and villages grew up along the Ohio River Valley, the future port cities of Milwaukee, Chicago, Detroit, and Cleveland languished as frontier trading centers and military outposts. At the conclusion of the War of 1812, fought largely to put to rest any illusions the British might have held concerning sovereignty over the Great Lakes and Upper Midwest, Detroit was still a largely French-speaking village of a few hundred (down from 800 before the war), economically dependent on the fur trade and the export of maple sugar. While Cincinnati boomed to the south, Cleveland was only just being incorporated as a village, with a population of 150. Chicago was rebuilding the ruined Fort Dearborn, and Milwaukee was little more than an intermittently occupied trading post.

Americans in general knew little of the Upper Midwest and the old French settlements of Detroit, Mackinac, Green Bay, and Prairie du Chien. In a time when cleared woodlands were held at a premium for farming, the vast prairies of Indiana, Illinois, and western Wisconsin were considered difficult to till and impossible to drain. The pine-forested sandy soil of Michigan was dismissed as wasteland. These attitudes were to change dramatically, however, in the nation's rush to advance "internal improvements" in the 1820s. As Ohio, Indiana, and Illinois in turn achieved statehood, a network of highways and turnpikes were built connecting major river towns with villages springing up to the north; the Cumberland, or Old National, Road stretched west from the Potomac, across the Alleghenies, Ohio, and Indiana, and into Illinois by the 1830s.

As the highways came to advance settlement into the interior, the Erie Canal, the first of a series of shipping canals intended to connect the Great Lakes with the nation's natural waterways was completed in the 1820s. Finished in 1825, the 363-mile Erie Canal connected the Great Lakes to the Hudson River and the Mohawk Valley. Four years later, the Welland Canal linked Lakes Erie and Ontario, bypassing Niagara Falls and opening the lower St. Lawrence River to shipping from the Upper Lakes. To the south, the 333-mile Ohio Canal, connecting Cleveland to the Ohio River at Portsmouth, was opened to navigation in 1832. Eleven years later the Wabash & Erie Canal joined the Wabash River at Lafayette to Lake Erie at Toledo, a distance of 187 miles. In Illinois work commenced in 1836 on the Illinois and Michigan Canal, which, when completed in 1848, linked Lake Michigan at Chicago with the Illinois River and, downstream, the Mississippi River. By the 1850s America's great period of canal development had largely ended as enthusiasm for overland rail transportation swept the country, once again shifting settlement patterns and opening up hitherto inaccessible regions to settlement and development.

The impact of canal development in the Northwest transformed the previously tranquil, isolated situation of Great Lakes outpost villages. Still considered an old French town when granted its city charter in 1824, Detroit reeled under the onslaught of more than 3,000 waterborne immigrant arrivals in 1825, the year the Erie Canal opened. Four years later there were more than 1,100 passenger arrivals during one 11-day period in May alone, and more than 5,000 were recorded for the season. Many of these arrivals passed on further west overland, but others stayed; by 1834 the city had grown to almost 5,000 inhabitants—and that number was to double in the next three years. According to one account, by 1838 this once-remote, French-inflected hamlet had become an "eastern city" built by easterners and full of eastern manners.

Buffalo was the great point of embarkation for immigrants moving west by boat. In the spring of 1835, fifty-six boats left Buffalo in one week bound for Cleveland, Detroit, and Chicago. Six to eight boats carrying 1,000 to 1,500 passengers passed Erie, Pennsylvania, daily; that season more than 200,000 would take passage at Buffalo bound for the west, according to the *Erie Observer*. The next year was similar. In October 1835 alone, nine boats carrying 4,000 passengers left Buffalo. With the completion of the Ohio Canal in 1832, Cleveland was a great beneficiary of this flood of immigration. By the mid-1830s the city was a lively trading and shipping center. By 1840 the population exceeded 6,000—a veritable metropolis by the standards of the day.

Chicago and Milwaukee also shared in the increased lake traffic in the years following the opening of the Erie and Welland canals. Although lagging somewhat behind their eastern rivals, both ports enjoyed steadily increasing populations and enhanced opportunities for trade. Lacking the early locational advantage of Chicago, Milwaukee was only mapped and laid out in 1833; nevertheless, by 1838 there were more than 244 steamboat clearings and 268 arrivals of sailing vessels. South along the Lake Michigan shore, Chicago was stirring in anticipation of the construction of the Illinois and Michigan Canal. Land and city lot sales were brisk as speculators bid up prices in anticipation of the explosive growth, which was sure to follow—as indeed it did.

The Port of Chicago—in fact, the Chicago River itself—historically had been blocked by a troublesome sandbar straddling the river's mouth, which was finally breached in 1834. In June of that year, the steamer *Michigan*, built by Oliver Newberry of Detroit, entered the port and tied up below Dearborn Street; on July 12, the schooner *Illinois* entered the harbor amidst great fanfare. The Port of Chicago had come into its own! Two years later work actually got under way on the promised canal, and by the time of its completion in 1848, Chicago was well prepared to become the leading entry point of the American interior.

In many ways the 1850s represented a pivotal decade for the Chicago and the Great Lakes. By the end of the decade, more than 1,450 commercial vessels were registered on the lakes, of which 1,122 were sail powered and 335 paddle-wheel and propeller powered. The arrival in 1857 of the British-built *Madeira Pet* out of Liverpool signaled the commencement of direct saltwater shipping on the lakes; by the next year, 15 vessels were to carry cargoes of lumber, staves, and grain from the Great Lakes ports to Liverpool (not forgetting that the steamer *Dean Richmond* is credited with inaugurating the service in September 1856). Far to the

north, completion of the ship canal at Sault Ste. Marie stimulated both immigration and the rapid development of iron ore mining in the Lake Superior region, the richest ore fields in the world.
The ready availability of cheap iron ore was to stimulate and support the development of steelmaking and heavy industry in the
Chicago area and across the Great Lakes for the next hundred
years. In 1852 the Michigan Central Railroad ran its first train into
Chicago, and two years later an all-rail connection was established
between New York and Chicago.

By the 1850s Chicago was a mature center of inland trade and
commerce. A lumber trade begun modestly in 1835 had grown the
extent Chicago in the 1850s was the world's leading shipper of
dressed lumber. By this time regional agricultural production had
made Chicago the world leader in the shipment of grains. Much
of this bulk commodity trade was carried in the holds of Great
Lakes vessels through the port of Chicago. The arrival of the railroads only enhanced the port's activities. Timber cut along the
shores of northern Lake Michigan arrived by boat for processing
and shipment out by rail, and grain, brought into the city by railcar and canal barge for delivery to the city's towering grain elevators, was shipped east in the holds of merchant schooners. Such
was the synergistic consequence of highway, canal, rail, and lake
port joined at Chicago, that commerce and industry thrived as
nowhere else in the country. Chicago was indeed the "miracle of
the prairies."

Throughout the remainder of the century, the Port of Chicago
was the vital center of the city's commercial life. An international
port of call since the days of the *Dean Richmond* and *Madeira Pet*,
maritime traffic continued to build. The port had clearly achieved
world-class status when, in 1882, more than 26,000 ship clearances and arrivals were recorded—substantially more than the
ports of New York, New Orleans, and San Francisco combined!

As our region's early settlers found it expedient to follow the

Grain was the early Chicago port's most important export. It typically moved on schooners in bulk—being poured into an open hold without being bagged—which gave the city a significant cost advantage over its steamboat rivals on the rivers. This drawing illustrates the first grain shipment from the city, in 1838, aboard the schooner Osceola, *bound for the Erie Canal at Buffalo. (A. T. Andreas,* History of Chicago*)*

nation's inland waterways in their search for furs, town sites, and cheap farm land, so, too, were the major Great Lakes cities founded on the basis of maritime advantage and prospects. As it is necessary to follow the Ohio and Mississippi rivers in tracing urban settlement patterns of the eighteenth and nineteenth centuries, for similar reasons we note the origins of Great Lakes cities founded on their harbor potential—as lake ports first of all. For Cleveland, Toledo, and Chicago, the fortuitous combination of both lake port and canal terminus offered an extraordinary advantage. Each provided more or less direct access from one mighty waterway system, the St. Lawrence—of which the Great Lakes form the headwaters—and another, the Mississippi. With the arrival of the railroads, these natural and built advantages were only enhanced, all combining to create perhaps the richest, certainly the most productive, region in the world. Underlying that early success and continuing prosperity are a common maritime experience and heritage. A thousand miles from our nearest saltwater shoreline, one finds a maritime perspective both useful and relevant in understanding even the interior of our great continent, beyond the mountains, the Northwest Territory of the nineteenth century.

Mud Lake

Mud Lake—a glacial slough on what is today the Southwest Side of Chicago—no longer exists. Like Fort Dearborn, it is buried beneath factories, railroad tracks, stores, and homes. But when the French explorers arrived in the seventeenth century, they learned that the occasionally flooded marshland between the Chicago and Des Plaines rivers could be used as a canoe portage and was, in fact, the shortest such route between the watersheds of the Great Lakes and Mississippi River.

This statue in a forest preserve at Harlem Avenue and 45th Street is at the western edge of what was once Mud Lake, where a small creek emptied into the Des Plaines River. The statue depicts the Jolliet-Marquette discovery of the Chicago canoe portage in 1673. (David M. Young)

Louis Jolliet almost immediately recognized that it would be an excellent place to dig a relatively short canal to connect those two waterways. Thus this obscure and now forgotten slough was the origin for Chicago's development as a maritime center, although its utility as a canoe portage had ceased by the 1820s.

Mud Lake—known variously as Portage Lake, Oak Point Lake, and Le Petit Lac—was actually an elongated marsh located intermediate between what are now Archer and Ogden avenues and extending from about Albany Avenue (3100 West) to Harlem Avenue (7200 West). The contemporary Sanitary and Ship Canal crosses much of what had been Mud Lake.

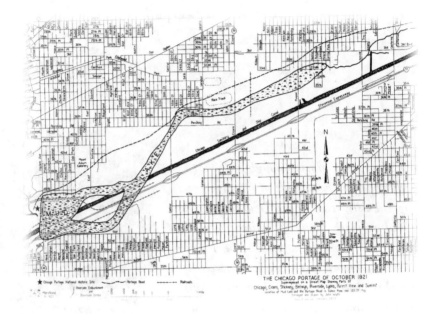

Mud Lake, an integral part of the Chicago canoe portage, in use until the early nineteenth century, is shown superimposed over a modern street map of Chicago's Southwest Side. The lake—a marsh, actually—extended from approximately Central Park Avenue south and west to Harlem Avenue, where a creek led to the Des Plaines River. The low-lying continental divide that separated the Mississippi River and Great Lakes watersheds is in the upper-right corner of the map, shown as a gap between two creeks at approximately 28th and Rockwell streets (extended). The portage road (shown as a dotted line) used at times of low water is just to the north of Mud Lake. (Philip E. Vierling)

Development of Chicago's Southwest Side resulted in the filling of Mud Lake. This remnant near Oak Park Avenue and 51st Street in suburban Forest View existed as late as 1988 but was subsequently filled in. (Philip E. Vierling)

This remnant of Mud Lake, along an Illinois Central Railroad yard in Forest View in 1974, has since been filled for development. The Sears Tower can be seen in the center of the photograph, above the parked freight cars. (Philip E. Vierling)

Chapter Two

From Eschicagou to Chicago

Louis Jolliet, accompanied by Father Jacques Marquette and five voyageurs, is generally credited as being the first French explorer to visit the site of Chicago when in 1673, on returning from his exploration by canoe of the Mississippi River, he was told by the natives of a shortcut to the Great Lakes by means of the Illinois River and a portage at a place that came to be known as Checagou. A few years later Cavelier de La Salle began trying to colonize Pays des Ilinois, as the French sometimes called the Illinois territory, and he and his successors established a small fort or outpost at Portage Checagou. It was abandoned apparently after the founding of New Orleans gave the French an easier and safer route to its Illinois outposts via the Mississippi River.

Charles J. Balesi, who holds a doctorate in history, is the author of the authoritative book The Time of the French in the Heart of North America: 1673–1818 (1996). *He condensed this account of Chicago's largely forgotten French period from that book.*

by Charles J. Balesi

The history of the founding of the City of Chicago, its dating and circumstances, long ago became a victim of terminal political correctness. It is accepted fact that more than two decades before the city was incorporated, Fort Dearborn stood on the banks of the Chicago River, and a few years before the fort was built a handful of buildings were erected on both sides of the river by such pioneers as Jean-Baptiste Point du Sable.

Yet long before any of that happened, the site was occupied successively by a long forgotten French Jesuit mission and a French fort. In fact, the selection of that marshy spot where a relatively small river met Lake Michigan was no accident: the Miami Indians and their cousins from the Illinois confederacy had used the area for seasonal rendezvous, a place for trade. The Miami were themselves a confederacy composed of four subgroups wandering along the southern shore of Lake Michigan. Their Illinois cousins, having lost by the end of the seventeenth century most of their power as rulers of the western Great Lakes region, had regrouped their dwindling numbers a little to the west—a daylong trip by canoe on the Des Plaines and Illinois rivers.

It was the French who discovered the site of Chicago from the Indians and first attempted a permanent settlement there. It was not successful for reasons that had more to do with French policy in the New World than the fact that they were ousted from America as a result of the French and Indian War. Chicago lay abandoned more than half a century before Versailles in 1763 relinquished its claims on America and for nearly a century before the first American settlers showed up.

The topography the French explorers encountered in 1672, if we believe that Nicholas Perrot was the first to reach the area, or in 1673 when Louis Jolliet and Father Jacques Marquette arrived, was a muddy and long portage between the Chicago River and the Des Plaines River more or less along the route of what is today Archer Avenue. The Jolliet-Marquette expedition left on May 7, 1673, from a French mission at St. Ignace on Michigan's upper peninsula, canoed down Green Bay, and continued on the Wisconsin River to reach the Mississippi River. They had traveled as far south as Arkansas before deciding to turn back on July 17, 1673, after hearing reports of white settlements further south that they feared would be Spanish.

On the return trip they used the Illinois River instead of the Wisconsin and were escorted by canoe from the "great Illinois Town," a large Indian encampment near the present town of Utica, Illinois, by one of the Kaskaskia chiefs and dozens of young warriors. Jolliet made a careful notation of the physiography of the area, which leads us to believe he and his companions spent several days there.

The portage fascinated Jolliet, and he was the first to recognize the potential implications of using it as a direct maritime link between the Gulf of St. Lawrence in Canada and the Gulf of Mexico. The distance between Chicago and the Des Plaines River was relatively short (four to five miles) and France had the technology to build canals of much greater magnitudes. It was precisely during the reign of Louis xiv that France dug the Canal du Midi linking the Atlantic Ocean to the Mediterranean Sea.

Jolliet, Marquette, and their party left Chicago for Sault Ste. Marie in August, 1673, and Jolliet continued on to Montreal the following spring to make his report to the governor of New France. However as he neared Montreal on July 21, 1674, he decided to shoot the dangerous La Chine rapids on the St. Lawrence River instead of portaging around them and lost all his documents when his canoe overturned. Thus it was from memory with the events still fresh in his mind that he dictated a memoir of his travels for Governor Frontenac and drew a map entitled *Nouvelle Decouverte de pluiiers Nations dans le Nouvelle France en l'anee 1674 et 1674.*

Jolliet also communicated his observations to Father Claude Dablon, who was then the Superior of the Jesuit Order for all of New France and who, as such, was the author of what were called *Relations*—diaries of a sort meant for publication back in France as a fund-raising tool. Today, Relations have proved to be a enormously useful tool for researchers on the history, politics, and scientific observations made in New France. In them, Dablon recorded Jolliet's observation about the maritime implications of the Chicago portage:

> The fourth remark which concerns an advantage, very consider-able and which will hardly be believed by one, is that we should be able quite easily to go as far as Florida in a bark and by very pleasant navigation. There would have to be made but one canal intersecting only half a league of prairie in order to enter from the foot of the lake of the Illinois [now Lake Michigan] into the river of St. Louis [now the Illinois River] which discharges into the Mississippi; being there the bark would navigate easily as far as the Gulf of Mexico.

Thus did Chicago enter the historical record, as a potential maritime project, not as a future metropolis. The French were divided on how or even whether to develop their corner of the New World. France was a nation that tended to favor central-ized government, and colonies deep in the inte-rior of North America so far from Louis XIV's palace in Versailles would be difficult to administer from the other side of an ocean, as the British dis-covered in 1775. On the other hand, many of the French who visited the New World realized its tremendous potential for development. Others only

The portaging of canoes between waterways was (and is) a laborious process that often involves two trips—one for the boat and a second for its contents. This photo shows the 1973 Jolliet-Marquette reenactors carrying their craft at the Chicago portage. (Ralph Frese)

wanted to save souls, and they were the first to attempt to develop something at Chicago.

In 1674, Marquette made a return trip to the Illinois tribe accompanied by two veterans of the previous voyage, Pierre Porteret and Jacques Largilier. They left the Mission St. Ignace during the last days of October, late in the year for a long canoe trip on the waters of Lake Michigan with its notorious rough autumn weather. They were escorted by a flotilla of nine canoes manned by fifty Illinois and Potawatomi Indians, and finally reached the Chicago site on December 4, 1674.

Marquette wrote in his journal:

We started to reach Portage River [Chicago River] that was frozen half a foot thick. There was more snow than anywhere else and also more track of animals and turkeys. Navigating the lake from one portage to the other is quite fine, but there being no traverse to make and landing being quite feasible all along providing you do not obstinately persist in travelling in the breakers and high winds.

After waiting several days at the Chicago portage for an improvement in the weather, on December 14 they moved about four miles inland to a spot between the Chicago and Des Plaines rivers and decided ". . . to winter here, as it was impossible to go further." Marquette by then was extremely sick, probably suffering from a chest ailment. As it turned out another Frenchman was already wintering in the area—one of those independent-minded voyageurs who traveled alone or in very small groups and integrated with the Indian tribes with whom they visited. His name was Pierre Moreau, known as "The Mole," and he was traveling with a partner known only as "Le Barbier." He traveled fifty miles to visit Marquette bringing corn and berries.

Once spring arrived, Marquette continued his trip downriver to the Great Illinois Town to keep his promise made to the Illiniwek

The Illiniwek Indians told Jolliet and Marquette of the Chicago portage—a shortcut between the Mississippi River and Great Lakes waterway systems. This 1973 photograph of the reenactment was taken during a simulated dog feast in Peoria in 1973. The Illiniwek, who did not have livestock, ate dogs at feast time. (Ralph Frese)

the year before to create a parish. However, Marquette decided to return to St. Ignace but died on May 18, 1673, on the return trip near what is today Ludington, Michigan. He was only thirty-eight years old.

While individual Frenchmen and occasional missionaries became a more familiar sight in northern Illinois, it was not until La Salle and his relatively numerous French and Indian followers arrived a few years later to try to establish a trading colony with the Illiniwek that Chicago once again appeared in the historical record. Robert Cavelier, the product of a wealthy merchant family in Rouen in Normandy, in accordance with the style of the time added to his surname the name of one of his family properties to give him the scent of nobility (later confirmed by the king) as Sieur de La Salle. He is a man who by sheer determination hoped to transform the small domain the French had acquired in North America into an empire the size of a continent.

It was during one of his multiple forays to Illinois to locate and navigate the Mississippi River that he wound up on January 4,

1682, at the uninhabited site of Chicago. Although La Salle was not enamored with the Chicago portage because of the difficulty of traversing it at times of low water, requiring the canoes and their cargo to be hauled four to five miles overland between the Chicago and Des Plaines rivers, he had chosen it for a rendezvous with his lieutenant, Henry Tonty. In this instance a particularly harsh winter that froze the rivers made for an easy transit by loading the canoes on sleds which were then pulled on the ice. Three months later, La Salle and his crew arrived at the mouth of the Mississippi, and on April 9, 1682, La Salle, surrounded by his officers, soldiers, clergy, Indian escorts, and a *notaire*, a royal officer of justice, claimed for Louis xiv all the land in North America that would be later known as the Louisiana Territory.

However, one of the intrigues that hampered France's ability to effectively colonize its North American possessions was unfolding. Frontenac, a proponent of colonization and La Salle's sponsor, was replaced with a new governor (De la Barre) who La Salle considered to be a creature of the Jesuit religious order. The Jesuits were more interested in converting souls than colonizing them. La Salle had built a fort (Fort St. Louis des Illinois) atop Starved Rock near the future site of Utica, Illinois, and La Barre promptly ordered another fort built at Chicago to divert the fur trade away from Fort St. Louis and La Salle.

In 1683 La Salle decided to travel to Versailles to defend himself at Louis xiv's court and on the trip wound up at Fort Chicago. A letter La Salle sent from there on June 4, 1683, confirms its existence. However, a few years later after La Barre was disgraced and replaced as governor, the fort was abandoned but had been replaced by a Jesuit mission. Two Jesuit priests named Binet and Binneteau had founded in 1683 the Mission of the Guardian Angel to minister to the indigenous Miami tribes. The mission consisted of a chapel surrounded by about 150 temporary cabins. According to a letter written years later by one of the priests of *Mission etrangeres* (Father St. Cosme), the Chicago mission was located on the north bank of the Chicago River between its fork and the lakefront. The mission had been closed for a year on the orders of the anti-Jesuit Frontenac, who had returned to New France in 1689 for his second term as governor, but was reopened after a strong protest by the bishop.

Meanwhile at Fort St. Louis ninety miles downstream, Tonty, the unsung hero of the French adventure in America, maintained the French king's power with a few *soldats d'infanterie de marine* and hundreds of Indian allies who lived just across the Illinois River. La Salle had left France for the New World with a new expedition, the purpose of which to this day remains unclear, and landed in Texas. The expedition met with disaster, and only a handful of French soldiers along with Father Jean Cavelier, La Salle's brother, eventually made the long and arduous journey back to Fort St. Louis des Illinois. La Salle had been assassinated by his own men in Texas on January 7, 1687.

Jean Cavelier was received with open arms by Tonty, but decided to continue on his way back to France without revealing the death of his brother. In his journal for September 25, 1687, Cavelier noted that he had halted in Chi-ca-gou, "which as we have been able to learn, has taken its name from the great quantity of garlic which grows in this area, in the woods." However, the weather had turned bad and Cavelier decided to return to Fort St. Louis for the winter. The following spring he set out again for France, and again on March 29, 1688, the weather forced him to delay his voyage at Chicago. He and his party spent a week camping in the remnants of the fort while waiting for the winds to abate.

Among the survivors of the Texas expedition in his party was a professional soldier, Henry Joutel, who like Jolliet saw the importance of Chicago as a connecting point between Canada and the Mississippi. "It would be very easy to connect the two rivers because the land is quite flat. . . . However, a large settlement would be necessary to support such an enterprise," Joutel wrote in his diary. Interestingly enough, neither Cavelier nor Joutel made any mention of a Jesuit mission at Chicago. It may have been temporarily abandoned at that time.

The situation of the French establishment in North America had been deteriorating largely as a result of a series of poor administrators who had succeeded the Marquis de Frontenac as governors of New France, so it was as a last resort that despite his seven decades of life, he was returned to Montreal as governor. The flamboyant and often controversial character, like La Salle, had been the driving force behind much of whatever development had occurred in the French colony. In spite of the adverse conditions he found, Frontenac quickly showed the brio that had earned him the nickname of *Montio*, "the Beautiful," from the Indians. He was capable of combining quick diplomacy with the Indian nations and daring military moves.

In the spring of 1690 to revive the dwindling fur trade he sent Captain Louis de Louvigny to Michilimackinac (present day Mackinaw City, Michigan) to rendezvous with the legendary voyageur Nicolas Perrot and representatives of the Indian nations Perrot had gathered. The fur trade resumed with a vengeance for the profit of the merchants of Montreal and their brigades of voyageurs.

At Fort St. Louis des Illinois the situation was becoming increasingly difficult for Henry Tonty and his old associate Francois de la Forest. They made the decision to relocate further downriver at a newly built Fort St. Louis Pimitoui near present day Peoria. They had been joined by Tonty's nephew, Pierre de Liette, who was put in charge of the Chicago site where a warehouse had been built. Despite their efforts, commercial success eluded them; the principal fur trade axis was far to the north, anchored at Sault Ste. Marie and Michilimackinac. In 1694, Antoine de la Mothe-Cadillac, the celebrated founder of Detroit but then the commander at Michilimackinac, was made chief administrator of the western territories and undermined Tonty even more by sending a lieutenant, Monsieur de Manthet to take command of Fort Chicago with orders to report directly to Michilimackinac.

On November 28, 1698, Frontenac died in the City of Quebec, and with him the informality and rough directness of an administration which had been more successful than many had wished. However, a month before his death an event was set in motion to establish a new colony that became France's promised land in the eighteenth century as Canada had been in the seventeenth century. On October 24, 1698, a four-ship convoy set sail from the Atlantic port of Brest with colonists bound for Louisiana. The eclipse of Canada by the new Louisiana colony ultimately would have a profound effect on Illinois.

For one thing, Illinois was split between the two colonies. New settlements founded along the Mississippi River were beholden to New Orleans. The founding on July 1, 1701, of Fort Pontchartrain au detroit des lacs Erie et Huron (now known simply as Detroit) by Lamothe-Cadillac contributed to a shift in trade patterns away from the Chicago portage and to the Ohio and St. Joseph rivers. St. Genevieve (Missouri) and Fort des Chartres at Kaskaskia (Illinois) became the center of French presence in the Midwest. Chicago, never more than a dream to Jolliet and Joutel, a secondary portage to La Salle and Frontenac, and a minor backwater mission to the Jesuits, disappeared sometime around 1700. So did the Peoria fort.

The revival of Chicago had to wait nearly a century until a couple of men of French heritage arrived to get things started again. Jean-Baptiste Point du Sable, likely the son of a French father and West Indian mother, showed up in Peoria in 1771, married a Potawatomi woman, and exploited a 35-acre farm. Sometime thereafter he moved to the Chicago portage to run a trading post for a few years before selling it to another Frenchman, Jean Lalime. In 1792, Du Sable's daughter, Suzanne, married Jean-Baptiste Pelletier in Chicago.

By then the place was a territory of the new United States, and it was up to the Americans to build the next fort there.

Chapter Three

The Canoe Age

*Until the 1820s what commerce there was on the Great Lakes was usu-
ally carried by canoe. Although both sailing vessels and steamships
began to appear on the lakes in the first two decades of the nineteenth
century, the opening of the Erie Canal across upstate New York in 1825
caused both the development of the Great Lakes basin and an explosive
growth in commerce that could not economically be served by canoe.*

This chapter on the canoe age was adapted from a Chicago Tribune
article published on October 17, 1999.

In the automobile age a person can drive the 851 miles from
Chicago to Montreal in a day or fly it in less than two hours, but
two centuries ago the trip would have taken the better part of two
months. And that was in favorable weather, since the only modes
of travel on that route were by foot or by canoe. For more than 130
years after the French first ventured into the western Great Lakes
from Canada in the 1670s, the local beast of burden was man. And
man used canoes to ease the task.

Scores of canoes—traveling singly or in convoys, laden with
trade goods for the American Indians and beaver pelts for
Europeans, and manned by French-speaking voyageurs—made
the trip each year between Montreal and wilderness outposts such
as Checagou.

CMS member Ralph Frese—owner of one of the nation's
largest private canoe collections and the organizer of the tricen-

One of the 1973 Jolliet-Marquette reenactors was teacher Jim Phillips, who gained fame anonymously as an environmental activist known as the Fox. He secretly plugged factory drains and dumped effluent in the offices of companies that polluted the Fox River. (Ralph Frese)

tennial reenactment of the 1673 voyage of Louis Jolliet (accompanied by Father Jacques Marquette) that resulted in the discovery of the site of Chicago—does not think that the role of the canoe has been given proper credit by historians. Jolliet, of course, was the first person to suggest that a canal could be dug at the Chicago portage to link the St. Lawrence River–Great Lakes and Mississippi River watersheds. The canal did not become a reality until 1848.

"The canoe is the only watercraft that is still with us in its original form," Frese once told an interviewer, referring to the primordial vessels used by neolithic man. "The only use we've added is recreation. But in the Third World countries, it's still an important watercraft because it's affordable and can be made from local materials."

Beginning in the 1600s and lasting until the end of the canoe age in the 1820s, flotillas of birchbark canoes, some in excess of 30 feet long and capable of carrying up to five tons of cargo, plied the rivers and lakes in what the French called *Pays d'en haut*, which the English-speaking colonists referred to as the Northwest Territory and we now call the Midwest. They hauled guns and trinkets for trade with the Wea (Miami), Potawatomi, and Illiniwek and returned to Montreal with beaver furs destined to become hats for the courtiers at the Versailles palace of the Sun King, Louis XIV.

South and west of Chicago, where birch trees were rare, the birchbark canoe gave way to the dugout—a hollow log tapered at both ends—which the French called *pirogues*. They were sturdier than bark canoes but were heavier and not as economical for carrying the big loads of the beaver convoys. Heavier canoes meant more men were required to carry them across portages, and larger crews took up valuable cargo space. However, Timothy J. Kent, who has written extensively on the subject of canoes, disputes the illusion that dugouts were big, clunky, heavy watercraft that could not be portaged. Some were quite sleek.

Birchbark canoes required more maintenance than dugouts. Birch canoes, which lasted only five or six years in normal service, had to be kept in sheds or buried during winter. Each year they had to be recaulked with gum. Dugouts weren't quite as fragile, but they tended to crack if not kept wet. The French also used a double-ended rowboat called a *bateau*, but it was too heavy and awkward for the frequent portages on the beaver route between Montreal and Chicago.

Although La Salle built the sailing ship *Le Griffon* for a voyage across the Great Lakes in 1679, sailing ships at 6,000 to 8,000 livres ($60,000 to $80,000) were too expensive to build for the early fur trade. The loss of the *Le Griffon* and its cargo of furs on its return trip from Green Bay to Niagara almost bankrupted La Salle.

Sailing ships after 1800 began to appear in appreciable numbers on the Great Lakes, which could create dangerous traveling conditions for canoes, and proved they were able to handle more cargo with fewer crewmen. Claiborne Skinner, who wrote his 1990 doctoral dissertation on the canoe age, once estimated that a small sailing ship with a crew of five or six could carry 40 tons of cargo. To haul the same amount of cargo by canoe would require eight vessels with a total of 64 men. The demise of the canoe was not abrupt, however. In the 1830s, long after the sailing ship replaced the canoe on the Great Lakes, a few French voyageurs still worked on the docks in Chicago, paddling their canoes over the bar at the mouth of the Chicago River to load and unload ships with too deep a draft to enter the river.

The canoe age developed its own lexicon, now largely forgotten, just as the age of sail did later. For example, *voyageurs* were Frenchmen with a legal license to trade or were paddlers hired by the trader. *Coureurs de bois* were bootleggers or illegal traders, and the *canot de Maitre* (literally "Maitre's canoe"), named after one of its French-Canadian builders, was the bulk freighter of its time, the workhorse of the beaver trade after 1729. At 32 to 36 feet long, it could carry four to five tons of cargo and a crew of up to eight. *Canots de Maitre* were known as Montreal boats at Mackinac, Michigan, and as Mackinac boats in Chicago. *Batard* (French for "bastard") was a slightly smaller (29- to 30-foot) version of the *canot de Maitre*. *Canot du Nord* (canoe of the North) was the mainstay of the beaver route in the early 1700s. It was 24 to 28 feet long and had a crew of four to six.

In the first half of the seventeenth century, the Indians did most of the beaver hauling in their own canoes. Fleets of as many as 150 Huron and Algonquin canoes loaded with pelts would descend on Montreal. After 1663 the French began sending voyageurs inland to trade, typically in two- or four-man canoes bought from the Indians. Within a few years scores of French canoes were paddled alone and in convoys between Montreal and the tribes that were settled along the Great Lakes.

Surprisingly, the route the French used largely skirted the Great Lakes. For one thing, the lakes had major storms that could keep canoes on the beach for three to four days. Jim Phillips, one of the tricentennial reenactors and an environmentalist known far and wide under his pseudonym, the Fox, recalled in an interview before his death that during the 1973 voyage retracing Jolliet's path, high winds on Lake Michigan kept his party on the beach for an entire day.

For another thing, despite many portages the river route across present-day Ontario was only about 900 miles long—about 300 to 400 miles shorter than the 1,251-mile route across the Great Lakes, which had fewer portages. Niagara Falls was the largest portage on the lakes; it was controlled by the Iroquois confederacy, which was not particularly friendly to the French. The Iroquois's bitter enemies were the Hurons, who allied themselves with the French. The Iroquois war parties also disrupted trade at the Checagou portage, as did the Fox tribe, which had a running war with the French between 1710 and 1730.

Voyageurs leaving Montreal each spring put their canoes into the St. Lawrence River just upstream of the dangerous Lachine Rapids and paddled up the Ottawa and Mettawa rivers in present-day Ontario, across Lake Nipissing, and down the French River and into Georgian Bay on Lake Huron. They then paddled across Huron to Michilimackinac (current Mackinaw City, near the top of Michigan's lower peninsula) and fanned out over routes deeper into the interior. It took Jolliet two months to travel by canoe from Montreal to the Straits of Mackinac in the autumn of 1672, prior to his famous voyage of discovery. He left Montreal a few days after October 1 and reached Michilimackinac on December 6.

The canoe routes from Michilimackinac south ran on both sides of Lake Michigan. One ran down the western shore to the Chicago portage. It was on the leeward side of the lake and more sheltered than the eastern shore, which was used to get to the St. Joseph River at present-day Niles, Michigan. The St. Joseph River in turn led to the portages to the Kankakee and Wabash rivers in Indiana and Illinois. The return trip to Montreal usually began in July.

The canoe trading route across Canada continued, however, even after the French were evicted from North America in 1673 following the French and Indian War, and the canoe remained the principal vessel of commerce in the Great Lakes region into the nineteenth century. The lore of the Great Lakes, albeit somewhat faded in the automobile age, has been kept alive by maritime enthusiasts. The rigors of the canoe age have been largely forgotten. For one thing, the voyageurs had a high mortality rate; at least half of them were unable to swim. Accidents were serious enough that trading companies forbade their employees from shooting rapids, requiring them to conduct laborious portages that involved unloading the canoes and hauling the craft and their cargo in separate trips over the gap, often of several miles. Jolliet himself was involved in one of the best known accidents when in 1674 he tried to shoot the Lachine Rapids on the St. Lawrence River above Montreal. His canoe overturned and he lost his belongings, diaries, and three companions.

There were more than 30 portages between streams or around rapids on the beaver route across Canada. The Chicago portage was favored at certain times of year when the water was high and Mud Lake full because it was the shortest and easiest route to the Illinois River. But when the water was low and during Indian wars, the French shunned it. The last battle between the French and Fox Indians was fought in 1730, and although it resulted in an overwhelming victory for the French, they were by then using the Mississippi River from New Orleans as their principal route to Illinois country.

The life of a voyageur was relatively good for a young man willing to endure the rigors of the wilderness canoe route. France was a nation of farmers, but Canada was too cold for many types of farming practiced in Europe, so some young men signed on as voyageurs. It was hard work, but they could earn 750 livres a season in wages and trade goods they could sell. A gun in Montreal at the time cost 20 livres and a shirt cost 2.

The decline of the canoe occurred abruptly in the 1820s as sailing ships came into use in greater numbers on the Great Lakes. Individual traders, such as Jolliet, couldn't afford expensive sailing

La Salle made his voyage of discovery to the mouth of the Mississippi River in 1676 and returned via the Chicago portage. This photograph of the 1976 reenactment shows canoes pulled onto a Lake Michigan beach with the modern Chicago skyline in the background. (Ralph Frese)

ships, but as trading companies came into existence in the second half of the eighteenth century and merged into ever-larger firms, they found schooners cheaper to operate than flotillas of canoes. By 1793 the Northwest Company of brothers Benjamin and Joseph Frobisher had a schooner on Lake Huron.

The death knell for the canoe occurred in 1821 when the Northwest and Hudson Bay companies amalgamated into an effective monopoly and over the next four years cut their payrolls by 58 percent. Although some canoes were still used on Canadian rivers or around ports like Chicago as lighters to get cargo over bars that had formed at the mouths of rivers, two-thirds of the voyageurs were out of work by 1830. Gurdon S. Hubbard, who ran the American Fur Company operations in Illinois country, gave up on the Chicago portage in 1824 and substituted pack animals for mules.

The Chicago Flood of 1849

The Chicago River, a rather sluggish stream navigable for only a few miles, somewhat surprisingly has been the site of a number of disasters over the years. The steamship Globe *blew up on the river in 1860, the Chicago Fire of 1871 was perhaps the single most destructive disaster on the Great Lakes in terms of vessels lost in a single incident, and the capsizing of the* Eastland *that took 844 lives in 1915 still reigns as the single worst calamity on the lakes in terms of loss of life. Then there was the bizarre subway flood in 1992 that caused an estimated $800 million in damage in Loop basements when a crew driving pilings poked a hole in the bottom of the Chicago River and into an abandoned freight tunnel system. The Chicago River's first disaster occurred way back in 1849 and was equally strange because it was caused by ice. This account of that incident is reprinted from A.T. Andreas's* History of Chicago from the Earliest Period to the Present Time (1885), *Vol. I, pp. 200–201.*

by A.T. Andreas

The flood which occurred March 12, 1849, was an event of most calamitous nature. For two or three days previous to that date the citizens of Chicago had been reading accounts of the remarkable rise of rivers in the interior of the State. The heavy snows of the winter had been followed by frequent and hard rains. Rock, Illinois and Fox rivers were threatening to burst their bounds and devastate the country. Their waters were higher than in 1838, and, in some localities, even than in 1833. The bridges on Rock River were nearly all swept away, and the Illinois had partially destroyed the village of Peru. The Desplaines River was also higher than it had ever been before. The following account of the flood, from the pen of Rufus Blanchard, is taken verbatim:

The last thing one might expect in Chicago, situated as it is on almost a dead level, is a flood, in one of the branches of the river. But this actually took place one fine morning in March, 1849. After two or three days of heavy rain, which had been preceded by hard snow storms during the latter part of the winter, the citizens were aroused from their slumbers by reports that the ice in the Desplaines River had broken up; that its channel had become gorged with it; that this had so dammed up its waters as to turn them into Mud Lake; that, in turn, they were flowing thence into the natural estuary, which then connected the sources of the South Branch of the Chicago River with the Desplaines. These reports proved to be correct. Further, it was also rumored that the pressure of the waters was now breaking up the ice in the South Branch and branches; that the Branch was becoming gorged in the main channel at various points, and that if something were not done, the shipping which had been tied up for the winter along the wharves would be seriously damaged. Of course each owner or person in charge at once sought the safety of his vessel, added additional moorings to those already in use, while all waited with anxiety and trepidation the result of the totally unexpected catastrophe. It was not long in coming. The river soon began to swell, the waters lifting the ice to within two or three feet of the surface of the wharves; between nine and ten a.m. loud reports as of distant artillery were heard towards the southern extremity of the town, the sounds proceeding from crashing timbers, from hawsers tearing away the piles around which they were vainly fastened, or snapping like so much packthread, on account of the strain upon them. To these in turn were succeeded the cries of people calling to the parties in charge of the vessels and canal boats to escape before it would be too late; while nearly all the males, and hundreds of the female population, hurried from their homes to the banks of the river to witness what was by this time considered to be inevitable, namely, a catastrophe such as the city never before sustained. It was not long before every vessel and canalboat in the South Branch, except a few which had been secured in one or two little creeks, which then connected with the main channel, was swept with resistless force toward the lake. As fast as the channel at one spot became crowded with ice and vessels intermingled, the whole mass would dam up the water, which, rising in the rear of the obstruction, would propel vessels and ice forward with the force of an enormous catapult. Every lightly constructed vessel would at once be crushed as if it were an eggshell; canal-boats disappeared from sight under the gorge of ships and ice, and came into view below it in small pieces, strewing the surface of the boiling water. At length a number of vessels were violently precipitated against Randolph Street bridge, then a comparatively frail structure, and which was torn from its place in a few seconds, forcing its way into the main channel of the river. The gorge of natural and artificial materials—of ice and wood and iron—kept on its resistless way to the principal and last remaining bridge in the city, on Clark Street. This structure had been constructed on piles, and it was supposed it would prevent the vessels already caught up by the ice from being swept out into the lake. But the momentum already attained by the great mass of ice, which had even lifted some of the vessels bodily out of the water, was too great for any ordinary structure of wood, or even stone or iron to resist, and the moment this accumulated material struck the bridge, it was swept to utter destruction, and with a crash, the noise of which could be heard all over the then city, while the ice below it broke up with reports as if from a whole park of artillery. The scene just below the bridge after the mate-

Photography was in its infancy in 1849, so the only images of the disastrous ice flood on the Chicago River were done years later by artists. This drawing of the disaster was originally published in the 1880s. (A.T. Andreas, History of Chicago*)*

rial composing the gorge had swept by the place just occupied by the structure, was something that bordered on the terrific. The cries and shouts of the people, the crash of timbers, the toppling over of tall masts, which were in many cases broken short off on a level with the decks of the vessels, and the appearance of the crowds fleeing terror-stricken from the scene through Clark and Dearborn streets, were sounds and sights never to be forgotten by those who witnessed them. At State Street, where the river bends, the mass of material was again brought to a stand, the ice below resisting the accumulated pressure, and the large number of vessels in the ruck, most of which were of the best class, the poorer ones having previously been utterly destroyed, helping to hold the whole together. In the meantime several canalboats, and in one instance a schooner with rigging all standing, were swept under this instantaneously constructed bridge, coming out on the eastern side thereof in shapeless masses of wreck, in the instance of the schooner, and of matchwood in the instance of canal boats.

Presently the ice below this last gorge began to give way, clear water appearing, while a view cut out into the lake showed that there was no ice to be seen. It was then that some bold fellows, armed with axes, sprang upon the vessels thus jammed together, and in danger of destruction.

Among the foremost and most fearless were: R.C. Bristol, of the forwarding house of Bristol & Porter; Alvin Calhoun, a builder, brother to John Calhoun, founder of the *Chicago Democrat* newspaper, and father of Mrs. Joseph K.C. Forrest; Cyrus P. Bradley, subsequently Sheriff and Chief of Police; and Darius Knight, still an employee of the city. These gentlemen, at the risk of their lives, succeeded in detaching the vessels at the east end of the gorge, one by one, from the wreck, until finally some ten or twelve large ships, relieved from their dangerous positions, floated out into the lake, their preservers proudly standing on their decks and returning, with salutes, the cheers of the crowd on shore. Once in the lake the vessels were secured, in some cases by dropping the anchors, and in others by being brought up at the piers by the aid of hawsers.

"Yesterday morning," says the *Democrat*, "the scenes in the river between Haddock's warehouse and Fort Dearborn, were most melancholy. Piles indiscriminately, in some places lay vessels, most of them as fine craft as float upon the lake, a mass of entangled wreck. Between them lay pieces of canal boats; a bow sticking out here and a stern there, and a mass of wreck in other places, ground up into pieces small enough for kindling wood. Tall spars here and there lay across the decks, and ropes, chains etc., in inextricable entanglement, lay knotted and twisted in all directions. Some forty crafts of various kinds were wrecked or injured, and formed one of the most costly bridges ever constructed in the West, and the only one that Chicago now boasts of crowds of people were at the wrecks yesterday, and crowded the decks of the various vessels. Many ladies were not afraid to venture over this novel causeway, beneath which the water roared, falling in cascades from the obstruction to another, the whole forming the most exciting scene perhaps ever witnessed. We understand several daguerreotype views of the vessels in their present position were taken.

The following additional particulars are gathered from the files of the Journal:

At about ten o'clock the mass of ice in the South Branch gave way, carrying with it the bridges at Madison, Randolph, and Wells streets—in fact, sweeping off every bridge over the Chicago River, and also many of the wharves. There were, in port, four steamers, six propellers, twenty-four brigs, two sloops, and fifty-seven canal boats, many of which have been either totally destroyed or damaged seriously. The moving mass of ice, canal boats, propellers, and vessels was stopped at the foot of Clark Street, but withstood the pressure only a moment, crashing vessels and falling spars soon giving note of the ruin which was to follow. A short distance below the river was again choked, opposite Kinzie's warehouse; vessels, propellers, and steamers were piled together in most indescribable confusion. A number of vessels are total wrecks, and were carried out into the lake a mass of debris. A boy was crushed to death at the Randolph Street bridge, a little girl was killed by the falling of a topmast, and a number of men are reported lost upon canal boats which have been sunk, and upon the ice and bridges as the jam broke up. The bridge over the lock at Bridgeport is gone. The wharves all along the river have sustained serious injury. A son of Mr. Coombs was lost at Madison Street bridge, and James L. Millard had his leg badly fractured while on board his vessel. One poor fellow on a canal boat waved his handkerchief as a signal of distress, about ten miles out, during the afternoon; but there was no boat which could be sent to his assistance. The vessels were without their riggings, and the engines of the steamers were out of order. The loss by the flood is thus estimated:

Damage to the city	$15,000
To vessels	$58,000
To canal boats	$30,000
Wharves	$5,000
Total	$108,000

The figures given are rather below than above the actual loss. The city went to work with a will to repair the great damage. In the meantime the river was crossed by a number of ferries. Besides the boat at Randolph Street, a canal boat lay across the river, upon which passengers were allowed to cross on payment of one cent each. The ferry at the Lake House, the safest and pleasantest on the river, was free. A schooner was used at Clark Street; fare, one cent. Mr. Scranton's old ferry was running at State Street; fare the same as the others. Other temporary appliances were brought into use to bridge over the inconveniences of the next few months. These ferries were generally overcrowded with passengers who, in their eagerness to cross, sometimes rushed aboard, recklessly, and it is a wonder that fatal results did not sometime follow.

Chapter Five

The Des Plaines River, 1673–1940

The Des Plaines River, now perhaps best known for the annual canoe races held on it, is certainly one of the nation's more obscure rivers. In fact, for much of its recorded history, it didn't even have a name on which everyone could agree. It was simply a stream that flowed from what is today the Chicago metropolitan area into the Illinois River near Channahon, roughly 45 miles southwest of the Loop. It had marginal utility as a navigable waterway, and as soon as the Illinois and Michigan Canal opened in 1848, it declined into the backwater it had been in pre-Columbian times. The I & M, of course, was superseded in 1900 by the existing Sanitary and Ship Canal. The Des Plaines, which flowed alongside the Sag for much of its route, became known because of its propensity to flood, an aggravation primarily to suburban residents who had built their homes on its banks.

Yet the Des Plaines made an important contribution to Chicago's history, first as part of a canoe portage and second as the route of the canals built for commercial navigation. The river is poorly documented, but CMS member Ralph Frese, the organizer of the canoe races back in 1957, sometime thereafter began a long search for background on the stream. He finally discovered the existence of a privately printed volume and obtained, on loan from the widow of its author, Hermon Dunlap Smith, the last remaining copy. This chapter is excerpted from that book.

by Hermon Dunlap Smith

The terseness of Juliet's rhetorical question, "What's in a name?" has implanted this thought so strongly in our minds, that we are almost ready to believe that there is little, if anything, in a name, although we are confronted with daily evidence to the contrary. In names, as in honorary degrees or military decorations, mere numbers add an impressive air of authority. Even the Governor General of the Bahama Islands sounds very important when he says, "I, Edward Albert Christian George Andrew Patrick David." If seven such rather common place names are enough for a Duke, a river which has had over forty colorful Indian, French, and English names can certainly claim a long and aristocratic ancestry.

The aristocracy of the Des Plaines River, however, does not depend on its many names, but rather on the important part it has played in the early history of the Continent. Interestingly enough, there is a close link between the two, in that the name of the River changed as its role changed, so that by following the development of the name, we also follow the history of the River.

The early importance of the Des Plaines arose from its being the connecting link in the Illinois-Chicago River route, by which it was possible for goods to pass from the Great Lakes to the Mississippi. As such, it was from earliest times one of the great "keys of the Continent." The importance of Chicago in the Twentieth Century has risen largely from the same geographical factors of strategic location which made the Des Plaines portage important in the Seventeenth.

The first white men known to have used the portage were Marquette and Jolliet in 1673, although Parkman believes LaSalle may have been there two years previous. Marquette's Journal provides the earliest record we have of the coming of Europeans to the site of Chicago, but in it neither the present Des Plaines nor the Chicago River are referred to by distinctive names. Marquette calls the Des Plaines simply the "river of the portage." The French priests and explorers for many years did not give it a name which was distinct from the two other rivers in the connecting water route, and usually called it "Illinois" or "Checagou." At this time, the Illinois, and hence the Des Plaines, was quite often called "La Divine," as a compliment to Count Frontenac, whose wife and her friend, Mademoiselle d' Outrelaise, were referred to as "Les Divines" at the Court at Quebec.

It was not for over a hundred years that the independence of the Des Plaines from the Illinois and the Chicago Rivers was recognized by a cartographer who gave it a designation of its own, "Plein." Curiously enough, this occurred during the same period in which the independence of the nation was established. This word, which can properly be used in French to refer to "high water" seems to be derived from the habit of the Des Plaines of overflowing its banks, a tendency which was as well known to Marquette by 1675 as to some of the modern "pioneers," whose cabins were flooded in the high water of 1938. Marquette has left a very colorful record of his unhappy experience. "On the 28th [March 28, 1675] the ice broke up, and stopped above us. On the 29th, the waters rose so high that we had barely time to decamp as fast as possible, putting our goods in the trees, and trying to sleep on a hillock. The water gained on us nearly all night, but there was a slight freeze, and the water fell a little, while we were near our packages. The barrier has just broken; the ice has drifted away; and, because the water is already rising, we are about to embark to continue our journey [March 31]....The very high lands alone are not flooded. At the place where we are, the water has risen more than twelve feet."

The first use of the modern name, Des Plaines, occurred about the time of the first serious consideration of the construction of a canal. Whether there was any connection between the two, it is impossible to say. The idea of a canal is as old as the knowledge of the River. In 1674, Father Dablon, quoting Jolliet's oral statement, had reported, "We could go with facility to Florida in a bark and by very easy navigation. It would only be necessary to make a canal by cutting through but half a league [one and a half miles] of prairie to pass from the foot of the Lake of the Illinois [Lake Michigan] to the River St. Louis [Des Plaines, Illinois]."

During the days of the French explorers down to comparatively modern times, there was, during periods of high water, a continuous passage from the Illinois River to Lake Michigan, through the Des Plaines River, the Chicago River, and "Mud Lake," a connecting slough about five miles long, located a little east of the site of modern Riverside.

In a letter of La Salle's written in 1685, which gives the first detailed description of the Portage, the situation is described as follows: "This is an isthmus of land . . . at the west of the Ilinois Lake. [Lake Michigan] which is reached by a channel [the Chicago River] formed by the junction of several rivulets, or

The Des Plaines River, used by the French voyageurs in the 1600s but not navigable to commercial vessels above the Sanitary and Ship Canal at Lockport in modern times, is the site of one of the oldest and largest paddle sports races in the nation. The Des Plaines River Canoe Marathon is held annually. (Ralph Frese)

meadow ditches [such as the Skokie]. It is navigable for about two leagues to the edge of the prairie, a quarter of a mile westward. There is a little lake [Mud Lake], divided by a causeway, made by the beavers . . . from which runs a stream, which, after winding about a half league through the rushes, empties into the River Checagou [Des Plaines] and thence into that of the Illinois. This lake is filled by heavy summer rains or spring freshets, and discharges also into the channel which leads to the lake of the Ilinois, the level of which is seven feet lower than the prairie on which the lake is. The river of Checagou does the same thing in the spring when its channel is full."

LaSalle realized, however, that such continuous navigation was possible for only a few days in the year, and for very small boats. He pointed out that in the summer there is often no water at all in the river, "as far as Fort St. Louis [Starved Rock]." Unfortunately, the tendency of the Des Plaines to extreme fluctuations in water level, which LaSalle's keen eye had noted, was not fully recognized by later engineers, with a consequent tendency to under estimate the length of the canal which would be required. Thomas Jefferson in his *Notes on the State of Virginia*, which was written in 1781 when Illinois was still part of Virginia, said, "The Illinois is a fine river, clear, gentle, and without rapids; insomuch that it is navigable for batteau to its source. From thence is a portage of two miles only to the Checagou, which affords a batteau navigation of sixteen miles to its entrance into Lake Michigan." Father Dablon's ditch through "about half a league of prairie" was ultimately found to require a canal of nearly one hundred miles at a cost of many million dollars.

It is a strange paradox that the relative importance of the Des Plaines as a highway of commerce should have begun to decline soon after the completion of the canal which was intended to crown its glory. The project for a canal was laid before Congress in 1808 by Albert Gallatin. In 1816 a treaty was negotiated with the Indians, under which they ceded a strip of land for canal purposes, extending from about ten miles on each side of the proposed route, from Lake Michigan to the confluence of the Fox and Illinois Rivers. This territory was surveyed by Captain John C. Sullivan in 1817 and 1818. The boundaries determined by him are still known as "the Indian Boundaries," and are commemorated by various road houses in the Chicago district, such as the Indian Boundary Tavern on the Skokie Highway near Niles Center.

After further surveys and many disappointing delays, construction and financing of the canal were finally voted by the Legislature in 1836. An additional appropriation was included in the notorious Omnibus Bill of 1837, which also provided an ambitious railroad and highway network to be built by the State, and, incidentally, for the transfer of the capital from Vandalia to Springfield. It is interesting to note that what is now the greatest railroad center in the world was entirely omitted from this extensive state railroad system, as its transportation needs were presumed to be cared for by the proposed canal. Any further action on these projects was indefinitely delayed when the banks suspended special payments in the spring of 1837 and the Panic ensued. By 1848, when the Illinois Michigan Canal was finally finished, the railroads were already beginning to overshadow the canals as arteries of commerce. In spite of the expenditure of over ten million dollars, the Canal was too small for lake boats, and connected with a river that was barely navigable during much of the year. It was nonetheless an important factor in the commercial development of Chicago.

Unfortunately, the Illinois and Michigan Canal channel was not of sufficient capacity to carry off the Des Plaines floods. On March 12, 1849, the year following the completion of the Canal, shipping was piled up in the harbor at Chicago by a severe flood in the Des Plaines. But what was more serious, the flow of the Canal was not adequate to take care of the increasing amount of sewage, even after the direction of the Chicago River had been reversed in 1871 by cutting down the summit level of the Canal. In spite of various makeshift efforts to improve the situation by auxiliary pumping arrangements, a serious Des Plaines flood in August, 1885, swept the sewage out into the Lake, and the city water pollution became so intolerable that a drastic remedy became necessary. This led to the creation of the Sanitary District of Chicago, under which the "Drainage Canal" was completed in January, 1900.

During the first quarter of the nineteenth century, while the fur trade was active in the Middle West, there were still frequent references to the River as a trade route, and to the terrific obstacles of the portage.

Gurdon Saltonstall Hubbard left in his autobiography [*The Autobiography of Gurdon Saltonstall Hubbard: Pa-pa-ma-ta-be, "The Swift Walker"* (1911)] a graphic description of the Mud Lake passage he made in 1818 as a voyageur of the American Fur Company.

Mud Lake drained partly into the Aux Plaines and partly through a narrow, crooked channel into the South Branch, and only in very wet seasons was there sufficient water to float an empty boat. The mud was very deep, and along the edge of the lake grew tall grass and wild rice, often reaching above a man's head, and so strong and dense it was almost impossible to walk through them.

Our empty boats were pulled up the channel, and in many places, where there was no water and a hard clay bottom they were placed on short rollers, and in this way moved along until the lake was reached, where we found mud thick and deep, but only at rare intervals was there water. Forked tree branches were tied upon the ends of the boat poles, and these afforded a bearing on tussocks of grass and roots, which enabled the men in the boat to push to some purpose. Four men only remained in a boat and pushed with these poles, while six or eight others waded in the mud alongside, and by united efforts constantly jerking it along, so that from early dawn to dark we succeeded only in passing a part of our boats through to the Aux Plaines outlet, where we found the first hard ground. While a part of our crew were thus employed, others busied themselves in transporting our goods on their backs to the river; it was a laborious day for all.

Those who waded through the mud frequently sank to their waist, and at times were forced to cling to the side of the boat to prevent going over their heads; after reaching the end and camping for the night came the task of ridding themselves from the bloodsuckers.

The lake was full of these abominable black plagues, and they stuck so tight to the skin that they broke in pieces if force was used to remove them; experience had taught the use of a decoction of tobacco to remove them, and this was resorted to with good success.

Having rid ourselves of the blood suckers, we were assailed by myriads of mosquitoes, that rendered sleep hopeless, though we sought the softest spots on the ground for our beds.

Those who had waded the lake suffered great agony, their limbs becoming swollen and inflamed, and their sufferings were not ended for two or three days.

It took us three consecutive days of such toil to pass all our boats through this miserable lake.

After experiences such as this, it is not surprising that Hubbard should have taken a leading part in the agitation for a canal.

In 1827, on his return to Chicago from some Indian negotiations in St. Louis, General Lewis Cass ascended the Des Plaines and reached Mud Lake at nightfall. According to his biographer:

It soon became so dark that they could not discern the bank. The lake was covered with the broad leaves of a kind of lily, favorite haunt of disgusting looking water snakes. A birch canoe cannot touch the shore without danger of having a hole broken through its slight material. . . . Finding they could not get to shore safely, the party spent the night upon that slimy sheet of water. Eighteen men in a small canoe, in a hot summer night, with the poles stuck

Canoeing has been a popular sport on the Des Plaines River for at least a century. This postcard from the early 1900s shows members of a canoe club based at west suburban Riverside. (Ralph Frese)

into the mud across the canoe to steady it, accompanied with the most intense rain and with the most intense thunder and lightning—such are the reminiscences which belong to that memorable night. And he who was not there, or has never been in such a place, if such another place there is, has little conception of what a formidable enemy a mosquito can be. During that long night—long in suffering, though short in the calendar, for it was in the month of July—their venomous attacks were beyond the power of description.

By 1835, the fur trade was rapidly passing, but the river was frequently mentioned by travelers, due to the necessity of fording it on the way to the west. Harriet Martineau, in her Society in America (1837), in describing a trip from Chicago to Joliet, writes:

A little further on we came to the River Aux Plaines, spelled on a sign board "Oplain." The ferry here is a monopoly, and the public suffers accordingly. There is only one small flat boat for the service of the concourse of people now pouring into the prairies.

Though we happened to arrive nearly first of the crowd of today, we were detained on the bank above an hour; and then our horses went over at two crossings, and the wagon and ourselves at the third. It was a pretty scene, if we had not been in a hurry; the country wagons and teams in the wood by the side of the quiet clear river; and the oxen swimming over, yoked, with only their patient faces visible above the surface. . . . As we proceeded, the scenery became more and more like what all travelers compare it to—a boundless English park. The grass was wilder, the occasional footpath not so trim, and the single trees less majestic; but no park ever displayed anything equal to the grouping of the trees within the windings of the blue, brimming river Aux Plaines.

In 1831, when John H. Kinzie made a trip from Fort Winnebago, Wisconsin, where Mr. Kinzie was an Indian Agent, to visit Mrs. John Kinzie, Sr. in Chicago, they pushed on so as to make the crossing at Barney Laughton's place (on the site of modern Riverside) by nightfall on a raw March evening. "It was almost dark when we reached Lawton's," Mrs. Kinzie writes in her Wau Bun, published in 1856. "The Aux Plaines was frozen, and the house was on the other side. By loud shouting we brought out a man from the building, and he succeeded in cutting the ice, and bringing a canoe over to us, but not until it had become difficult to distinguish objects in the darkness. A very comfortable house was Lawton's after we did reach it—carpeted and with a warm stove, in fact, quite in civilized style. . . . Mrs. Lawton was a young woman and not ill-looking. She complained bitterly of the loneliness of her condition and having been 'brought out there into the woods' . . . but we tried to comfort her with the assurance that things would grow better in a few years."

With steady emigration to the west and southwest, highways to a large extent displaced the undependable Des Plaines as a route of travel in those directions. However, in the 1830s the valley of the Upper Des Plaines was still the best way to reach the undeveloped region to the north, especially as the Green Bay trail was still in a primitive state. In 1834, Daniel Wright, the first white settler in what is now Lake County, built his house a short distance west of the Des Plaines River, about a mile south of the site of Half Day. Within a short time, a respectable colony of several families had settled along the relatively open west bank of the River in this neighborhood and further north. By September, 1835, Hiram Kennicott had opened a general store near the mouth of Indiana Creek (below Half Day). This river settlement is credited with most of the "firsts" of Lake County—the first wedding, the first death, the first sawmill, and the first Negro, who used to boast that he was the first "white man" to plant corn in the County!

Conjecture as to the origin of the present name of the River has been a favorite pastime of historians. Hurlbut, for example, says, "It is understood to receive its name from a variety of maple, which the Canadians call 'Plaine.'" Professor Keating, the historian of Major Long's second expedition (1823), also brings the maple tree into his report that "in Potawatomi the river is termed Sheshikmaoshike Sepe (which signifies *flumen arboris quae mingit*). This appellation," he explains for the benefit of mediocre Latin scholars, "is derived from the great quantity of sap which flows from this tree in the spring." To this day these sugar maples are landmarks of great beauty, especially in the fall, when they turn a gorgeous yellow-orange.

Since the River was call "Plein" for some thirty years before it was called "Des Plaines, " it seems a reasonable supposition that the latter was derived from the former, particularly in view of the similarity of their French pronunciations. In days when written references to the River were infrequent, a change from "Plein" to "Des Plaines" would not be improbable. The latter name, the River of the Plains, would be appropriate for a river which was about to be cut through the prairies, as Father Dablon had suggested one hundred and fifty years earlier.

There seems to have been an easy transition from the old name of "Plein," via "De Plein" (1817) and "Desplain" (1817) to "Des Plaines" (1819). It may appear strange that a period of about sixty years should have elapsed before this latter name was generally adopted. During these sixty years we find over a dozen corruptions in frequent use. In the leading early American atlas (Carey & Lea), the River is designated in different places in the same volume by four different names. The many variations are readily accounted for by the fact that this was the period during which the River was encountered by illiterate fur traders, emigrants, and travelers whose spelling would be entirely phonetic. This is in contrast with the earlier period when reference to the river would be largely by learned priests and cartographers, and the later period when, with the extension of its settlement, standardization of the name would be expected.

By a parallel tracing of the history of the River and its names, we find both divide themselves into three main periods. (See Table 1)

Throughout these changes in name and significance, covering nearly three centuries, the River has held faithfully to the characteristics which have given it an individuality—almost a personality—to those who have used it as a means of transportation, or more recently, as a playground. These characteristics are the extreme variations in its water level, from "Plein" to mud hole, and the peaceful beauty of the "grouping of its trees," which Harriet Martineau admired over a hundred years ago.

Table 1

SOME HISTORIC NAMES OF DES PLAINES RIVER

Date	Cartographer* or Historian	Designation
1674	Dablon, *The Jesuit Relations*	Saint Louis
1674	*Joliet or Raudin	La Divine or L'Outrelaize
1675	Marquette, *The Jesuit Relations*	River of the Portage
1682	La Salle	Checagou
1720	*Moll	Ilinese
1778	*Hutchins	Plein
1795	*Mann	Maple
1814	*Carey	Kiccapoo
1817	Storrow, *The Northwest in 1817*	De Plein
1817	Major Long, "Report"	Desplain
1819	*Melish	des Plaines
1822	*Carey & Lea, *American Atlas*	Riviere des Plaines
1825	Schoolcraft, *Travels in the Central Portion of the Mississippi Valley*	Des Plaines
1830	*Goodrich	Despatch
1831	Kinzie, Waubun	Aux Plaines
1835	Shirreff, *A Tour Through North America*	Oak Plains
1846	*Mitchell	des Pleines
1880	Hurlbut, *Chicago Antiquities*	Desplaines

Chapter Six

Summer on Our Lake of Many Colors

Margaret Fuller (1810–50) was a New England writer (author of Seeress, Caged Eagle, *and* Bandit's Bride, *among others) who enjoyed travel, an avocation that led to her untimely death when a ship on which she was returning from Italy was destroyed in a hurricane near New York. In 1843 she made a voyage from Buffalo to Chicago and wrote about it in her book* Summer on the Lakes. *Passages from this book, excerpted here by CMS member John Heinz, give not only glimpses of lake travel in the first half of the nineteenth century, by which time the canoe had been replaced by the steamboat as the preferred method of passenger travel, but also a picture of Chicago as a small yet bustling port. On this journey Ms. Fuller also visited the future suburb Geneva, Illinois, and found in it some of the same characteristics that charm women in the twenty-first century. Among the other places she visited on this trip were Milwaukee and Mackinac Island.*

Summer on the Lakes was originally published in 1844 in New York and was reprinted in 1999 by the University of Illinois Press. The excerpts begin with her arrival in Cleveland.

by Margaret Fuller

Next day, when we stopped at Cleveland, the storm was just clearing up. Ascending the bluff, we had one of the finest views of the lake that could have been wished. The varying depths of these lakes give to their surface a great variety of coloring. And beneath this wild sky and changeful lights, the waters presented kaleidoscopic varieties of hues, rich but mournful. Coming up the river St. Claire, we saw Indians for the first time. They were camped out on the bank. It was twilight, and their blanketed forms, stealing along the bank with a stride so different in its wildness from the rudeness of the white settler, gave me the first feeling that I really approached the West.

The people on the boat were almost all New Englanders, seeking their fortunes. They had brought with them their habits of calculation, their cautious manners, their love of polemics. It grieved me to hear these immigrants talking not of what they should do but of what they should get. We reached Mackinaw the evening of the third day, but to my great disappointment, it was too late and rainy to go ashore.

The fourth day on these waters, the weather was brighter, so that we could see to some purpose. At night was a full moon, and from the upper deck I saw one of the great steamboats come majestically up. It was glowing with lights, looking many-eyed and sagacious. In its heavy motion it seemed a dowager queen, and this motion becomes these smooth waters. In the afternoon we went ashore at the Manitou Islands, where the boat stops for wood. No one lives here except woodcutters for the steamboats. I had thought of such employment from its profound solitude, with service to the world, as possessing an ideal beauty. I think so still, after seeing the woodcutters and their slovenly huts.

We reached Chicago on the evening of the sixth day, a rather longer passage than usual.

Chicago, June 20, 1843.

There can be no two places in the world more completely thoroughfares than this place and Buffalo. They are the two valves that open and shut as the life blood rushes from east to west and back again. Since it is their office to be the doors, it would be unfair to expect from them much character. To make the best transmission of produce is their office, and the people who live there are suited for this—active, complaisant, inventive, business people. There are no provisions for the student or idler. To know the place you should be at work with the rest. The mere traveler will not find it profitable to loiter there as I did.

In Chicago I read again Philip Van Artevelde, and certain passages in it will always be associated with the deep sound of the lake. The moon would be full upon the lake, and the calm breath, pure light, and the deep voice harmonized well with the thought of the Flemish hero. When will this country have such a man? No thin idealist, no coarse realist, but a man whose eye reads the heavens while his feet step firmly on the ground, and his hands are strong and dexterous for the use of human implements. . . .

In Chicago I first saw the beautiful prairie flowers. They were in their glory the first ten days we were there. The flame-like flower I was taught afterwards, by an Indian girl, to call wickapee, and she told me too that its splendors had a useful side, for it was used as a remedy. Beside these brilliant flowers, which gemmed and gilt the grass in a sunny afternoon's drive near the blue lake, I enjoyed a sort of fairyland exultation never felt before. At first the prairie seemed to speak of the desolation of dullness. After the vast monotony of the Lakes, to come to this monotony of land— to walk and walk and run but never climb—oh it was too dreary for any but a Hollander to bear. How the eye greeted a sail or the smoke of a steamboat; it seemed that anything so animated must come from a better land where mountains gave religion to the scene.

We set forth in a strong wagon with the look of those used for transporting caravans of wild beasts, loaded with everything we might want—for buying and selling were no longer to be counted on—with a guide who knew by heart the country and its history and whose clear hunter's eye needed neither road nor goal to guide it. The first day brought us woods rich in the moccasin flower and lupine, and plains whose soft expanse was touched by the slow moving clouds. We came to the Fox River, a sweet and graceful stream. We reached Geneva [Illinois] just in time to escape being drenched by a violent thunder shower whose rise threw expression into the scene. Geneva reminds me of a New England village, as indeed in the neighborhood are many New Englanders of an excellent stamp. Such seem like points of light among the swarms of settlers, whose aims are sordid.

Next day, travelling along the river's banks, was an uninterrupted pleasure. We closed our drive at the house of an English gentleman, who has gratified his wish to pass the evening of an active day amid the quiet of country life. The young ladies were musicians and spoke French fluently, having been educated in a convent. Here in the prairie they had learned to take care of the milk room and kill the rattlesnakes that assailed their poultry yard.

Next day we crossed the river. We ladies crossed on a little footbridge, from which we could see the wagon pass over at the ford. A black thunder cloud was coming up. The sky and waters heavy with expectation. The motion of the wagon, with its white cover, and the laboring horses, gave just the due interest to the picture. We were a mile or two on our way when the violent shower obliged us to take refuge in a solitary house. In this country it is as pleasant to stop as to go on.

No heaven need wear a lovelier aspect than earth did this afternoon, after the clearing of the shower. We traversed the blooming plain, unmarked by any road. Our stations were not from town to town but from grove to grove. These groves floated like blue islands in the distance. In the afternoon of this day we reached the Rock River, and crossed at Dixon's ferry. To these beautiful regions Black Hawk returned with his band "to pass the summer," when he drew upon himself the warfare in which he was finally vanquished. No wonder he could not resist the longing to return to this home of beauty.

Chicago again. Chicago had become interesting to me now that I knew it as the portal to so fair a scene. I had become interested in the land, in the people, and looked sorrowfully on the lake on which I must soon embark. Now was the time to see the lake. The July moon was near its full, and night after night it rose in a cloudless sky above this majestic sea. The heat was excessive, so that there was no enjoyment of life, except in the night, but then the air was of that delicious temperature, worthy of orange groves.

The most picturesque objects to be seen in Chicago on the inland side were the lines of Hoosier [covered] wagons. These rude farmers travel along, sleeping in their wagons by night, eating only what they bring with them. In the town they look like foreign peasantry and contrast well with the Germans, Dutch and Irish. On the lake side it is fine to see the great boats come panting in from their rapid and marvelous journey. Especially at night the motion of their lights is very majestic. When the favorite boats, the *Great Western* and the *Illinois*, are going out the town is thronged with people from the south and west to go in them.

At Milwaukie as at Chicago, are many pleasant people, drawn together from all parts of the world. There are lures enough in the West for people of all kinds—the enthusiast and the cunning man, the naturalist, and the lover who needs to be rich for the sake of her he loves. During the fine weather the poor refugees arrive daily in their national dresses, all travel soiled and worn. The night they pass in rude shanties, then walk off into the country— the mothers carrying their infants, the fathers leading the little children by the hand, seeking a house where their hands may maintain them.

The bank of the lake is here a bold bluff, eighty feet in height. A little narrow path wound around the edge of the lake. Here, standing in the shadows I could appreciate its magnificent changes of color, which are the chief beauties of the lake-waters. It was fine to ascend into the lighthouse, above this bluff, and watch from thence the thunder-clouds which so frequently rose, or the great boats coming in. Approaching the Milwaukie pier they made a bend and seemed to do obeisance in the heavy style of some dowager duchess entering a circle she wishes to treat with especial respect.

These boats come in and out every day, and still afford general excitement. The people swarm down to greet them, to receive and send away their packages and letters. To me they seemed such mighty messengers, to give, by their mighty motion, an idea of the power and fullness of life, that they were worthy to carry dispatches from king to king. It must be very pleasant for those who have an active share in carrying on the affairs of this world to see them come in. It must be very pleasant to those who have dearly loved friends at the next station. To those who have neither business nor friends, it sometimes gives a desolating sense of insignificance.

Mackinac. Late at night we reached this island, so famous for its beauty. It was the last week in August, when the Chippewa and Ottowa tribes are here to receive their annual payments from the American government. As their habits make traveling easy and inexpensive, neither being obliged to wait for steamboats or to write to see whether hotels are full, they come hither by thousands.

As our boat came in, the captain had some rockets let off. This greatly excited the Indians, and their yells and wild cries resounded along the shore. Except for the flash of the rockets it was dark, and as I walked with a stranger to a strange hotel, through the midst of these shrieking savages, and heard the pants and snorts of the departing steamer, which carried away all of my companions, my sensations were somewhat of the dismal sort. Although it was pleasant too, in the way that everything strange is.

PART II

Inland Navigation on the Canal

Illinois and Michigan Canal boats originally were pulled by mules or horses but within a couple of decades made the transition to steam power. The steam barge Nashota *is shown loading grain at an elevator. (I&M Canal Archives, Lewis University)*

Chapter Seven

The Illinois and Michigan Canal

From the standpoint of the twenty-first century, when jet aircraft span the nation in hours and a tractor-trailer full of merchandise can travel round-trip between Chicago and La Salle in a single morning, the Illinois and Michigan Canal seems almost like ancient history. The idea of mules pulling boats for nearly 100 miles between those two cities is not something prominent in our collective memory more than a century and a half later. Yet when the I&M was planned in the 1820s, it represented the best that transportation technology could offer. When it finally opened in 1848, at the very end of America's canal age, however, it was already threatened by a superior technology—the railroad—that would within a few decades render it obsolete.

Nevertheless, the I&M Canal and its sister in the East, the Erie Canal, more than any other natural or man-made project caused the development of Chicago by linking together the two halves of the North American continent with a continuous transportation corridor. Professor John Lamb, a CMS member, is the leading scholar of the canal. This article was written by him for this book.

by John Lamb

The concept of a canal to connect the Great Lakes and the Mississippi River goes back to the seventeenth century, when in 1673 Louis Jolliet first suggested the possibility. It would be a while before the concept was fulfilled—a century and a half until the new state of Illinois finally got the project rolling and another quarter of a century until the canal actually opened for business. However, the increasing interest in the Illinois and Michigan Canal project in the nineteenth century stimulated the development of Chicago and northern Illinois. The I & M Canal took its name from the fact that it linked the Illinois River, a Mississippi tributary, with Lake Michigan.

The first survey of possible routes for the waterway was completed in 1825. In an effort to finance this ambitious project in the sparsely settled frontier of northern Illinois, the U.S. government granted the state and its canal commission not only the land needed for the canal and a 90-foot strip on each side but alternating five-mile sections of land on either side of the route. The idea was that the mere prospect of a canal would stimulate land sales that would finance its construction.

In 1830 two towns were laid out by the canal commissioners: Chicago at the eastern terminus of the proposed waterway and Ottawa at the confluence of the Fox and Illinois rivers at the canal's western end. That same year an auction of lots was held for both of the new towns, but the resulting revenues didn't even cover the cost of the survey. This was typical of the boom-and-bust cycles that dominated the canal's early history.

By 1833 Chicago was an incorporated town, however, and a land rush was on. In June 1836, when the reconstituted canal commission was ready to start building the canal, its land auction in Chicago produced markedly different results. For example, a lot on South Water Street sold for $21,000, and overall the auction produced several million dollars.

On July 4, 1836, Colonel William B. Archer, one of the three canal commissioners, turned the first shovel of dirt at Bridgeport where the canal would diverge from the Chicago River. The festivities of the day were highly stimulated when a barrel of whisky was poured into a nearby spring. But by 1839 the recession had set in and work stopped on the canal for six years.

The I&M Canal declined in importance as a commercial waterway late in the nineteenth century but increased in importance as a sanitary sewer. For that reason it was replaced in 1900 by the Sanitary and Ship Canal east of Lockport. The Calumet Sag Channel was dug for sanitation and shipping about two decades later and joined the Sanitary and Ship Canal at a junction (behind the lighthouse) just east of Lemont. The waterfalls are man-made— built to aerate the water treated upstream at sewage plants. (David M. Young)

Despite the economic ups and downs, the canal from 1830 to 1850 was responsible for encouraging settlement in the City of Chicago, the population of which grew faster than any other city in the nation. The I&M also helped the city become a transportation center. When the canal opened in 1848, the center of trade in the Midwest almost immediately shifted from St. Louis to Chicago.

Once construction started, the canal project itself was responsible for a great deal of the population growth. A large number of workers had to be hired, and those itinerant, unskilled laborers lived in workers' towns close to the project. They were mostly Irishmen forced to leave their native land because of such agricultural failures as the potato famine, and when the depression hit in their adopted country in 1839, canal construction halted, and many workers found themselves unemployed. This in turn created bad blood between two factions of the workers, the Corkonians and the Fardowners, who began attacking each other on the canal line. The townspeople and other settlers who felt threatened by the unarmed immigrants proceeded to take up arms and attacked the Irish gangs, killing several members and arresting others.

By 1845 the economy had improved to the point that construction resumed. The state had placed the canal in the hands of a three-man board of trustees—two appointed by the bondholders and one by the state—who were able to raise money and restart construction on the I&M. The canal would remain under the trustees' control until its debt was paid off in 1871.

The trustees in 1845 hurriedly hired hundreds of workers, again mainly Irish, to rush the completion of the canal. The result once again was worker unrest. On the Summit Level (Chicago to Lockport), the workers decided to strike, or have a "turn out," demanding a pay raise from $1 a day to $1.25 a day. The strike failed when the workers in the other two sections stayed on the job. Once the canal was completed in 1848, some of the workers settled along the canal as farmers or laborers, but most moved on to other jobs in construction.

Construction of the canal had an almost immediate effect on the landscape. The plats of Chicago and Ottawa were influenced by the rivers that served them. In Chicago's case the junction of the north and south branches of the Chicago River defined the heart of the town, and Ottawa was planned around the junction of the Fox and Illinois rivers.

But the canal towns that sprang up after construction began were influenced by that new waterway. For example, Lockport, the town selected as canal headquarters, had its principal streets running east and west parallel to the canal instead of north and south. The Des Plaines River (the canoe route that served the Chicago portage) just west of the canal was not much of an influence on Lockport's development and served mainly as an overflow reservoir for the canal.

Engineer William Gooding (1803–78) designed the canal so that it could generate hydraulic power from power basins in order to encourage industry powered by waterwheels to locate along its banks. The largest of these hydraulic basins was at Lockport, where entrepreneur Hiram Norton developed a large flour mill and other industries powered largely by water power. Norton was born in New England, immigrated to Canada (where he was involved in public works projects), and came to the Chicago area to take advantage of the new canal.

On April 17, 1848, the canal finally and officially opened when the General Fry arrived in Chicago from Lockport. It was one of the few locally built boats to ply the canal in its first year. Most were brought in from other canals, like the Erie. Captain Elisha Sly's 1848 journey to Chicago on his newly acquired Erie Canal boat turned into an adventure when he was hit by a storm on Lake Erie and was forced to put into Cleveland when his towline threatened to break. (See Chapter 9.)

In the first years of operation, the boats plying the 96-mile waterway from Bridgeport to La Salle carried mainly passengers. In 1850 the number of passengers that traveled from La Salle to Chicago was 17,000, while 22,614 traveled in the other direction.

There were various types of canal boats, but the packet boats carrying passengers got the most attention from contemporaries. The packets carried about 100 passengers; were usually hauled by horses at the brisk pace of six miles an hour; and traveled day and night on a 22-hour schedule to go from the Chicago River at Randolph Street to the Illinois River at La Salle, where paddle-wheeled steamboats would take travelers downriver to Peoria and St. Louis. In fact, the trips were typically somewhat longer than the schedule said.

Packet boats, as well as all other boats on the canal, were 98 feet long and 18 feet wide—the maximum dimensions determined by the size of the lock chambers. They were invariably wooden boats and were hauled by horses plodding at six miles an hour on the towpath adjacent to the canal. About every 15 miles the teams had to be changed, so mule barns to supply fresh teams were built at intervals along the canal.

The packet boats were towed by horses controlled by the driver and hitched to the boat by a 150-foot towrope. Evidently, the horses didn't always stick to the towpath, as a reporter from the *Chicago Democrat* recounted a show put on for some canal official and bankers from the East on a leisurely inspection trip in 1848:

> As though it was necessary to make the scene complete, and give the eastern gentlemen a full exhibition of canal performances on Friday morning, during a fine shower, the driver let his team get into "the drink" ahead of the boat, and they all swam to the opposite shore. There was some little alarm for the moment; but the driver managed with so much skill and coolness, that all was soon right again. He stuck by the teams and made them swim back, saying 'it was a matter of no consequence, nobody hurt, and it was all necessary to make up a life on the ditch, all confessed he was a perfect rough and ready.'

Canals built before or in the early years of the Industrial Revolution invariably were flanked by towpaths on which teams of draft animals pulled the canal barges. This drawing shows mules towing a barge on the I&M Canal. (I&M Canal Archives, Lewis University)

In the late nineteenth century, after the packets had disappeared and mules were the principal source of power, a mule boy could start at age 13. A future captain on the canal, William Schuler started driving mules for his uncle's boat. The four or five mules on each team were hitched in front of one another or in tandem. Schuler reported that he worked 13 or 14 hours a day and could either walk along the towpath or ride the last mule, which was called the saddle mule.

Although canal boats were generally preferred by the traveling public over the slower and less comfortable stagecoaches of the day, these packets were hardly luxurious. They were designed with one long cabin that ran most of the length of the boat—the place where meals were served and passengers slept. Luggage was stored on the roof. For sleeping the cabin was divided by a curtain, with the women and children on one side and the men on the other. The sleeping accommodations were bunks attached to the cabin walls and stacked three high, and because the cabin was less than seven feet high, the sleepers were stacked cheek by jowl. The atmosphere was noxious as the windows were tightly closed for fear of the night mists, which were believed to cause malaria or the ague.

It was not always smooth sailing on the canal. Some of the boats carried few supplies and ran on a schedule that depended on the mood of their operators. Describing a trip from Lockport to Chicago in 1848 in which a storm caused delays, canal engineer William Gooding said that vigorous reaction by the passengers was required to get the one-horse operation going. (See Chapter 10 for Gooding's full account of the trip.)

The regular packet boats were more orderly than what Gooding experienced. A Swiss engineer traveled on the canal in 1849 and noted that the packets had a crew of four: the captain, a cook, and two steersmen, one of whom had to be constantly on duty. However, he didn't mention the fifth crewman—the person who drove the horses along the towpath. This was an irregular job that required walking along the towpath at a pace brisk enough to keep up with the animals and was sometimes given to a passenger for free passage.

In 1850 an English Army officer, Arthur Cunyngham, anxious to shoot some native birds, took the canal boat *Queen of the Prairie* from Chicago to La Salle. He complained that at dinner the beefsteak was "tough as usual" and found sleeping difficult in such close quarters, with the one fellow passenger over his face, constantly threatening to fall through the canvas mattress. The air was stifling, but he recovered by rising early and going on deck to wash with fresh water from the canal.

The history of transportation technology suggests that passengers are the first traffic to develop on a new transit system—and the first to abandon it when an even newer rival appears, leaving the older system to subsist on freight. That is what happened in 1853 when the Chicago & Rock Island Railroad was built alongside the I & M from Joliet to La Salle. Although the Rock Island continued from Joliet to Chicago over a different route, the Chicago & Alton Railroad was built next to the canal from Joliet to Chicago in 1858.

The railroads, which were able to operate even during winter when the canal was frozen, very quickly took away the vast majority of the I & M's passenger business. The Rock Island even bought up some of the packet boats to discourage the competition. But the canal continued to thrive from the 1850s through the 1890s by carrying heavy freight: grain, lumber, coal, cut stone, and flour. Water transport, while usually slower than such land carriers as railroads, is invariably cheaper when it comes to hauling heavy commodities in bulk, material like stone and sand, which are not time sensitive.

The I & M's freight boats could carry about 150 tons and often were designed for the cargo they carried. For example, grain boats had two hatches, fore and aft of a central cabin where the crew lived. The boats that carried stone had the cabin in the stern and a lowered deck so the stone blocks could be carried on and off. The lake boats, which were towed from the canal out onto Lake Michigan, had upswept sterns to protect them from waves and a cabin and crew quarters below deck.

Freight crews were the same as those on the packets: a captain, a cook, two steersmen, and a full-time mule boy. Frequently, all crew members were related, so that the captain's wife was the cook and the steersmen might be his brothers, cousins, in-laws, or sons. The captain often owned the boat. This was true of the crew of Joseph Foster, who was born in the 1850s on the canal somewhere between Morris and Seneca. He operated a boat on the canal until the 1890s; then he captained the converted canal boat *City of Henry* on the Illinois River. It was steam powered and had a high pilothouse that prevented it from clearing the bridges on the canal. Foster continued on the waterways until his death in 1916.

Grain was the most lucrative traffic on the I&M after the passenger trade shifted to the railroads, and its movement in increasing quantities from the developing prairie had a profound effect on trade patterns in the United States. In 1848 when the canal opened, most of the grain from America's heartland was shipped down the Mississippi River through St. Louis to New Orleans. Once the I&M opened, Chicago became a major player in the trade. Grain moved east, not south, via the Great Lakes, Erie Canal, and Hudson River to New York.

The new route was able to handle grain more efficiently than the river steamboats that passed through St. Louis. On the rivers grain was still transported in sacks, which had to be laboriously and expensively loaded and unloaded by hand by large gangs of workmen. On the Illinois and Michigan Canal, the newly developed warehouse steam elevator meant grain could literally be poured into canal boat and ship hulls. The first elevator on the canal—a 100,000-bushel-capacity stone structure in Lockport—was built by Hiram Norton in 1849–50. The grain was hauled to the elevator in wagons by the farmers, dumped into an underground hopper, and transferred by belt scoops to a head house on the roof, from whence it was transferred to various bins by gravity. It was then dumped, again by gravity, into the holds of canal boats headed to Chicago or points west. By 1854, as a result of this innovation, the Chicago Board of Trade was measuring grain by weight instead of by the bushel. The railroads eventually broke into this trade but on a large scale only after the Civil War.

Another Illinois product that was hauled into Chicago on the I & M was coal. The canal had begun tapping this resource in the 1850s, when mining began in La Salle County. Another canal commodity was lumber. The demand for precut lumber in the growing towns in the interior fueled this industry.

The horse-and-buggy era ended on the canal long before it did on America's highways. In the 1870s the canal boats were converted to steam. Screw propellers, then coming into wider use on the Great Lakes and oceans, were ideal for the canal because they created very little wake compared with the side or stern wheelers that had been navigating the rivers and lakes for years. Wakes tended to erode the canal banks. The result of the introduction of steam power was that fewer boats were hauling more freight, because a steamer could tow or push as many as two other boats. The highest tonnage hauled on the canal was in 1882.

The professions associated with the canal were diverse. The lockkeeper was responsible for opening and closing the lock gates. There were 17 lift locks on the canal when it opened in 1848, but in 1871 the ones in Bridgeport and Romeoville were removed. The lockkeepers (or lock tenders) were paid $300 a year and had free use of the lockkeeper's house. When the canal was frozen over in the winter, they did other work on the canal.

A lockkeeper's job was not as sedate as it sounds. In 1849 a mob in Joliet threw the lockkeeper there into the canal when he refused to close the gates on Lock No. 5. In 1851 the lockkeeper at Marseilles had a disagreement with the crew and passengers of the packet *Montazuma* and contrary to canal rules they locked their boat through the lock, all the while verbally abusing him. After the demise of the packet business, the life of a lockkeeper was much more leisurely, as the boats did not usually run at night.

There were other sundry jobs on the canal. From 1870 to 1904 James Flavin worked as a caulker at one of the Lockport yards

Gates on the original locks on the I&M Canal were operated by hand. This drawing is of the lock at Summit, the highest point on the canal. (I&M Canal Archives, Lewis University)

that built or repaired boats. New construction of canal boats ended in the 1880s as the canal went into decline, but Flavin stayed at the Western Stone Company yard repairing that company's vessels. It was seasonal work; he spent his winters, when the canal was closed, as a brewery caulker in Chicago.

No sooner was the canal completed than its supporters began agitating to enlarge it. Because the state of Illinois did not have the finances for this, advocates naturally began looking to the federal government, which at the time didn't support internal improvements in the states unless they were deemed important to the whole nation. The pleadings of then Illinois Congressman Abraham Lincoln, who told the House of Representatives that although the I&M traversed only a portion of the state, it was used to transport sugar and other products from New Orleans to the East Coast and was thus a national canal, fell on deaf ears. Lincoln continued to support the canal into the 1850s by acting as a paid lobbyist.

When the Civil War came along and Lincoln was president, national defense was cited as a reason the federal government should enlarge the canal. According to one somewhat tenuous argument published by the Chicago Board of Trade in 1862, English gunboats could easily take control of the Great Lakes, but by enlarging the I&M Canal, the United States could have gunboats ready to defend Lake Michigan and other ports from the potential depredations by an English fleet in Canada.

By the time this photograph was taken on the I&M Canal in Joliet in 1890, the canal was in serious decline. (I&M Canal Archives, Lewis University)

In 1863 the National Ship Canal Convention held in Chicago endorsed the enlargement of both the I&M and Erie canals for purposes of national defense; however, no federal support was forthcoming. In 1866 Congress finally appropriated some money for a survey of the I&M and the Illinois River to determine how to make them navigable by the largest steamboats. In his 1868 report on the survey, Brevit Major General J.H. Wilson made no bones about the continued threat from the English to the north and recommended that the government must either enlarge the I&M to accommodate gunboats or "prepare for the annexation or conquest of Canada." Despite the dire warning from Wilson, neither recommendation was acted on.

Ultimately, sanitation, not national defense, was the issue that precipitated action. In 1871 the continental divide that separated the Chicago River from the Des Plaines was breached by the so-called deep-cut excavation, reversing the flow of the Chicago River so that it carried Lake Michigan water (and Chicago

sewage) inland to the Mississippi River. The river initially emptied into the lake. Although sanitation rather than navigation was
the principal reason for the improvement, it also aided navigation
on the I & M Canal and the Illinois River and eliminated the two
summit locks at Bridgeport and Romeoville.

The newly formed Metropolitan Sanitary District of Chicago
launched an even bigger project in the 1890s to shift sewage
downstate. This was the Sanitary and Ship Canal, a massive project to dig a new waterway 18 feet below the level of Lake
Michigan to divert enough water from the lake to prevent
Chicago sewage from contaminating the city's drinking supply
from Lake Michigan. Despite the name, Sanitary and Ship Canal,
no navigation was possible west of Lockport when it opened in
1900. That resulted in objections being raised in both the United
States and Canada, the opposition claiming the new canal violat-
ed federal statutes dating back to the Northwest Ordinance of
1785, which said that water from navigable waters could only be
diverted for the purpose of navigation.

As a result, the S & S Canal in 1906 was extended a couple of
miles, and a lock and hydroelectric plant were added. That resulted in the I & M Canal east of Lockport being deprived of water
and closed to navigation. Navigation continued on the I & M west
of Lockport, but it was difficult because the water supply was limited and the canal depth was reduced to four feet (from its original depth of six feet), reducing the carrying capacity of the canal
barges. Nevertheless, some traffic remained. In 1913 Sterling
Morton experimented with the barging of salt between Chicago
and Rock Island via the I & M and the newly opened Hennepin
Canal across western Illinois. He found the experiment was successful, costing less than transporting by the railroad, even though
the shallower canal limited the cargo capacity and the docking of
barges.

In the 1920s Illinois decided to replace the western section of
the I & M (Joliet to La Salle) by making the Des Plaines and
Illinois rivers navigable between those two cities. That was done

by building a series of locks and dams to create a slack water navigation channel on the two rivers. However, Illinois ran out of money for the project during the Depression, so it was taken over by the federal government and completed in 1938. The Illinois Waterway, as the project is still called, put the I&M Canal out of business, but since the early twentieth century there had been proposals to put the rapidly declining canal to other uses by converting it from commerce to recreation.

There were even proposals to turn it into a superhighway. In a 1905 pamphlet the Lockport Woman's Club proposed using the canal right-of-way for a below-grade limited-access highway. It would be a highway below grade with no crossroads. Although the bulk of the canal couldn't be dried up elsewhere because its construction had irreversibly altered the natural drainage, a short stretch of the Stevenson Expressway near Summit was ultimately built on the canal bed.

The alternative proposal to develop the canal for recreation dated back to the late nineteenth century. At Rock Run, a few miles outside of Joliet, an amusement park served by excursion boats on the canal and trains was built in conjunction with the Rock Island Railroad. At Channahon a number of recreational facilities, including a racetrack and dance hall, were built alongside the canal. However, these facilities went out of business with the rise of automobile transportation.

A different concept of recreational use came during the Depression and the New Deal era. Under Governor Henry Horner, the state was able to get a large commitment from New Deal agencies like the Civilian Conservation Corp (ccc) and the Works Project Administration (wpa) to launch an ambitious regional program to link together by means of the I&M such state parks as Starved Rock and Buffalo Rock, as well as forest preserves in Cook and Will counties and municipal parks. The program included building lodges, canal picnic shelters, canoe landings, and hiking and bicycling paths. Many of the locks and lock houses were rebuilt and restored. The canal office at Lockport was designated as a museum.

The New Deal projects ended in 1941 when the United States entered World War II, and after the war the state of Illinois turned its attention away from recreational to industrial development. The accomplishments of the 1930s were left to rot. However, in the 1970s and 1980s recreation became important again. In 1984 the Illinois and Michigan Canal was declared by Congress to be a National Heritage Corridor, the first in the country. The I & M's emphasis once again became recreation and historic preservation.

Chapter Eight

Days of Old on the Canal

Due mainly to the movies, the popular image of the Wild West is one of stagecoaches rumbling across the plains being pursued by Indians, brawls in saloons in one-horse towns, and desperados robbing unwary travelers. Decades before the West was settled, Chicago was at the nation's western frontier, and the environment along its new canal was a precursor of the type of activity that Hollywood screenwriters later recounted ad nauseam. There were saloons, fights, and robberies.

This article from the Chicago Tribune *of May 21, 1899, describes the wild and woolly nature of Bridgeport, now a Chicago neighborhood but once a town at the eastern end of the canal, and the competitive shenanigans of the men who made their living on the Illinois and Michigan Canal. CMS member John Lamb dug up this old clip from the* Trib *and presented it for reprinting in this volume.*

"Is there any bottom to this road?"

"If you had larger wagon wheels you'd be in a fair way of findin' out. Bound for China?"

"No; Joliet."

"Well, keep your spirits up."

"That's what I'm tryin' to do. I've got two barrels of the best whisky in this wagon that ever left Chicago by Archer road, but how to keep em is the question that's worryin' me."

"This conversation led to the establishment of the first business house in Bridgeport," said John Scanlan, the oldest boatman on the Illinois and Michigan canal, who, hale and hearty, despite his fifty years of service, still braves the treacherous waters of the "raging canawl" and commands the *Terror*, one of the Western Stone company's boats.

One of those barrels of whisky constituted the first stock of goods ever offered for sale in what is now one of the most populous and enterprising sections of the great City of Chicago.

"Doubtless I'm the only living witness to that conversation," continued Mr. Scanlan, smiling complacently as he surveyed the comfortable fittings of his little cabin. "Probably I don't remember it at first hand, though I've heard it so frequently repeated that I seem to, for it took place in the spring of '38, when I was only one year old.

"My parents came from Ireland, and, after stopping long enough in Albany to make me a native-born American, moved on to Chicago. Ground for the first great improvement in the West— the Illinois and Michigan Canal—had been broken on July 4, 1836, amid a wonderful display of oratory and an almost equally surprising disappearance of whisky, and my father, Michael Scanlan, who had no great love for work but felt obliged to live, went there to seek employment.

"On the Archer road, near the present canal locks, there was a small house that had been erected by a German laborer, who, under the combined influence of ague and rheumatism, offered to sell it for $20. My father borrowed the amount from three Irish friends, purchased the property, moved in, and went to work with a pick and shovel on the canal.

Bridgeport's First Business House

"Within a month the conversation I have quoted was carried on between an enterprising liquor dealer and my mother. She helped the man unload one of the barrels and he managed to get through the mud with the other one. Returning a little later, he sold the barrel that stood in front of our door to my mother, on exactly what terms I cannot say, and resumed his journey. My mother rolled the cask into our front room, borrowed two glasses and a tin cup from our nearest neighbor, hung out a rude sign and the first business house of the future Bridgeport was open to the public.

"Archer road was the great thoroughfare connecting the recently incorporated City of Chicago with the towns and farms to the south and west, and many thirsty travelers stopped at our door. My father was a peculiar man; he had no great liking for hard work, and when he came home on Saturday night and found my mother possessed of nearly $40, he promptly threw up his job, took charge of the business, and became one of the pioneer tavern keepers of Bridgeport."

The history of the Illinois and Michigan canal has been many times written, but the present residents of Chicago have little conception of its importance in early days; of the manner in which it was operated, the unique characters it gathered together, and the excitement and sport it afforded. From John Scanlan, already quoted; P.E. McDonald, chief engineer of the Bridgeport pumping station, who worked on the canal as a boy nearly half a century ago; Fernando Jones, who was present at the grand powwow sixty-three years ago, when the orator of the day was dragged from the platform for prophesying that in 1900 Chicago would be a city of 100,000 people; and other "old-timers" much curious and interesting information touching Bridgeport and the early days of the canal has been secured.

The Illinois-Michigan canal had its inception in an act of Congress passed March 2, 1827, through the efforts of [U.S. Representative] Hon. David P. Cook, for whom Cook county was named, by which some 284,000 acres of public land, a considerable portion of which lay within the limits of the future City of Chicago, were granted to the State of Illinois for the purpose of constructing a canal from Lake Michigan to the Illinois river.

After much agitation and several unfortunate beginnings an act of the Illinois Legislature was adopted February 10, 1835, which authorized the Governor to negotiate a loan of $500,000 with which to begin the work. It was the original design to construct a ship canal and a portion of it was dug deep. The small tax provided by the act did not produce money enough to pay the interest, and, after a time, scrip was issued, which soon became worthless.

State Disgrace Averted

"To the genius and farsightedness of Justin Butterfield, one of Chicago's earliest and ablest lawyers," said Fernando Jones, "the ultimate completion of the canal must be ascribed. The major portion of the bonds were held in England, and, when a scheme for reorganization was under discussion by the leading men of Chicago and the State, it was proposed to repudiate these obligations. To this policy Mr. Butterfield strenuously objected, and through his efforts state disgrace and ultimate failure of the enterprise were averted. In the revised scheme a tax of two mills was levied to pay the interest on the old bonds, and Englishmen became liberal buyers of the new issue."

Bridgeport, which owes its name to the first bridge built over the river in that section, near Ashland avenue, was purely a creation of the canal, the eastern terminus of which was located there. As a preliminary to the great work, it was decided to build a road from Chicago to what is now Lockport. This diagonal thoroughfare, which involved an outlay of some $40,000 of canal funds, was styled Archer's Road, in honor of William B. Archer, one of the commissioners. This soon became Archer Road, and later the Archer avenue of the present day.

Founded at a time when the advisability of running a daily stage from Chicago to Twenty-second street was being gravely discussed as a business venture, and finding a few supporters, Bridgeport speedily became a great attraction, far more generally visited by townsmen and strangers than is the Drainage Canal of this day. As the work progressed, a struggling village grew up around the Locks, which many predicted would eventually become a rival of Chicago. Originating in the venture of Mrs.

Michael Scanlan, business rapidly increased, the line of trade in which she engaged continuing to lead all others. Indeed, from the day when the mud of the newly constructed road compelled the unloading of the first barrel of whisky, Bridgeport has never been regarded as a temperance place.

Among the business houses and popular resorts of those early days are the following, the names of many of the proprietors having been perpetuated in that section of the city: The Bowes Saloon, ever popular with the canal men; the Joice House, near the locks, which was opened by William Joice, an old-timer, who maintained, in addition to the regulation saloon, a handball court and bowling alley; the saloon and grocery of Ed Butzer, which became the recognized headquarters of boatmen; the Walsh House, built in 1848 by an Eastern man named Wheelock, and sold two years later to Peter Walsh, who bestowed upon it his name; and the saloon and grocery of John Flemming.

The Canal House, built by Sargent in 1848, was the great resort of Bridgeport, being to that village what the Sherman was to Chicago. It was a large frame structure of two stories and stood at the corner of Ashland avenue and Levee street, near the spot where the horses stopped towing. This speedily became the political headquarters—Lincoln, Douglas and other prominent leaders holding many meetings and conferences there. Here many notable persons, including the Prince of Wales, were entertained—for no caller at Chicago thought of leaving without paying a visit to Bridgeport and the great canal.

"Bridgeport was a wild spot in my boyhood," said Engineer McDonald. "Wolves were numerous and many a man has had the run of his life to escape them. My father, Terrence McDonald, was the justice of the peace, and the lawless element brought in by the canal gave him plenty of employment. The country was but sparsely settled for the most part by struggling farmers. I recall one notable exception. This was Daniel Burke, who may well be described as the magnate of that section. He owned an immense farm, located in the vicinity of California avenue and the canal.

Burke was a most hospitable man, keeping open house to all comers. He had a fine home, splendid stock and maintained a coach and four. The days when he drove into Bridgeport on his way to the city were notable ones, for he was a royal entertainer. His fine turnout and portly figure were almost equally well known in Chicago, where he used to sometimes stay for a week, spending the proceeds of the sale of a bunch of cattle with veritable prodigality. Traditions of this remarkable and eccentric man are still current in Bridgeport, while some old residents, like myself, remember him well."

The pumping works at Bridgeport are not, as many people believe, a comparatively new institution; they are as old as the canal. The necessity of pumping water into the canal that a sufficient level to properly float boats might be maintained was recognized by the engineers and formed a part of the original plan. The first plant, which raised the water by means of immense wheels, was installed by Engineer Guthrie, father of Ossian Guthrie, well known in mining and engineering circles. It was first put into operation on February 10, 1849, after the canal had been practically completed.

The greatest day that Bridgeport ever saw or is ever likely to see was April 10, 1848, when the first boat, the General Fry, arrived from Lockport. All of Bridgeport, and a large proportion of Chicago, was there to witness the final triumph of an undertaking that had been before the people for a quarter of a century and had met with manifold delays, disappointments and failures. There may have been times when Rome howled louder and consumed more drink than did Bridgeport on this occasion, but not in proportion to the number of people engaged. It is still a day from which old settlers make their reckonings.

Rival Canalboat Lines

The winter and early spring preceding the opening of the canal was a season of great activity. Companies were organized, horses

Although northern Illinois is relatively flat, there is a difference in elevation of more nearly 150 feet (up and down) in the 97 miles between the Chicago River and the Illinois River at La Salle. That required the construction of 17 locks to raise and lower canal boats over the terrain. This one at Lockport, CA. 1896, with the steam canal boat Niagara *towing a barge, began the 140-foot descent to the Illinois River. (I&M Canal Archives, Lewis University)*

purchased and boats built. Most of the latter work was carried on at Chicago and Lockport. Three lines of canal boats were put into operation—the John L. Chapin line, the Charles Walker line, and the Chicago and St. Louis line. In 1850 these were consolidated into what was commonly known as the "Big Line," of which Henry George was the agent. During the two years that the sharp rivalry continued a great deal of trouble occurred, the agents, captains, drivers and crews of the different lines all struggling for advantage and stopping at nothing to attain it.

"The boatmen, who were made up of almost all nationalities, were a rough set," said Mr. Scanlan, "and fighting was extremely common. For the most part the captains were Eastern men and were about the most dishonest and unscrupulous lot with whom I ever came in contact, though there were, of course, some exceptions to this rule. They turned everything to their own advantage, and were always collecting something in the way of extras. To get a boat through on time was often an important matter to the owner of the cargo and money was freely paid to expedite matters.

"Scaling was the means principally employed to effect this. Scaling was the giving of tips to the drivers to induce them to work their horses up to a higher rate of speed. No set of men and boys ever better understood the importance of their position, or were better qualified to turn it to account than the drivers on the old-time canal. They were natty, well-dressed fellows, with sweethearts in every canal village. Their pay was not large, drivers of three horses receiving $13 per month and their board; but a lad who knew how to quicken the lagging feet of a lazy horse earned more than that amount in tips. Sleeping at the relay houses, they took their turns in going out with boats. It was a happy-go-lucky life, monotonous at times, yet on the whole affording a great deal of excitement."

The packet lines were made up of green and red boats, from the lights displayed. The green boats, of which there were five originally, carried the mails. They were drawn by three horses, which were changed more frequently than those on the freight boats; about every twelve miles. The time from Chicago to La Salle was 24 hours. There they connected with a line of steamboats on the Illinois River for St. Louis. The time from Chicago to St. Louis was five days. The fare, which included good board, was $3 to La Salle and $8 to St. Louis. These boats often made from eight to ten miles an hour, the horses, under the inspiring influence of liberal scaling, being driven at a trot and gallop.

Racing Was Exciting Sport

The freight boats made slower progress. In the early days all sorts of goods and products were carried on the canal; grain, cordwood, cattle, sheep hay and all kinds of farm produce being transported to the city, while almost every conceivable variety of merchandise was shipped in the opposite direction. Under such circumstances jams and blockades were matters of every day occurrence, and it was often possible to cross the canal by stepping from one boat to another.

Racing was common and it was not unusual for one boat to pass another, particularly when a packet overtook a slow-running freighter. This was accomplished by urging the rear boat forward at the highest speed, then slackening the line and permitting it to pass under the leading boat. Under the most favorable conditions this was not easily done, and the difficulties were multiplied when the captain and driver of the obstructing boat were averse to the proceeding, as they generally were, in the case of rival lines coming in conflict. In such an event the line was liable to become tangled or mysteriously cut, and almost innumerable fights resulted from such attempts.

Traveling on the canal at this period was decidedly interesting. The boats were roomy, the sleeping accommodations good, and the meals excellent. At one time fully 250 boats were engaged in the grain trade alone, and an enormous traffic was carried on.

The canal attracted large numbers of rough characters; swindling and robbery were quite common, while gambling was the almost universal recreation of many and the regular calling of a goodly number. The hotels along the line were always well patronized

The long-abandoned I&M Canal locks in down-town Lockport have been preserved and can still be seen in the twenty-first century. (David M. Young)

during the boating season. Among the popular hostelries were Morse's Hotel at Lockport, the National at Joliet, and the Hopkins at Morris.

"As a rule, from captains to scullions, canal boatmen were honest among themselves," said Mr. Scanlan, "but it was an altogether different matter where outsiders were concerned. I've seen many a man towed in the water behind a boat for stealing from a mate, but never for robbing, short-changing, or in any manner wronging an outsider. Peddlers were the delight of boatmen; that is, they delighted to misuse and rob them, and a pack of goods marked a peddler as common prey. Indeed, after the first year, few of the craft patronized the canal."

Crowded Out by Steam

For a few years boating on the Illinois and Michigan canal was a profitable business and everybody connected with it, from owners to drivers, made money. Chicago was growing rapidly and the canal became a great public thoroughfare, open to all boats that were operated in accordance with the regulations and which paid the quite modest mileage charges. These conditions challenged competition and boats rapidly multiplied. In 1852 R.G. Parks of Cleveland, O., the owner of twelve boats in the old crosscut canal of Pennsylvania, brought them through the canals of Ohio to the Ohio river, then down that stream, and up the Mississippi and Illinois rivers to La Salle, where they went into service on the canal as freight and passenger boats. On this long and winding voyage they were towed by the steamer *Beaver*, which was afterwards taken back to the Ohio.

The Illinois-Michigan canal was constructed many years too late, and when it was opened railroads had already begun to invade Chicago and the West. These, particularly the Chicago and Alton, speedily absorbed the great bulk of the passenger and carrying business and the canal sank back to a secondary place, from which it has never emerged. A large amount of building stone and some grain is still brought in by steam-propelled boats, but the days of jams, scaling, gambling, robbing countrymen, towing thieves, and despoiling paddlers are gone forever.

Bridgeport has become an important portion of the mighty city, and from the spot beside the old locks, where brawny smiths once swung heavy hammers and sang and swore in a discordant melody as they shod canal horses, the eastern terminus of the great drainage canal can be seen.

Chapter Nine

Life on the Canal

Because Chicago was a small frontier town and northern Illinois was sparsely settled, the state in the 1830s had to import laborers to build the Illinois and Michigan Canal and then a decade later had to bring in boatmen to operate it. One such import was Elisha Sly, who had worked the Erie Canal in New York State since he was a boy in 1834 and decided to seek his fortune on the new canal in Chicago when it opened in 1848.

CMS member John Lamb found in the canal archives in Lockport, Illinois, Sly's December 14, 1896, account of his adventures as an early boat captain. It is reprinted from the winter/spring 1996 issue of the Chicago Maritime Society's newsletter.

by Elisha Sly

I commenced boating on the Erie canal when a boy of ten years old, in the year 1834. I worked along up until I got a boat to run and then I owned several boats off and on, and the last boat I had built was called the "Leg Boat," I run from Buffalo to New York city. In the winter of 1847 I laid in New York city, in the spring of 1848 I loaded with merchandise for Buffalo and when I got to Buffalo the boys were talking about the Illinois and Michigan canal. Then I got it in my head I wanted to see that canal and I made a bargain with Capt. Sprige, steam boat "Onider" for $200 to tow my boat to Chicago and if he lost me before he got me there he was to charge me for as far as he towed me. We run into Cleveland with three feet of water in my boat. On account of having a head sea, it worked the oakum out of her bottom. I put her on the dry dock and had her caulked and then started out for Chicago again. I had 350 feet of tow line out behind the steamer.

I rode every rod from Buffalo to Chicago on the canal boat "G.B. Danles." There was not money enough in the country to get a man to come with me to spell me. There had to be a man on the canal boat all the time when she was running. She was in all shapes on the takes. I landed in Chicago on the Fourth day of May, 1848. There wasn't much yet doing on the Illinois and Michigan Canal. I took some salt on for La Salle.

I had the second boat that locked through the La Salle locks. There was only three feet of water in the canal then. I seen that my boat was no use here, she drew to much water. I got my salt off at LaSalle and then went along side of a steamer off of the river and loaded with Mexican soldiers [ed. prisoners of war]. I took on 255 for Chicago most of them were down with the yellow fever. That was in the spring that the Mexican war broke up. I made four different graves from La Salle to Chicago. When I had seven or eight of them dead I would run to the bank and dig a hole and put them in.

Then next I sold the boat to a Wisconsin man, but never got anything for it. Then I was busted. I commenced packet boating. Here I boated on packets until the Rock Island railroad got built then the Rock Island road bought the packet company out. Then all the boys on the packets wanted to go on the railroad; I could go, but I went lock tender at lock they called No 2, then I staid there until Horace Singer went into the stone trade in Lemont. Then I took a boat to run for him. After I had left him I bought a grain boat and have been boating ever since off and on and have owned and built boats and rebuilt boats. Then I made another wild trip where there never was a canal boat. I made a contract to take 250,000 feet of lumber from Chicago to Osage City within seven miles of Jefferson city with two canal boats, where there never was a canal boat and never will be again. After making that trip I run out of boats and was busted again.

Then I went to work ashore and got a start again, then I went and seen all the merchants along the canal, they were paying their railroad from 16 to 35 cents a hundred for freight, I told them I could take it for 15 cents a hundred all around; and then I went and had a boat built, a steam boat 95 feet long and 12 feet wide that run 10 miles an hour, after the second year the railroads went around and contracted with them for 10 cents a hundred, that shut me out, I could not pay the tolls and warehouse rent in Chicago for that, then like bucking along until I bucked out all I had; and then I was busted again.

At that time the Lockport Marshal was elected by the people. I ran for Marshal and was elected and had to be elected every spring. I got elected 7 different times and

The I&M Canal was abandoned in stages in the early twentieth century and eventually became an archaeological site. This long-abandoned canal boat hull was excavated at Morris late in the century. (Fever River Research and the Illinois Department of Natural Resources)

there was nothing in it. This yearly election I got sick of, and after that I went to what they called the twin locks under Superintendent Capt. J. M. Leighton, and staid there until [Illinois Governor John Peter] Altgeld was elected, and then had to get out. Then I came back and found that there was people enough going to and from Romeo to the drainage canal to pay a man with a boat about $15 a day. Then I went and had a boat built on purpose for that trade, and then the canal officers run in one of their state boats to keep me out of it, because I was a republican.

Chapter Ten

A Letter to Ann

Perhaps the most famous account of a ride on a canal—certainly the most humorous—was contained in Charles Dickens's American Notes, *based on a trip he took in 1842 on Pennsylvania's Main Line of Public Works canal. The Illinois and Michigan Canal carried passengers in significant numbers for only a few years, until the railroads came along, but there are a few surviving accounts of travel on it. Surprisingly, one of the most delightful was written by an engineer, a member of a profession not known for its literary skills, who worked on the canal.*

William Gooding (1803–78), the engineer (and later secretary of the Canal Trustees), wrote this account of his early canal travels in a letter to his wife, Ann, in Lockport. Passengers on the canal packets did not travel in luxury; indeed, as Gooding recounts, getting something to eat was sometimes an ordeal. This account of a trip taken about seven months after the canal opened for business in 1848 originally appeared in a family history that was privately published in the 1880s and most recently reappeared in the winter 1996–97 issue of the Chicago Maritime Society's newsletter.

by William Gooding

Chicago, Nov. 30, 1848

Dear Ann,

After countless perils "by flood and field" I arrived here yesterday at four o'clock P.M. precisely, and having now so far recovered my faculties that I can again wield the pen, and Mr. Saltonstall being absent at his Thanksgiving dinner I seized upon the present moment to let you know how I got here.

When we first left port [ed. the western terminal at La Salle] there was nothing in the heavens above or the earth beneath, or in the waters under the earth, so far as we, with our limited vision could perceive, which portended such awful calamities as befell us. It is true that we had one horse in our team [ed. pulling the boat] "vot vouldn't go" and a driver as obstinate as the horse and a great deal less sensible. It is true, also, that the hands on board, and the man called Captain, were awful hard cases and did not seem to be very anxious about getting along; and further, that there was a villainous smell of whiskey and tobacco not at all agreeable to one like myself, not in the constant use of them; but all this we could have borne until we ascertained that there was not a mouthful of

Although many canal barges were manned by families—including husbands, wives, and children—there were also hired hands. Like lake ship crewmen, canallers could be a rowdy breed, working during the canal season to make money until they found something better to do. (I&M Canal Archives, Lewis University)

provisions on board except a little ginger bread, which a poor, half-starved, cadaverous looking passenger had thoughtfully stuffed into his pockets.

What was to be done in this fearful emergency? There we were upon the "raging canal," making headway occasionally at the rate say, of one knot per hour, with threatening skies overhead (for night had set in dark and gloomy,) and frowning rocks on both sides! Such was our condition when we arrived in sight of the classic village of Athens. As soon as the boat touched shore Lem Norton and myself, guided by a dim and distant light, pushed forward under a full press of sail to Brown's, resolved to get something to eat or sink in the bottomless mud through which we were up to our knees in the fluid, plowing our way. Here we got a cup of tea, some bread and head-cheese, which forcibly reminded me of Roscoe and Board's Hotel. Some of the other passengers and the boat's crew laid in supplies here, but only in such moderate quantities as their stomachs would hold, poor credulous souls, fondly believing, no doubt, that in the morning they would be where provisions could be easily obtained.

During the night the obstinate horse and driver had various tantrums which greatly retarded our progress and when we got to Summit our lights went out and we laid by till morning, fearing that we should be cast away if we proceeded, the wind having, in the mean time, freshened to a gale. Nearly an hour after daylight I succeeded in rousing the boat's crew, who seemed strongly inclined to take a Rip Van Winkle snooze, and having secured a pocket full of crackers at an Irish grocery, I again embarked and we proceeded on our voyage.

By this time the rain descended in torrents, the driver swore like a man-of-war's man and the stubborn horse, after getting within a mile of Bridgeport, refused to budge an inch further. In process of time, however, we made another start, reached Bridgeport, got some more head-cheese of extremely doubtful quality and the boat was laid up for the day. Here was a fix, but I succeeded in getting a horse and one wagon and got to the city precisely at the time mentioned at the commencement of my epistle, having faced the worst storm I was ever out in.

Chapter Eleven

Trials and Tribulations on the Chicago River

Tort litigation resulting from accidents occurring in traffic congestion is not a phenomenon confined to automobiles in the twentieth and twenty-first centuries. Although Chicago's bridge problem—the conflict between maritime traffic that needed open bridges and street traffic that wanted them closed—probably was the biggest source of complaints about traffic in the middle decades of the nineteenth century, fender benders on the waterways were also a problem. Some of the accidents also resulted in litigation—perhaps not as famous as Abraham Lincoln's Rock Island Bridge case, where a steamboat plowed into a railroad bridge, but interesting just the same.

This is an opinion of a judge in a lawsuit filed by the owner of a canal barge that was struck on September 16, 1856, by a sailing barque on the Chicago River at Polk Street. Both vessels were being towed at the time. Although a barque (also known as a bark, or barkentine) is a three-masted sailing ship with square sails on the foremast and fore-and-aft-rigged sails on the other masts and was quite capable of moving under its own power, sailing vessels were generally towed on the Chicago River because of the traffic congestion. The December 1857 opinion of Judge J. Drummond of the Federal District Court in Chicago was reprinted from American Canals, *No. 92 (February 1995).*

Drummond, J.—On the 16th of September, 1856, the canal boat *Buffalo*, in company with several other canal boats, two abreast, was coming down the south branch of the Chicago River, on her way from Bridgeport to this city, in tow of the steam tug *Hiram Warner*. The canal boat was loaded with oats and corn, and was owned by the libellant. It was between eight and ten o'clock in the morning, and the tug, with its tow, was proceeding at a moderate rate, keeping close to the right bank of the river, and not far from Polk Street bridge. The barque *B.S. Sheppard* was going up the river in tow of the tug *Walter M'Queen*. Near the place where they met there is a bend in the river, the South Branch sweeping round somewhat to the west in its course to the lake. It will be seen therefore, that a tug proceeding up the river with a tow hugging the left bank of the stream at that point, would naturally head-reach across the river towards the right bank in turning the bend, and the tendency would be in proportion to the speed of the vessel. This is what actually occurred in the case before the court. The barque did not seem to be under perfect command, or from some cause, she headed too much towards the east, and came in collision with the *Buffalo*, and with her anchor knocked a hole in the larboard bow of the canal boat, doing considerable damage to the hull and cargo; for which the libel is filed. The *Buffalo* was next to the *Hiram Warner*, and as the danger of the collision became imminent, word was passed on those on the barque to let go the anchor. This, however, was not attended to, and, as already stated, the collision took place. The anchor of the barque was hanging from the cat-head on her larboard bow, by the ring-stopper, with the flukes in the water. It had been previously slacked down, but was not, in fact, let go until after it had struck and fastened into the canal boat, when its weight carried it to the bottom. The river at the place of collision is quite narrow, and there was, besides, a vessel lying on each side moored to the dock. A short time before the collision, the barque had a stern line out, fastened ashore, and was in the act of checking her speed at the time; and the weight of the evidence seems to be, that at the moment of actual collision her motion was inconsiderable.

The first question is, was there any fault on the part of the *Buffalo* or on the part of the tug that had her in tow? After an

The Chicago River was the eastern outlet for the I&M Canal and the place where cargo was transferred between canal boats, barges, and lake ships. Because Chicago was the busiest port in the world for a time after the Civil War, the river was choked with schooners, steamers, tugs, canal boats, and barges. (I&M Canal Archives, Lewis University)

attentive consideration of the evidence, the court cannot say there was. The speed of the *Hiram Warner*, with its tow seems not to have been unusual or improper. They were well over to the right bank of the river. The only complaint made is that the canal boats ought to have had their lines out as the barque had, and it is insisted if this had been done no collision would have taken place and such appears to be the opinion of some of the defendant's witnesses. But we must not lose sight of the distinction between a canal boat and a barque like the *B.S. Sheppard*. This court has already frequently ruled that when a vessel is passing up or down the Chicago River, whether in tow of a tug or not, a boat astern with a line ready to be thrown ashore in case of emergency, is a proper and necessary precaution. The court has no doubt of the soundness of this rule; it is a salutary and practicable one with vessels which are and shall be provided with boats. Canal boats are different; they are not usually attended by row-boats, and it would in the nature of things be impossible that they should always be able to meet such a requisition. The court does not intend to intimate but that there may be circumstances where it would be a fault for a canal boat not to throw out a checking line to arrest its way. That is to be determined when the case arises. In this case, I do not consider that those on the canal boat were bound, under the facts as established, to have lines astern. I do not well see how it could have been availing to prevent the collision; that is, there was no sufficient time, with the means at the disposal of the canal boat, after the collision seemed probable, to accomplish the object proposed—that of checking with a line astern. It is to be observed that it was but a moment, as it were, that they could count on, and the thing to be determined is whether they did all they could at the particular juncture to avoid the collision with the barque. On the whole, I cannot say that they could have prevented it at the time; nor do they appear to have done any act immediately preceding which tended to bring about the collision.

With the barque it was different. The evidence is of course conflicting. To those on board of the barque it was the canal boat that ran against their anchor and into their vessel. The passion and excitement of the moment give form and color to the statement of each witness. It is only by taking some leading facts, and by placing ourselves as cool spectators in the midst of so much confusion, that we can judge fairly of the event. How much reliance is to be placed upon the account of this or that witness as to what occurred in the great tumult, need not be determined. There are some facts which are free from doubt. The *B. S. Sheppard* with its tug was approaching a turn in the river; the river itself was there quite narrow; a vessel was lying on each side; it was at a time when they were likely to meet vessels coming down. It is manifest, under these circumstances, extreme caution should have been used. If, as is stated by some of defendant's witnesses, it was impracticable for the two tows to pass at that point without coming in contact, the greater the necessity for caution and vigilance. Now it may be conceded that on the instant before the actual collision the barque was not moving at too rapid a rate, but I think it clear that in approaching the bend her speed was too great under the circumstances. The result was, in attempting to turn she had so much headway on her that with all their efforts, aided by a line fastened ashore, she would not mind her helm quick enough, and in the language of some of the witnesses, she head-reached across the stream and thus caused the collision. That this was the fact is made the more apparent from the circumstance that the fellow of the *Buffalo* sheered over to the starboard side of the barque, the latter in her progress dividing, as it were, the two canal boats which were towing abreast. It matters not that the motion of the barque was moderate at the time, provided, by a want of care immediately prior to the collision,—as for example, by too much headway,—it was out of their power to check their vessel at the proper time. No doubt as soon as they saw the probability of a collision they did all that they could to avoid it, the fault consisted in their putting themselves in such a condition they could not soon enough stop their vessel. The error, therefore, I think, on the part of the *Sheppard* and of her tug, was not using the needful precaution in approaching the bend of the river.

Again, there was serious fault on the part of the barque in relation to the anchor. I had occasion fully to consider this point in the case of the *Palmetto* decided about a year since in this court. It is true the facts in that case were somewhat different. There the vessel was lying at the wharf discharging her cargo, and while there the collision took place; but the main ground upon which the *Palmetto* was held to be in fault in that case, was because the anchor was not out of the way. No doubt the case is much stronger against a vessel at the wharf when the anchor is permitted to remain where it may strike a passing vessel, because when the craft is in motion it may be right and proper for the anchor to be in such a position that it can be let go on the instant. It is said that the ordinance of the city required the anchor of the *Sheppard* to be hanging at the forefoot. I do not consider myself bound in all cases by the city ordinances as to these matters. If the anchor was in a proper place and the proper conduct had been observed in relation to it, I should not, in this respect, hold the barque responsible, because technically it had not complied with the ordinance as to the anchor. The *B. S. Sheppard* had her anchor at the cat-head. The ordinance requires it to be dropped under the forefoot. There was therefore a clear violation of the ordinance, even if we take the opinion of one of the witnesses, that the anchor is under the forefoot when it is suspended from the ring stopper at the cat-head, a foot or two from the bottom of the vessel. However this may be, it is clear the anchor should be where it can be let go without delay. If this had been done in this case, most if not all the injury and damage would have been avoided. They let go of the anchor after it had struck the canal boat; but then, as one of the witnesses told them, and the same one who had shouted to them to drop their anchor, it was too late; the thing was done. The truth seems to be that there was the feeling on board of the *B. S. Sheppard*, so common on these occasions, that theirs was the stronger and heavier vessel, and they, at any rate, would not be likely to suffer. This feeling not infrequently produces carelessness and indifference at that time, and it certainly should not be countenanced by courts of justice. One objection made to the anchor hanging under the forefoot, or by a chain from the hawse-pipe, by the mate of the barque is, that if it had been suspended there it would have been likely to come in contact with something and thus endanger the vessel which bore it. And yet this same witness insists that the barque had no motion at the time, "not over two feet an hour." It is manifest that if an anchor is permitted to hang at the side of the vessel as it comes in contact with another, the risk of loss is immensely increased, and the only safe rule to adopt is to require it to be dropped out of harm's way, and if need be to the bottom, in all cases where it is practicable. Here is clear it could and ought to have been done, and for not doing it the *B. S. Sheppard* was in fault.

I shall therefore pronounce a decree for the libellant for the amount of damage which has been proved together with costs.

Steamers navigating crowded harbors or channels, or entering ports in the dark or in fogs, are bound to move with the greatest care, and to keep themselves under a headway at all times controllable, and sometime to stop entirely.

PART III

The Golden Age of Sail

Chapter Twelve

Great Lakes Sailing Ships

A certain nostalgia is attached to the age of sail, and the Great Lakes are no exception. The continuing popularity of the fictional saltwater captains Horatio Hornblower and Jack Aubrey caused British writers C.S. Forester and Patrick O'Brian to grind out 11 and 20 novels, respectively, about them. Closer to home, America's great novelist of the sea, Herman Melville, paid homage to the Great Lakes sailing in a passage in his classic whaling novel Moby Dick. *These days sailing on the Great Lakes is limited primarily to yachtsmen, but in the nineteenth century the lakes were dotted with the sails of plodding schooners carrying lumber to Chicago and grain from it. The schooner, a predominantly two-masted, fore-and-aft-rigged ship, did not have the literary glamour of the square-rigged ships on the oceans, but it was the workhorse of the lakes.*

The article that follows initially appeared as the introduction to Great Lakes Sailing Ships (1947), *by Henry N. Barkhausen, as the second in a series of albums on ships and sailing produced by Kalmbach Publishing Co., a firm more recently known for its authoritative interest in railroading. Barkhausen is a resident of north suburban Lake Forest.*

by Henry N. Barkhausen

Few can recall the heyday of sail on the Great Lakes in the late 1860s and early 1870s, when sailing vessels outnumbered steamers four to one; when big "barks" and schooners might repay their owners in two seasons, carrying grain from Chicago and Milwaukee to Collingwood and Buffalo; when lake ports were forests of masts and yards, and when on a single day in 1873, 135 lumber-laden schooners arrived in Chicago.

Vessels were sailing the lakes, of course, for many years before the first photographer set up his clumsy apparatus on the water front. The growth and evolution of the lake sailing fleet really started with the opening of the Erie Canal in 1825 and kept step with the expansion of commerce that followed. Not too much is known of the vessels that comprised the small lake marine just prior to and for some years after the war of 1812, but they were schooners, brigs, and sloops of small displacement and shoal draft. That many of their designs and rigs left considerable to be desired is indicated by the recollection of a contemporary captain who recalled that "most vessels upon the lakes at that day (1816–1818) were dull sailers; some of them could hardly claw offshore under canvas."

During this period the centerboard was developed, which innovation greatly increased the efficiency of these vessels to windward, particularly without cargo or ballast, and permitted the design of larger vessels of still moderate draft.

As lake commerce, competition, and confidence developed, the size of the sailing vessels tended to increase as well—a tendency that was naturally tempered by the existing conditions of harbors, channels and canals. For instance, until a cut was made through the St. Clair flats in 1855–1858, a ship could carry only 6 feet across the bar in normal weather. Another factor, in addition to river and harbor improvements, that permitted larger vessels was the appearance of the steam tug about 1860. Once tugs were available for towing through the rivers and in the large harbors, less emphasis had to be put on maneuverability of the vessel, and the 1860s and early 1870s saw the schooners and barks develop to around 200 feet over all, with a displacement of 700 to 800 tons.

In general, vessels larger than this proved too expensive and unhandy to sail and soon found themselves sailing continuously on a towline behind a steamer, although they carried their spars and canvas for many years.

In 1870, an official tabulation of vessels on the upper lakes listed 214 barques, 159 brigs and 1,737 schooners. [Ed. On the lakes, most vessels called "brigs" were actually brigantines, that is, they were square rigged only on the foremast, whereas true brigs were square rigged on two masts. Similarly, so-called "barques" or "barks" were actually barquentines, square rigged only on the foremasts with fore-and-aft sails on the main and mizzen masts. Many of the early schooners were actually topsail schooners with fore-and-aft sails on all masts, but carrying cross yards and square sails on the foremast as well.] Although schooners were always in the majority throughout the whole period of sail, until the early 1870s the accepted and conventional rig for the largest three-masters was the barquentine, inaccurately called "barque" (or "bark") on fresh water. After the 1870s, the simpler, more efficient topsail schooner rig prevailed.

Fore-and-aft-rigged schooners were by far the most common type of sailing ship on the Great Lakes in the nineteenth century. They were built with two to five masts. This three-master is shown docked on the Chicago River. (CMS Collection)

Only three full-rigged ships are known to have been built for service on the lakes — the *Superior,* the *Milwaukee,* and the *Julia Palmer.* These ships were launched in the 1830s and lost the following decade, the *Palmer* having been converted to a steamer.

Brigantines, called "brigs" by lake men, formed a considerable fleet up until the 1870s, but were likewise displaced by the fore and aft rigs after that.

In laying out a vessel, the owner or builder had to decide whether he wanted to trade on all the lakes or confine himself to the upper lakes. In the first case, he was limited to Welland Canal dimensions, which until the late 1870s meant a vessel not to exceed 142.5 x 26.25 x 10 feet. Efforts to develop the most capacity within these limits resulted in a very distinctive class of schooners called "canallers" — relatively narrow, wall-sided ships, with straight stems and flat transoms.

The voyages of vessels from fresh to salt water comprise a colorful chapter in lake history, although this commerce never bulked very large in relation to the total. The brigantine *Pacific* made what is thought to be the first such trip in 1843, carrying wheat and flour from Toronto to Liverpool. The bark *Eureka* achieved considerable fame in 1849 by voyaging from Cleveland to San Francisco, and a small but steady stream of sailing vessels left the lakes in the following years for European, South American, and South African ports. In 1856, the bark *Dean Richmond* made the first direct trip abroad from Lake Michigan, leaving Milwaukee July 19 loaded with wheat, and arriving at Liverpool September 5. Fifteen lake vessels sailed for foreign ports in 1858, 30 in 1860.

In foreign waters and American saltwater ports, lakers were quickly distinguished from conventional ocean-going types by their straight-sided, shoal-draft hulls of center-board construction, their square sterns and their stumpy mizzenmasts. The barquentine rig was strange to Europeans in the early days of this commerce, and it is believed that this rig originated on the lakes. The same can definitely be said of the raffee topsails carried by the fore-and-afters. The reason that the mizzenmast of the three-masters was inevitably shorter than the forward two spars has never been satisfactorily explained, but the fact that this convention was generally followed by builders can be observed throughout this album.

Old lake sailors like to tell of fast passages made by some of the famous schooners—and there were many remarkable runs. The schooner *Bonnie Doon* went from Milwaukee to Detroit in 56 hours in 1865, the *Redington* sailed from a Lake Superior port to Cleveland in four days, and the *Fayette Brown* made a round trip from Escanaba to Cleveland and back in eight days. With fair, hard winds, grain schooners sometimes went from Chicago to Collingwood in a little over two days. These passages were, of course, exceptional. Two weeks was considered fast time for a trip from a Lake Michigan port to Lake Erie and return, while the average was perhaps a month.

It was the average lengths of these trips that induced Captain James Norris of St. Catherine's, Ontario, to try an experiment that was to have a profound effect on the sailing fleet. He hired the powerful American tug *Samson* to tow three of his schooners to Chicago and back late in the fall of 1869. By

The Rouse Simmons, *shown in this painting by Charles Vickery, was arguably the most famous schooner to sail out of Chicago. The Christmas tree ship of legend hauled a load of Christmas trees to Chicago late each autumn but disappeared with all hands during a storm on the lake in November 1912. (Clipper Ship Gallery, La Grange)*

fueling the tug from deckloads of cordwood on the schooners, the caravan made a successful and fast round trip before freeze-up. This was the beginning of schooner towing which increased in volume each year as more powerful steamers were put into service. The conversion of schooners to tow barges was accelerated in the 1880s, when a seaman's union enforced a higher rate of pay in fully-rigged vessels.

If they survived the considerable hazards of lake operation, the big schooners all ended their days as tow barges behind tup or steamer. It was the smaller schooner that wrote the last chapter in the history of sail on the lakes in the 1920s, living on borrowed time, earning an uncertain livelihood in the coal and lumber trade until her aging timbers gave way, or there was no more money to replace the rotten sails or rigging.

Chapter Thirteen

Wooden Shipbuilding in the Windy City, 1836–90

Shipbuilding in the wooden vessel era is usually associated with communities in Wisconsin and Michigan where large amounts of timber were available, even though many of those hulls were built for owners in Chicago. However, a number of ships were built in yards in Chicago even into the age of steam and steel.

This is a paper that was given by Professor Richard J. Wright, professor of history at Bowling Green University, at a symposium in March 1984, at Loyola University in Chicago, which was jointly sponsored by that school and the Chicago Maritime Society. Unfortunately, as Wright noted in his introductory remarks, many of the city's early maritime records were lost in the Great Fire of 1871, making a historian's job more difficult.

by Richard J. Wright

Shipbuilding began in Chicago in 1835 when Nelson R. Norton commenced construction of the sloop *Clarissa*. She was launched on May 12, 1836, but apparently was too small to be recorded in the district custom house at Detroit. Norton's greatest contribution to Chicago prior to his boat building effort was the "lifting leaves" drawbridge at Dearborn Street, built in 1834. The *Clarissa* represented his only shipbuilding endeavor. Two years later, in 1838, Samuel Ellis built the seventy-foot, two-masted schooner *Hiram Pearson*, named after a prominent Chicagoan. She was the first vessel built in Chicago to receive federal recognition, vis-a-vis custom house enrollments, to engage in Great Lakes commerce.

Following the loss of the early steamboat *Detroit* in 1837, an association of Chicago citizens formed to build a replacement steamer for the Chicago–St. Joseph cross-lake run. During the interim and to connect with the stage and mail line, the small Lake Erie steamer *W.F.P. Taylor* was brought to Lake Michigan. Captain Calvin H. Case came from Buffalo to superintend construction of the new steamer at a shipyard established on Goose Island. The *James Allen* was launched on March 30, 1838, and by late summer she was running to St. Joseph with the *Taylor*. Her twin horizontal low-pressure engines were built by William H. Stow of Chicago.

Unfortunately her boilers proved too small. On her trial trip, she covered fourteen miles within the first hour. Then she began to slow down. Total time for the trip was ten hours. Her captain said that she "ran like a skeered dog" for the first thirty minutes, then her speed would slacken to about seven miles per hour. She maintained this same pattern for two years on the St. Joseph run, and then was sold for service on Lake Erie. In September 1838, the *Taylor* was driven ashore near Michigan City, so the *Allen* carried on as the lone steamboat on Lake Michigan until a second side-wheeler, also under construction by Case on Goose Island, could join her. By October the slightly smaller *George W. Dole* joined the Allen on the St. Joseph run.

The next fifteen years saw shipbuilding in Chicago pick up, but it did not gain a prominent place along the river front. [ed. While shipyards may have been dispersed along the north and south branches of the Chicago River, ship chandlers sought visible waterfront locations. Notable early establishments were Hugunan & Pierce, Foster & Robb, and Dodge & Tucker. In 1837 George F. Foster opened a sail loft on North Water Street, expanding into a ship chandlery in 1839; the firm survived through 1886.] In 1843 the first propeller to be built in Chicago, the 231-ton *Independence*, was launched. She later would cross the isthmus at Sault Ste. Marie, Michigan, on rollers to become the first steam-propelled vessel on Lake Superior. The *Independence* was lost in 1853 when her boiler exploded and she sank just above the present-day Soo Locks. R.C. Bristol signed her master carpenter's certificate.

Several two-masted schooners, ranging in length from 60 to 110 feet, also were built during this period, but only three builders appear with any consistency. In 1842, Captain James Averell began a shipyard on the north

Shipbuilders in the nineteenth century used broadbladed axes to hew timbers into the shapes necessary to build their vessels. (A.T. Andreas, History of Chicago*)*

side of the main river channel just below the Rush Street bridge. His first vessel was the schooner *Maria Hilliard*, built in 1844. She was followed by at least one schooner and four brigs between 1844 and 1848.

George Allen appears as a master builder on documents in 1846 with the launching of the schooner *N. C. Walton* and the brig *Ellen Parker*. The following year he built a schooner and the propeller *A. Rossiter*. For lack of biographical information, one must wonder whether Allen was in business for himself, or perhaps he was complying with federal bookkeeping requirements while in the employ of Averell. Such a practice was not uncommon in other Great Lakes shipbuilding communities.

In 1847, John Connor reportedly built a set of boxes—a small floating dry dock capable of lifting vessels out of the water for repair purposes. He was located at Van Buren Street on the east side of the South Branch. Connor built the schooner *Mount Vernon* in 1850. Shortly thereafter he reportedly formed a partnership with Riordan & Dunn and engaged exclusively in the ship repair business. Also in 1847 John Lillie built a schooner modestly named *John Lillie* at Gross-Point [ed. the present-day North Shore suburb of Wilmette]. He followed her three years later with the schooner *Arrow*.

Beginning in 1853, the Chicago shipbuilding scene took an upswing, not because of the lake trade, but rather through the prospects offered by the construction of the Illinois and Michigan Canal. In 1853, the partnership of Doolittle & Miller was formed. This was followed the next year by another partnership, Jordan & Olcott. These two firms would dominate shipbuilding in Chicago for the next decade.

Andrew Miller was born in Londonderry County, Ireland, in 1820. He came to Oswego, New York via St. John, New Brunswick, in 1841. In Oswego, he learned the shipbuilding trade by working for his uncle, also named Andrew Miller. In 1846, he went to Cleveland, Ohio, to superintend the building of a floating dry dock. Two years later he moved to Chicago, where he ultimately formed a partnership with Edgar M. Doolittle. They built a set of boxes and conducted business on the North Branch. In 1854, they purchased a dry dock that had been started by George Wicks, completing it in 1855. The site was located at the North Halsted Street bridge. In 1860 the firm name was changed to Miller & Hood and in 1863 to Miller Brothers & Clark. Through 1860 this firm built a few small sailing vessels, but specialized in canal boat construction. Miller & Hood, in 1861–1862, built two tugs and a schooner. Miller Brothers & Clark specialized in the construction of tugs, a vital component to the mixed canal, river, and lake trade of Chicago in the 1860s.

Francis Jordan first appears on the Chicago shipbuilding roll in 1847 with the construction of the schooner *Buena Vista*. By 1856 he had joined forces with Orville Olcott. Olcott was born in 1814 into a farm family in Lenox, Madison County, New York. At the tender age of fourteen he went to Utica to learn the canal boat building trade with his uncle. By 1835 he was in this business for himself. However, by 1848, the depressed conditions along the Erie Canal forced him to look west, attracted by the prospects of the Illinois and Michigan Canal. A trip to Chicago resulted in a contract to build a line of canal packet boats. He would remain in the shipbuilding and repair business in Chicago for the next thirty years.

During the period 1851 through 1866, canal boat building was by far the most prominent feature of new ship construction in Chicago. A simple head count of canal boats identified as built in Chicago during that time numbers merely 101. There undoubtedly were more than this built, but either they did not get into the federal enrollments or the enrollments themselves were illegible. Several other individuals and firms built canal boats during the 1850s and 1860s. They include Hewitt & Judd, Stephen Gosselin, Matthews & Kenefick, and Akhurst & Douglas. Unfortunately nothing is known of a biographical nature or of the site locations of their yards. The canal boats averaged between 96 and 102 feet in length.

This writer can only pursue these evasive builders through 1866, as their names appear only on the first enrollment issued to a new vessel. An examination of the abstract of enrollments for the Chicago Customs District (established in 1847) for the years succeeding 1866 shows an interesting change in the construction profile. In 1866 the first steam canal boat specifically identified as such, the *Chicago*, appears. In 1873 another one shows up. By 1875, new non-propelled canal boats (or barges) drop completely from the abstract. By 1885 an estimated twenty-five steam canal boats [were] listed in the Chicago District abstracts with the assumption that most were built in Chicago. Identification of their builders awaits further examination of the Chicago District vessel enrollments currently housed in the National Archives in Washington, D.C.

One other interesting observation is the predominance of what appears to be the French origin of names of the builders. Obviously Chicago shipbuilders were supplying a local/regional need and depended upon shipyards in other lake ports to supply the needs of new ship tonnage on the Great Lakes.

The meeting of local needs is exemplified by a small shipyard started in 1861 by the renowned Buffalo, New York shipbuilder Jacob W. Banta. Banta and his partner, Benjamin Bidwell, built some of the largest and most ornate "palace" side-wheelers on the Great Lakes in their Buffalo shipyard during the 1850s. Bidwell was killed in the Civil War, and Jacob Banta moved to Chicago. There he started a small shipyard on West Charles Street near Harrison Street. He built a few tugs to service the demands of the Chicago River. In 1865 he sold his facility to Green Bay, Wisconsin, shipbuilder John Gregory. Gregory, with a connection to the marine contracting firm of O.B. Green & Company, continued to build tugs and engage in the ship repair business at least through 1883. He also continued to maintain his shipbuilding interests in Green Bay. Most of the tugs produced in this yard were familiar sights along the Chicago River for many years in the towing and dredging business.

William Bates, probably the most famous schooner builder on the Great Lakes, moved his operations from Wisconsin to Chicago for a time after the Civil War. (CMS Collection)

The shipbuilding picture for Chicago from 1870 to 1890 is one of confusion because of interlocking business interests and problems brought on by the need for greater amounts of capital to build and maintain more elaborate repair facilities such as dry docks. Sometime prior to 1871, the well-known Manitowoc, Wisconsin, shipbuilder William W. Bates, along with his son Stephen, moved to Chicago and started a dry dock company along the South Branch. They were in business with Edgar M. Doolittle, and the company was called W.W. Bates & Company. Bates ultimately purchased Doolittle's half interest in the company for $11,000, providing as security mortgage notes on the working property and capital. Unfortunately the facility was wiped out in the great conflagration of 1871. After the fire, Doolittle advanced Bates $3,000 from the insurance payments to enable him to rebuild. John A. Farrow apparently had succeeded Doolittle as a financial partner. Farrow sold Bates his interest in August 1874 and later engaged in the ship repair business as Burns & Farrow on the North Branch.

In December 1874, Bates along with Andrew Miller and his brother Thomas E. Miller and Orville Olcott organized a new company, the Chicago Dry Dock Company. The Miller brothers already operated two dry docks in their facility on the North Branch. In November 1875, Doolittle filed suit to recover his losses from the now defunct W.W. Bates & Company. After much legal confrontation, Bates was forced from the Chicago Dry Dock Company. Further confusion resulted when it was divulged that the Chicago Board of Education owned the dry dock property along the South Branch, but Andrew Miller owned the boilers and engines required to furnish power to the facility. After more legal wrangling, the school board leased the property to the firm of Miller & Olcott for $3,000 per year. By 1877 Doolittle was running the yard alone and finally closed it down. The Millers continued to run their shipyard on the North Branch, as did another of the financial partners, Captain Ben Eyster, who had a ship repair business adjacent to the Millers' on North Halsted Street.

In August 1879, the Chicago Dry Dock Company was reorganized. Milwaukee vessel owners William H. Wolf, David Vance, and James Sheriffs, along with Chicagoans Andrew Miller, Edgar Doolittle, William Bates, James Higgie, Ben Eyster, and O.B. Green comprised the major stockholders. Bates again was appointed manager, and the dry dock was enlarged by thirty feet. Milwaukeeans Thomas Davidson and Oliver Mowatt later became financially involved.

Bates again left the fold and was succeeded by Mowatt. The company was healthy enough as late as 1887 to declare a twenty percent dividend [but] again closed, and the site was sold for $90,000, thus ending the stormy career of the Chicago Dry Dock Company. In 1881, another dry dock was built just east of the Miller brothers' yard on the North Branch. It was incorporated as the Vessel Owners' Dry Dock Company. Orville Olcott, William Bates, and Ben Eyster were principal stockholders. This property was sold to the Miller brothers in 1885, giving them three adjacent dry docks on Goose Island.

Captain Benjamin Eyster first appeared as a Chicago shipbuilder in 1863 with construction of the tug *J.A. Crawford*. He operated a set of boxes in the North Branch called the Union Dry Dock Company. By 1871 he was involved financially with William Bates and later with the Chicago Dry Dock Company. Captain Eyster dropped from the scene in 1881 as a result of a scandal. On June 28, 1881, as he [drove his carriage into] an alley leading to his barn, he encountered a hackman coming the other way. A fight ensued in which Eyster was thrown to the ground. Enraged, he ran into his house, came back with a revolver, and shot his antagonist in the neck. He later contended that he was defending himself from a pitchfork, which was not seen by witnesses or found. The man, John B. Schumacher, brother of a Chicago police lieutenant, died a few days later. Eyster was found guilty and sen-

Lumber remained the major cargo for schooners in the late nineteenth century although steamships had supplanted them for hauling bulk material, like ore. As seen here, the ship moored at the railroad docks was a lumber hooker, and the one at the breakwater had her masts cut back and was used as a barge—a fate of many schooners as the century waned. (CMS Collection)

tenced to fourteen years in the state penitentiary. He received a second trial in May 1882, based on legal technicalities, which resulted in a hung jury. However, he emerged so discredited that he slipped into obscurity.

There were other shipbuilding and ship repair firms that appeared in the daily marine news columns of Chicago newspapers, including Mowatt & Rice in Lighthouse Slip, Burns & Farrow, Jacob Arville, Paul Pouliot, and J.S. Williams, to mention a few. But these must remain mysteries until further investigation once again brings them to life.

Through the first blush of research, a definite profile of Chicago's wooden boat building era peeks through. [There was] very little wooden construction after 1850 [and the industry] looked to the lake for its rewards. New construction was heavily influenced by Chicago's unique geographic relationship to canal [heavy traffic that required repair yards], and, to a lesser degree, package freight trades on Lake Michigan. Canal boats and tugs serviced this trade and situation. One very important facet of the shipyard business, that of ship repair, reaped mightily from the benefits of Chicago's location. Vessel repair constituted the real nugget of the shipbuilding business in Chicago. It was a rare day during the shipping season that one could not find reference to vessels going into, coming out of, or waiting to gain space in Chicago dry docks from about 1865 through 1890.

Chapter Fourteen

The Port of Chicago in the 1880s

Chicago in the second half of the nineteenth century had already become the nation's railroad center, a position it still holds, but at the same time, the Windy City was also one of the busiest ports in the world in terms of the number of vessels it handled. A synergy had developed between the growing rail network and the Great Lakes maritime industry in which the railroads acted as gatherers and distributors of produce and products hauled to and from the city by ship. The competition between rail and sail kept shipping tariffs lower in Chicago than in rival cities, and shippers favored whatever routes were the cheapest.

CMS member Philip R. Elmes in the 1980s originally wrote for a maritime trade publication this essay on the influence of its port on the city. He reprised the essay for this book.

by Philip R. Elmes

Standing at Chicago's Clark Street bridge a young traveler from New Jersey was astounded by the sights and sounds of the nation's leading inland port. "There I saw," he was to write years later, "a large steamship that would compare favorably with such vessels as I had seen in New York, making her way with the assistance of tugboats up the river, with a load of grain from Lake Superior. Small towboats, noisy and smoky, were rushing up and down the river tipping their smoke stacks as they passed under the bridges.

I saw two schooners loaded with lumber with yards hauled aback and 'cockbilled' so as to pass through the traffic. That type of vessel was new to me and a casual acquaintance told me that they were 'Lumber Luggers' from northern Michigan."

The nineteen-year-old F.E. Coyne returned to Chicago in 1883 to "try his luck" in the booming metropolis and in the years to follow was to become a prominent businessman and politician. His timing was exquisite. Chicago in the eighties was just hitting its stride, a world leader in the shipment of lumber and grain since the 1850s, and an important center for meat packing, iron and steel production, and heavy manufacturing. Much if not all of this trade passed, at one time or another, through the Chicago River— the nineteenth century port of Chicago.

In the early 1880s, the port of Chicago was arguably the busiest in the country. In the year 1882 alone, over 26,000 ship clearances and arrivals were registered, according to one historian substan-

Lumber was one of the commodities that for a time in the nineteenth century made Chicago one of the busiest ports in the world. This photograph shows the river choked with lumber hookers, as the schooners that handled the commodity were called. (CMS Collection)

tially more than those counted at the salt water ports of New York, New Orleans and San Francisco combined!

Until the turn of the century, the Port of Chicago was in fact the Chicago River, beginning at the river mouth and extending along both banks north and south along the river's two main branches. Coyne recalls South Water Street, Chicago's downtown waterfront, "absolutely jammed with wagons and trucks, loading up with produce for outlying stores. The commission houses at that time were thickly located on both sides of the street, from LaSalle to State Street." Being "bridged" was a common daily experience as wagons, "horse cars" and pedestrians alike waited for blocks in every direction for bridges raised to accommodate the continuous river traffic to be lowered once again. As late as 1890, Coyne was to report, "There were lumber, coal and steel barges being towed, and quite frequently large steamships under their own power passing at all hours. It was a common occurrence for a large steamer to get stuck in the draw and hold up traffic for hours at a time."

Where downtown landmarks such as Tribune Tower, Marina City and the Merchandise Mart stand today, waterfront docks and lumber yards stood in the decades before 1900. As the shorelines of northern Lake Michigan were being clear-cut by lumber barons of the period, Chicago stood ready to receive countless cargoes of dressed lumber for transshipment by rail across the country. Lumber yards dominated Goose Island and the banks along both sides of the north branch, and along some twenty miles of slips and canals dug on the south branch of the river to 35th Street. Lumbering was big business. In the twenty years following the Chicago Fire, Chicago alone built nearly 100,000 buildings. The states of Wisconsin, Michigan and Minnesota were effectively defoliated as each year's harvest cleared hundreds of square miles of virgin timber. But, while receipts were still to peak in the early nineties, by the mid-eighties lumber markets were beginning to

Canal barges before the advent of steam power on that waterway had to be towed up and down the Chicago River by tugs, adding to congestion. But they were vital to the emergence of Chicago as a break-bulk center where traffic was interchanged between rail, lakes, and canal. This scene was downriver from the Clark Street bridge. (A.T. Andreas, History of Chicago)

shift to Minnesota and the soft wood stands of southern states. Chicago's days as a lumber capital of the world were drawing to a close.

It is said the Board of Trade Building, the city's center for commodities trading, was adorned in the 1880s with a two-masted schooner at the top of its tower, a symbol of that industry's dependence on waterborne transport in the 19th century. As with lumber, Chicago in the 1850s had become a world leader as a primary market in the shipment of corn and wheat; but, as the population shifted westward, the city's role shifted to that of a transfer market, accepting trainloads of grain for storage, sale and shipment out of the city by boat. In 1880, Chicago was accepting two and a half times the tonnage as St. Louis, Chicago's nearest competitor; and by 1890, Chicago was receiving 41 percent of all grains taken in by the ten chief primary markets in the country. Before the day of the skyscraper, grain elevators dominated Chicago's skyline: huge 5–10 story structures, crowned by tower attics of 30 feet and more. In the grain elevator business, speed was crucial. In 1891, one elevator could unload 1,500 railcars in a day and, in an hour, load 300,000 bushels into waiting vessels. Waterborne shipping dominated grain transport during the period, with lakes carriers handling twice the tonnage as the six leading rail carriers combined. As with the lumber yards, grain elevators clustered along the south branch of the river until, late in the century, the activity shifted south to the developing Lake Calumet harbor facilities.

During the 1880s a perceptible shift was underway from sail-powered vessels to faster steamers, but the relatively inexpensive to operate 200-foot sailing schooners of 700–800 tons burden continued to serve effectively as bulk carriers well into the 20th

century. With hundreds of vessels registered out of the Port of Chicago, the local seaman's union reported a thriving membership of 2,500 in the mid-eighties, with sailors of Scandinavian birth predominating (with Irish, English and Scots making up the remainder). Chicago's waterfront stretched for miles along the river and yet we're hard put to locate a waterfront "district." The gaming parlors, saloons, bordellos and boarding houses that once

Chicago's port suffered from traffic congestion as bad as anything on land in the nineteenth century. The steamer Arabia *is shown negotiating the bend in the south branch of the Chicago River ca. 1900. (CMS Collection)*

clustered close about Cap Streeter's establishment at the harbor's mouth had been torn down decades before, forcing shore-bound sailors to seek their entertainment in working men's taverns scattered across the city. But as the lumber yards and grain elevators moved south to Lake Calumet, so too did the sailors and the last vestiges of Chicago's dynamic and colorful waterfront.

The docks, lumberyards, granaries and warehouses of the nineteenth-century port of Chicago gave way to concrete, steel and glass. In the name of progress, Chicago became another thing—stockyard, rail center, manufacturer, banker and broker. Only in the spring and again for a little while in the fall, when the occasional sailboat with its mast not yet stepped obliges the tenders to, one by one, raise the bridges, the City is reminded . . . reminded what it was like to be "bridged in Chicago." Now, that was something. . . .

Chapter Fifteen

The Chicago Harbor a Century Ago

The wintry Chicago River a century ago had an unreal, almost surreal look to it — a huge, linear parking lot for abandoned ships, sometimes moored as many as three and four abreast from each riverbank. The only indications of life in the otherwise deathlike scene was an occasional wisp of smoke from a cabin stove or bark of a guard dog. The river port was only hibernating. Come April 1 each year, after the insurance policies went into effect, the port became a beehive of activity. It was for eight months one of the busiest ports on earth. Then on November 30 the insurance policies expired and the port resumed its hibernation. Shipowners could get insurance for the dangerous winter months, but it wasn't worth the cost.

This story, by Theodore S. Charrney, was originally published in the summer 1988 issue of Sea History *magazine. A printer by trade, Mr. Charrney, in his early seafaring career, held such positions as cabin boy and cook's helper on lake boats and as purser and steward for Cunard and Swedish-American Lines. A self-educated historian of Chicago and the Great Lakes, he has written extensively on both subjects.*

by Theodore S. Charrney

Between the Civil War and the classic brilliance of the White City of the Columbian Exposition of 1893, Chicago knew a most unusual maritime bustle centered on the Chicago River, the sluggish stream that runs through its central district. These years paralleled the golden age of sailing ships on the Great Lakes, and nowhere was the greatness of that age more conspicuous than on the main channel and branches of the Chicago River.

The Chicago River is an unlikely candidate for a major port, and it was not until 1835 that the mouth of the river was broken and the river became navigable to anything of deeper draft than a lighter. Although the main channel is less than one and a half miles long and the north and south branches were navigable for only two and three miles respectively, the waterfront was so honeycombed with slips and channels that the shore measured about twenty-five miles. For eight months of the year this teeming watercourse, the greatest inland port in the history of waterborne commerce, was an empire of its own. During the 1880s, more than 20,000 ship clearances were recorded each year. In 1892, Chicago's incoming and outbound waterborne commerce was surpassed only by London, New York and Hamburg. The majority of lake vessels were still schooners which, even in the late 1880s, numbered more than 1700. They would continue to ply the Great Lakes carrying lumber, grain, coal and other bulk cargos well into the twentieth century.

The port of Chicago shook itself awake in early spring to begin the season's refit of the fleet for summer sailing. As the ice began to break up with the first warm breezes of April, there was a beehive of activity along the docks, for fully 20 percent of the sailing fleet of the entire Great Lakes and its tributary canal system wintered in the river. Insurance came into force on April 1st and the setting out of the first ship of the year was an event of great importance.

The lumber business was spread out among all the branches, canals and slips in the river. From the busy lumber centers of Muskegon and Manistee on Michigan's lower peninsula, Escanaba, Wisconsin, and the numerous havens, piers and landing places on the shores of Lake Michigan and Green Bay, lumber hookers carried dressed lumber to the city at the foot of Lake

Except for such bulk commodities as grain, lumber, and ore, cargo on the Great Lakes typically moved in sacks, barrels, and boxes, as shown in this drawing of Chicago's waterfront in the nineteenth century. The cargo was hauled to and from the docks on horse-drawn drays. (CMS Collection)

Michigan where it would be transshipped by rail to the west to supply building materials for the rapidly expanding but treeless plains states.

Issuing from the harbor, the grain fleets moved the golden riches of the breadbasket to the hungry mouths of the East, returning with coal to stoke the furnaces of commerce and industry and warm the hearths of Midwestern homes. Initially grain was sent to Buffalo, the first of the major Great Lakes ports, where it was off-loaded onto canal barges. After the Civil War, Europe became a major importer of United States wheat, and when railheads were established at Sarnia (opposite Port Huron), Goderich, Kincardine and Owen Sound on Georgian Bay, grain was taken by train for delivery to transatlantic ships sailing from Montreal and Quebec.

The grain ships had to wait for the opening of the Mackinac Straits before they could sail. (In the later part of the nineteenth century, the straits had their earliest opening on March 25, in 1889, and their latest on May 4, only the year before. The norm was late April.) Waterborne shipping dominated grain transport during the latter half of the century, and Lakes carriers handled twice the tonnage of the six leading rail carriers combined. In 1880, Chicago cleared two and a half times the tonnage of St. Louis, her closest rival, and ten years later she was transshipping 41 percent of all grains taken in the ten chief primary markets in the country. Her supremacy as a grain port would not be challenged until the opening of the fertile Red River Valley in the Dakotas and Manitoba, and the consequent emergence of the Port of Duluth. The grain elevators dominating the skyline along the south branch of the river were something of a Chicago innovation. The pre-fire structures were the work of the transplanted eastern architect John Mills Van Osdel, who borrowed the basics from the early depots first developed at Buffalo.

Each granary, gaunt and windowless, was capped by an attic of thirty or more feet and their total height often equalled that of a ten-story building, taller than the commercial buildings in the downtown area and surpassed in height by only a few church spires. In the grain elevator business, speed was crucial. By 1891, one elevator could unload 1500 rail cars in one day, and in one hour, an elevator could load 300,000 bushels of grain into waiting vessels. Despite this tremendous capacity, the port could not always keep pace with the bumper crops that poured into the city. The elevators began to accept grain in midsummer and the schooners were unable thereafter to keep up with the harvests. By December, when navigation on the lakes ceased for the year, the elevators were still loaded almost to capacity. The railroads continued to bring late crops throughout the winter, while the laid-up ships themselves were used for grain storage.

The harbor master and his assistant were responsible for keeping the river open and free from crowding due to delays and accidents. The great number of bridges crossing the river was the chief cause of river jams and delays. Nowhere was a major shipping center bridged by so many *ponts*. By the late 1870s, there were thirty-five pivot bridges in operation, five in the main channel and thirty on the branches. Four more were added in the following decade.

The tugmen made most use of the river, and their dependence on a clear and open stream was a bread-and-butter

Maritime traffic on the Chicago River and its branches was so heavy in the 1870s and 1880s that vessels double- and triple-parked, leaving a very narrow channel. (CMS Collection)

matter. As a consequence, the bridge tender developed into his natural enemy and feuds between the two groups were not uncommon. The three-mile stretch of the river most travelled was spanned by sixteen pivot bridges involving an aggregate of some 1200 openings daily, or more than 200,000 each year. In a stream as congested as the Chicago River, only a few minutes delay would create a jam that frequently was not resolved for an hour or more.

Navigating a river crossed by so many bridges required a certain type of seamanship on the part of the tugmen. Once a schooner in tow gained way, it generally could not be halted should there be some delay at the bridge. Tugs usually were paced from one bridge to the next to allow sufficient time for the tender to open the span. Still, there were a hundred or more fights between bridge tenders and tugmen in any given year.

The sound of a breaking jib boom against the framework of a bridge brought together a considerable crowd of people and the verbal exchange between bridge tender and tugmen was a drama few cared to miss. These scrimmages had a tendency to block the waterway for all moving craft as well. As soon as the harbor master was notified of an accident, he hurried to the scene in a tug to get commerce moving again. To the tugmen, accidents were no small matter because they were responsible for any damage to ships in their care. Since the bridge tenders were political appointees (which in those days meant Irish), if it could be proven that the bridge tender was at fault, the city was made to pay the damages.

Stiff competition for tows brought on frequent tug wars. In the spring of 1881, a particularly vicious tug war, in which the tugmen scoured lower Lake Michigan seeking tows, disclosed voyages of such distances that lake men shook their heads in disbelief. Tows of twenty-five miles or more were common, despite the fact that the tugs received no more compensation for all this additional effort than if the vessels had been picked up just outside the breakwater. Some tugs went northward as far as Racine, a distance of 70 miles, and returned without a tow only to re-coal for another sortie. Often schooners were picked up in mid-lake, a full day's sail from Chicago. In the tug war of 1890, some tugs went as far as Sheboygan, a matter of 125 miles. Some even waited outside the breakwaters at Milwaukee hoping to pick up Chicago-bound vessels as quickly as the beer city tugs dropped them in open water. With such an abundance of free rides abounding, the schooner-men were not anxious to have the wars come to a speedy conclusion.

Violence also erupted from time to time among lumber shovers, dock wallopers, grain trimmers, loafers, roustabouts and stevedores that congregated on the docks. The rivalries between trades were exasperated by two factors. On the one hand, the unionized trades were dominated by a single ethnic group. On the other hand, most of the longshore jobs were filled by drifters hired to do instant work for instant pay. There was always a milling throng of men, seeking employment or awaiting a certain vessel's arrival to perform some service. The lumber shovers were mostly Czechs who had migrated from the old crown land of Bohemia in Central Europe. Many of them lived in the area along Canalport Avenue, hard by the lumber district, known as Little Bohemia. They had their own union and few other ethnics were able to join its membership. Working in gangs of between four and eight people at so much per thousand feet, the average worker earned $1.50 to $2.00 per day. It was a sight to see a gang of lumber shovers attack a vessel and strip it of its cargo. According to underwriters, a ship of 200 tons could carry 200,000 board feet of lumber (give or take between 10 and 20 percent depending on the season), and a gang of four could unload a ship in a single day, all by hand.

As the Port of Chicago was one of the busiest in the world during the summer, in winter it became one of the most deserted. In no other place did the power of cold weather work such a dramatic change. When the insurance rates ran out at noon on the last day of November, the fleets began stripping down for the winter.

Before the development of bascule (draw) bridges, the large center pier required for swing bridges left little room for ships to maneuver. (CMS Collection)

Although insurance could be continued into December, the rates were usually too high to sail in profit.

The last ship to arrive at the end of a season gained something of a reputation. There were always those late birds whose owners would run every risk in order to secure the last freight at the best rate. As the season came to a close, those whose livelihood was dependent upon the fleets were forced to seek other work. It was said that fully one-fifth of the entire population of Chicago was dependent on the shipping interests, either as a business or for employment. Many of the day laborers would head for the lumber camps in the neighboring Lakes states during the winter to earn a living with hands more accustomed to the shovel, hook or sling than the axe helve. Some scattered to river and saltwater ports, while others remained in the city and sought temporary employment to carry them through the winter.

In the off-season, river pirates preyed upon the idle shipping, and tugs were a prime target. Equipment, cordage and even coal was often taken from the tugs, particularly in the fall and late sailing season. The press dramatized the situation and cautioned against the menace. An editorial in *Inter-ocean* warned, "We will have from 2,000 to 3,000 idle sailors in Chicago this coming winter and the desperadoes among them will, without doubt, work the fleet of fine large vessels laid up in the harbor. Owners should strip their craft of everything movable and where this is not possible shipkeepers should be left aboard."

Now the stormy gales could howl their loudest with no anxious ones waiting for tidings from overdue ships on the Lakes. The insurance men could sleep in peace while the ship owner counted his profits or computed his loss on the season's business. The columns of the press devoted to marine intelligence also went into hibernation, but not before printing a list of vessels and their whereabouts in the harbor so that postmen could make deliveries where onboard habitation post continued. The river was now lined with craft stripped of their sails and rigging and showing only their bare outlines. But not all were deserted. Some captains took up residence in the cabins with their families until the Straits opened again in spring, and a few lucky sailors were retained to tend the ships during the winter. The seaman turned caretaker, with a supply of fuel, an old armchair, plenty of coffee and tobacco, was ready for a long winter of easy living. The pay was small but the housing went with the job and a ship's cabin could be a very cozy home.

In their solitude, the boats at their winter roost seemed to tower more darkly and immensely, crowded together, side by side, mile after mile along the river's edge, the mightiest freighter held as helplessly as the smallest harbor skiff. Nothing moved except an occasional fire boat trying to keep a way open, often in vain. No one stirred on the docks. The rumble of the pivot bridges was stilled, for no boat passed.

Commerce had stopped. Business was dead. The grain vessels lay motionless, laden with corn and wheat. The lumber hookers covered with ice and snow presented a far different picture than when under sail. The black colliers rested darkly on the white snow more grim of aspect even than in summer.

It would be months before the cycle began anew and the return to harbor industry brought with it the welcome promise of economic prosperity to the laborer and the city at large.

Chapter Sixteen

Masters of the Inland Seas

The life of a seaman or master on the Great Lakes was perhaps not as brutal as that of their counterparts on salt water, but it could be just as dangerous and sometimes just as lonely. Because ships and crews were smaller on the inland seas, there was a greater familiarity between captain and crew, who often ate at the same table. As Herman Melville said, "Lakemen were as much an audacious mariner as any."

This chapter and the next, on the captains and crews of Great Lakes sailing vessels, are adapted by the author from Schooner Passage: Sailing Ships and the Lake Michigan Frontier *(2000), by Loyola University historian Theodore J. Karamanski, a CMS member.*

by Theodore J. Karamanski

With the wind blowing a gale and the ship overloaded, the brig *Indiana* pitched on her side. Cold lake water foamed over the bulwarks and the little ship looked as if it might capsize. Under a leaden October sky the winds lashed the ship first from the bow then from the beam, counter punches that threatened passengers and crew with a sudden tragic end to their voyage to Chicago. It was upon Captain McKenzie, the master of the *Indiana*, that their fate depended. On a ship, in the extreme peril of the sea, only one opinion mattered, only one will prevail, only one voice stood between the passengers and their doom. But the swirling winds of the gale clearly "baffled all the captain's skill," and his faulty orders had helped to pitch the ship on its beam ends.

"Profane beyond degree," was the way one terrified passenger recalled the master. Seemingly unable to control himself any better than the sailing ship, McKenzie hurled his oaths against the storm and heaped profanities upon his crew, "but his free-flowing curses availed him nothing." Careening over the lake a few inches of freeboard from disaster, Captain McKenzie acted decisively to save his ship. He ordered the crew to cut away the deck cargo. Heavy barrels of whiskey, densely packed at midship, were pitched over the side. The brig slowly righted itself and stood steady before the waves. The Captain's decision was nothing more than good seamanship, but made at the right time and executed properly it prevented a deadly shipwreck.

Captain McKenzie of the *Indiana* was no hero. From the slender leaves of the historical record he appears to share little with Horatio Hornblower, Jack Aubrey, or other fictional personifications of the stalwart master of a vessel. In fact no sooner did McKenzie save his ship from careening to destruction than he himself was careening about the deck drunk. Two of the whiskey kegs, their heads opened, had remained lashed to the mast. The Captain announced that it was henceforth free to all and all made freely of it, quaffing liquor from pails and water dippers. All but two of the men on the ship imbibed. One of those was a young man from the temperance state of Maine named William Folsom who was shocked by the behavior of the captain and crew. "They got ingloriously drunk; they rolled unsteadily across the deck; they quarreled, they fought, they behaved like Bedlamites, and how near shipwreck was the goodly brig from that day's drunken debauch on Chicago free liquor will never be known." In spite of the "wraughling of crew and captain" the *Indiana*, borne on a "tempest of profanity," safely reached Chicago after a fifteen day passage from Detroit.

As young William Folsom stepped on to the Chicago dock, dizzy from the constant pitching of the ship, he was grateful to leave the *Indiana* and her master behind. But the very human picture of a lake sailing master Folsom recorded in his memoir, *Fifty Years in the Northwest* (1888), provides a sobering look at a historical figure all too easily romanticized. Sailing the lakes, especially in 1836, when Folsom made his journey to Chicago, could be a hard, tough business. In addition to almost continuous heavy seas throughout the voyage Captain McKenzie had to contend with a quarrelsome crew, complaining passengers, and a cook who literally tried to poison everyone aboard the vessel. He had the latter fellow flogged and turned over to police authorities. To top things off one of the passengers tried to leave the ship without paying his full fare and Captain McKenzie laid the deadbeat out with a hard right cross.

These challenges, when joined with the complete absence of charts, the lack of navigation aides, and the few harbors of refuge, clearly meant that commanding a Lake Michigan sailing ship was not a job for the fainthearted. A sober look at the masters of Lake Michigan sailing vessels reveals that a diverse array of men commanded the more than 1,000 ships that scudded across the inland seas during the nineteenth century. They were neither Hornblowers nor Wolf Larsons, but sailing men drawn to the lakes by opportunity, small businessmen carving out a place in a frontier economy, heartlanders contending as best they could with what Rudyard Kipling called "a fully accredited ocean."

The masters of the first Great Lakes ships were saltwater men. Many quickly learned the particular chal-

Great Lakes crewmen's uniforms consisted of whatever they had in their wardrobe, which was minimal because employment was seasonal. Headgear varied from bowlers to rain hats. (CMS Collection)

lenges of the inland seas. Those who did not perished quickly. The pilot of the *Griffon*, a man named "Luke" who was described as a "malcontent," was the first saltwater man to misjudge the power of Lake Michigan. The Recollet missionary Louis Hennepin reports that Indians warned Luke to remain anchored in a sheltered bay as there was "a great storm in the middle of the lake." The pilot raised sail anyway and the ship was last seen "tossing in an extraordinary manner, unable to resist the tempest. . . ." This first account of a Great Lakes shipwreck reveals a consistent theme in the maritime literature of the region: the unwillingness of saltwater sailors to truly respect the inland seas.

Several of the skippers of the first United States vessels on the Great Lakes were also former saltwater men. The master of the schooner *Porcupine* in 1815 was a Lieutenant Packer, who had served under Oliver Hazzard Perry on Lake Erie. Jacob Varnum, the government factor at Chicago, described him as "a Virginian as well by overbearing hauteur as by birth and with all a perfect tyrant." As the little ship neared Mackinac, Packer gave a demonstration of the type of discipline which while common on the oceans, would not be long tolerated on Great Lakes ships. He felt the helmsman was not doing a good job holding the ship on its course in the face of the contrary winds and currents of the straits. This "raised the ire of Packer against the helmsman. He ordered a fresh hand to the wheel and the former man to receive a dozen lashes. Scarcely a minute elapsed when she went to the opposite tack and then he made another change at the wheel and gave another dozen or so [and] on successively until every seaman on board took his turn at the wheel and received his quota of lashes." Packer was a military man on a military vessel, yet Varnum and the other passengers were shocked by his harsh discipline which they found out-of-place on the lakes and "unworthy" of an American.

During the frontier period, while its own maritime culture was taking root, the Great Lakes territories needed men with seagoing experience, even if all of the traditions of the sea, such as brutal punishment, were not appropriate. James Fenimore Cooper's novel *The Pathfinder*, which is set on Lake Ontario, contrasts the arrogant and potentially dangerous actions of a saltwater mariner, with the intuitive talents of the young hero, born and raised on the shores of the inland sea. "Just as I expected," blustered the sailor upon seeing the lake for the first time. "A pond in dimensions, and a scuttlebutt in taste . . . This bit of a pool look like an ocean!"

In *Moby Dick* Herman Melville, who had personal experience with Lake Michigan, tried to put this prejudice to rest. Through the character of Steelkilt, a Great Lakes sailor, Melville had a chance to warn that the inland seas were "swept by Borean and dismasting blasts as direful as any that lash the salted wave; they know what shipwrecks are, for out of the sight of land, however inland, they have drowned full many a midnight ship with all its shrieking crew." Lakemen, Melville concluded, were "as much an audacious mariner as any."

Newcomers from the ocean only needed, as one old mariner recalled, "a trip or two" to have the "conceit of them." Captain John Kenlon, a veteran salt water man trusted with his first Lake Michigan command, had the starch taken out of him before his ship cleared sight of Chicago. He demanded to know why the water casks were empty at the start of the voyage. The cook just looked at him and exclaimed, "By the Heavens! Fresh from the salt water." Kenlon was handed a bucket and told, "Throw it overboard and help yourself to some of the finest drinking water you ever tasted." After meekly tasting the cold, sweet water Kenlon "walked aft and could literally 'feel' the silent laughter of the crew as they followed me with their eyes."

Leonard Withington Noyes was a twenty-two year old Newburyport Yankee who emigrated to the Lake Michigan frontier in 1841. He proudly wrote home that after serving only a year before the mast he had been made a master. Back home, he com-

Schooners were favored by Great Lakes shippers long after steamships came onto the scene because of their relatively low operating costs. They could be sailed by as few as five people. (CMS Collection)

plained there was little opportunity for a young man without means. "Show me the Man in Newburryport that would give me a vessel to saile, they have Sones enough for all their vessels there." He admitted that the schooner was "a homley Craft" but quickly added that "I have the promise of a better one next Spring." Young Captain Noyes' rapid assent, however, was not universally appreciated. He complained that "the Old Captains and Sailors on these Lakes" were "very jealous of me." Noyes' experience revealed the tension between the lakemen and the saltwater sailors.

> They think I am getting along too fast for a boy, and consequently reported all sorts of Stories about me last season (such as he is no Sailor but a Sail-maker; Knows nothing of the Lake. Nothing but a green Yankee Boy, and even Reported me Drunk to the Owners several times). . . . I weathered it out in spite of them. Made two more trips than any vessel in the same trade and weathered out gales that some men were lost in. I found one

friend among them Capt. Peterson of the Schooner *St. Joseph* he is the finest man in Grand River fleet, and a sailor too more than I could say of many of them, they all appear to be friendly this spring as they cannot bluff me off.

Even after commerce was well established on Lake Michigan there was a constant flow of saltwater sailors into the ranks of lake mariners. Timothy Kelley, who grew up in Manitowoc during the 1850s, looked up to the saltwater men for their skill and experience. "They made A-1 seamen of the boys and every branch of the sailor's craft," he recalled, "was thoroughly ground into us not at all uncommonly with the aid of the traditional rope's end." Kelley particularly identified this group as likely to produce the vessel's "fo'c'sle lawyer whose talk, to his own satisfaction at least, showed a more intimate knowledge of sailor's rights than any admiralty lawyer could boast." Kelley believed that saltwater sailors made up a "large part of the crews of the big sailing boats." There is no direct evidence to either support or contradict that assertion. Historian Jay Martin, based on a statistical sample of biographies, estimated that just under fourteen percent of vessel officers had saltwater experience. Certainly, as the nineteenth century reached its end and sailing ships declined, the need for an influx of saltwater seamen all but vanished.

The world of the lake schooner was male dominated. Women who broke this barrier were most often ship's cooks. John Kenlon described his cook on the schooner *Resumption* as a "broad-shouldered" hard-working woman, able "to take care of herself in almost any emergency." Her only vice in Kenlon's opinion was her penchant for "borrowing" the captain's cigars. In 1884 the Chicago *Inter-Ocean* tried to insinuate that schooner cooks served more than hot food to the masters and mates. The names of many Chicago vessels with female cooks were printed in the newspaper. One captain tried to squash the "slander" by threatening the *Inter-Ocean*'s marine reporter: "I swear by all that's good and great that if he prints me, I'll kill him." The newspaper also drew a quick reaction from captains' wives. The wife of one master condemned the practice of allowing women on ships and contended that, "If the wives would be a little more watchful, they might drive these women from the fleet themselves." Several vessel owners shared with the newspaper their orders to put the cooks ashore. Little sympathy was expressed for the working women who lost their jobs. Schooner captains and sometimes even mates would occasionally take their wives and children along for a trip. "This is the season of the year when the wives of vessel captains turn out in full force and take possession of cabins," the *Inter-Ocean* reported in July, 1884.

Children relished such visits, "tripping over deck loads of lumber seeking the best amusement they could find," while "the proud fathers carry their youngest and introduce them to their friends." In 1872, when he first became a vessel master, Timothy Kelley took advantage of the good weather in June and brought his wife along for a run. That occasion was an exception and normally there were no women aboard his ships. Mary Ames, wife of the master of the schooner *Pride*, took a trip with her husband from Saugatuck to Chicago. With virtually no wind the trip took three days and she labeled the whole business a bore. More often the lake's unpredictable weather would cause sea sickness or worse. In July 1891 the scow schooner *Silver Cloud* was lost near Sheboygan. A northeast gale raised rib-cracking heavy seas and the old scow fast took on water. When the captain went down to the cabin to see to his wife and child the swamped vessel suddenly capsized. Had they been on deck they might have scrambled into the rigging, as did the crew, and survive. As it was, the family perished in the cabin.

A mother and three children trapped in the cabin of the schooner *Experiment* survived after the captain and crew were swept away to their deaths. An air pocket formed in the cabin and for twenty-four hours the mother tried to keep hold of her children in the icy blackness. Her infant was at one point washed out of her arms. The other children were rescued when curiosity seekers rowed out to the upturned ship and after hearing the mother's pounding on the planks, chopped a hole through the hull. While some masters, particularly those who owned their own ships, wanted to share with their families at least a part of their sailing life, most captains would have agreed with the marine reporter who argued that in a storm "a woman is only in the way, or worse, for she often unnerves the crew by her very presence and alarm." With only a few exceptions the deck of a schooner was a male preserve.

The day-to-day duties of a commander of a Lake Michigan schooner consisted of blending the need to get the most speed possible out of the vessel, with the need to keep up with the regular maintenance of the ship. A skilled mariner knew numerous ways to squeeze a bit more speed out of any weather condition. Able seaman Nels Palmer had a nightmare experience with a staysail when he shipped out of Chicago on the *Ellen Williams*. To keep the schooner cracking on the captain would order set every inch of canvas she could stand. His "lucky sail" was a topmast stay sail. "This sail was way up aloft, close to the moon." As the *Ellen Williams* worked its way down Lake Michigan, tacking against a contrary wind, a crew member had to go aloft and take in and reset the topmast staysail after each tack:

We came about west of South Manitou Island. It was my turn to go aloft to shift over the sheets and a strong wind was blowing, but I went out on the triangle stays. I got a good hold on the staysail and was about to throw the sail and her sheet over the top stay when a strong puff of wind lifted the sail up in the air like a balloon, me hanging on to the sheets, was lifted up in the air and off the stay I went. I was a long way from home dangling between heaven and earth. Here again the Good Lord was with me, the sail made one great sweep and came back very gentile [*sic*] and

landed me close to the topmast . . . coming down from the rigging
I found that my knees were shaking and shivering to let me know
how close I had been to the Davy Jones Locker.

When Palmer discovered that several of his shipmates had similar
encounters setting the dangerous sail they conspired to cut its line
and let the wind shred it to pieces.

While ordering men into danger was part of a master's duty, a
bigger challenge could be keeping the crew busy with the drudg-
ery of maintaining a sailing
ship. Scraping, painting, and
polishing were the day-in-
day-out duties of an able seaman. Indeed it was the mind-
less repetition of these tasks
which likely made men
embrace the danger and thrill
of fighting a gale or working
aloft.

The smell most lakemen
associated with their days
before the mast was the odor
of tar. "Many an hour and
many a day have I spent midst
our shipping," a Milwaukee

The fresh fruit trade from western Michigan to the markets in Chicago accounted for a substantial amount of Lake Michigan traffic well into the twentieth century. (CMS Collection)

lake captain recalled, "and the aroma from pitch and tar is as sweet
smelling today as in days of youth." Tar was used in a variety of
concoctions to help seal the seams of the hull, deck, and to preserve the masts and bulwarks. During the 1870s it was possible for
ships to obtain all the coal tar they wanted from municipal gas
works in large towns such as Milwaukee or Chicago. Tar was used
so extensively in vessel upkeep that it sometimes looked as if the
schooners were glued together by the stuff.

So good were officers at keeping the crew busy that few Great Lakes vessels did not look neater and cleaner after a trip than before. While most of the busy work was scraping, washing, and painting, good mariners learned how to conduct even more serious repairs while underway. On the *City of Grand Haven* the mate showed the crew how to plug leaks in the old ship's hull while under full sail. Old rope was chopped into small pieces and placed in a bushel basket. The basket was then pushed by long poles over the leaky planks. The inrushing water sucked the fragments of hemp out of the basket and into the seam, caulking it temporarily. Other ordinary tasks which consumed a sailor's day were patching sails, helping the cook peel potatoes, or oiling the windlass.

Chapter Seventeen

Captains and Crews:
Management of the Sailing Ships

The lash—a punishment familiar to any watcher of Hollywood sea sagas—was a rarity on the Great Lakes, but booze was not. Drunken sailors seem to have been a problem on the five lakes as well as the seven seas. Unlike the oceans, where ships might be weeks from the nearest land, the Great Lakes were close enough to land that masters could quickly put ashore any crewman who misbehaved.

This chapter, like the one immediately preceding it, is from Schooner Passage: Sailing Ships and the Lake Michigan Frontier *(2000), by Loyola University historian Theodore J. Karamanski, a CMS member.*

by Theodore J. Karamanski

The nature of discipline on Great Lakes ships bore little comparison to what took place on ocean going ships. Ordering a seaman who was slow or sloppy with their duties to be lashed was neither an option nor a necessity for the captains of Lake Michigan schooners. A problem sailor could be discharged within a matter of days, sometimes within hours. The small size of the ships and crews on the Great Lakes bred a much greater degree of familiarity between officers and crew on schooners. This generally worked to smooth relations between the ranks, but it also meant that sometimes an officer had to be prepared to enforce his will with his fists. Isaac Stephenson, a sometime schooner captain, enforced discipline among his lumberjacks with "a strong arm and a heavy fist." While there are documented cases of vessel masters doing the same, such as in 1885, when the captain of the *H.P. Murray* settled a labor dispute with his crew with his fists, it was not generally necessary. Timothy Kelley remembered mates and experienced seamen employing "the traditional rope's end" on boys slow to learn their job.

Most Great Lakes officers seem to have tried to avoid physical punishment yet insisted upon a sailor's obedience and respect. Seaman Duncan McLeod recalled that his skippers invariably were referred to as "Sir" and the mate as "Mr."

The most persistent cause of problems between officers and crew on Great Lakes vessels was alcohol. Heavy drinking was part of the culture of Great Lakes sailors. Like construction workers and lumberjacks, sailors lived in a male subculture which valued physical prowess aboard and conviviality when in port:

> Now the Bigler she's arrived at
> Buffalo port at last,
> And under Reed's elevator
> the Bigler she's made fast,
> And in some lager-beer saloon
> we'll take a social glass,
> We'll all be jolly shipmates,
> and we'll let the bottle pass.

Drinking was hard for a sailor to avoid. Saloons were an integral part of the shore-based marine establishment. It was at a saloon that a sailor new to a port could locate a boarding house or leave messages for friends. They served "free" bar meals for drinkers, and most important of all it was the best location for landing a berth on an outgoing ship. "The sailors had two headquarters those days," recalled one Chicago schooner man, "one was the saloon at the South Water Market dock, operated by a large and powerful Norwegian, the other was the sailors' Union Hall. The saloon at South Water Market was a real home for the sailors, and you could obtain a berth on some vessel in need of a sailor or two."

Crews raised in a saloon often were a challenge to the captain, as the test of wills which took place on the *Ellen Williams* indicates. Nels Palmer was one of a group of six sailors hired out of a Chicago sailor's dive. "Some of the old-time sailors noticed that the captain was very anxious to get a crew and they took advantage by making the captain buy the drinks." When he finally convinced them to head for the *Ellen Williams* they insisted that he get a wagon in which they could ride. "We all piled on the dray and started to sing some of the old-time sailor songs." Even though the Captain, Alver Swanson, waited until the next afternoon to leave port, many of the men were still roaring drunk. In trying to raise the main sail several of the inebriates hauled on a line when they should have stopped and fell in a tumble on the cook, who was lending a hand. The cook was injured seriously enough that it was necessary to have the ship towed back into the Chicago River so he could be sent to the Marine Hospital. Needless to say, this made Captain Swanson "real sore" and he "promised he was going to sober the boys up."

All the way down Lake Michigan he drove the men hard, demanding that every possible piece of canvas set. Palmer and another crew member retaliated by cutting a line on one of the topsails. "We waited as long as we could to give the wind a good chance to do a good job ripping up the sail." The skipper suspected what had happened and after dressing down Palmer and his accomplice, ordered them to spend their off watch time mending every rent in the canvas. By the time the *Ellen Williams* reached Manistique [Michigan] "the whole bunch of us were sore to the core, and we were all going to jump ship. . . ." But here the magic of drink worked to Captain Swanson's advantage. After helping to load the ship with lumber the crew repaired to a saloon. Several other crews were also in port and the men "met many of our old-time sailing pals and friends." After a "few cans of beer" the men "forgot all about their sorrows and troubles." Not only did none of the men quit but Palmer decided "I admired the captain, he sure knew how to handle men and also knew how to get the best of men."

The experience of the *Ellen Williams* reveals the latitude sailors had within the disciplined framework of shipboard life. Rather than openly defying an officer, disgruntled sailors could resort to sabotage or simply a work slowdown to vent their anger. On the other hand sailors took pride in their skills as seamen, and by extension in the sailing qualities of their ship and the skill of the captain. A hard-driving captain might be a source of complaint among the crew during a run and something to boast about in a saloon afterward.

For most of the schooner era on Lake Michigan the relationship between officers and crew was structured by federally mandated "Articles of Agreement." Articles were a written contract between the vessel master and a seaman. They specified how much the man was to be paid, where the ship was going, what the sailor's duties were and generally listed certain prohibited activities such as fighting, drinking, and sleeping on watch. Masters could purchase books of blank articles, so that all he had to enter was the date, wage, and destination, and all the sailor had to do was sign his name or make his mark. Articles were a legal contract and could be enforced by police action. In October 1860, Martin Busher, master of the schooner *Rapid*, had five of his crew tracked down and arrested for deserting the ship. After the men were behind bars Busher had no trouble convincing them to return to the ship.

Earlier that year, in Chicago, the master of the brig *Walbridge* had the city police arrest seaman James Gerot "for refusing to do his duty in violation of the articles which he had signed." The use of articles, however, in spite of the law, was by no means universal on Great Lakes ships. In 1856, the Milwaukee Board of Trade issued a special resolution condemning masters who did not require articles.

The failure of many Lake Michigan captains to make use of Articles of Agreement reflects the fluidity of the labor situation during the schooner era. Some ships seem to have gathered a new crew for every run. "Plenty of sailors and plenty of ships in those days," one sailor recalled. If a sailor who had not signed articles wanted a few days off or wished to go on another ship they would simply grab their sea bag and leave as soon as they got to port. Captains arriving at busy ports also liked the freedom to discharge the bulk of the crew. Lumber ships entering the Chicago River frequently had to wait for dock space at the Lumber Market. Rather than keep the whole crew under pay for two or three idle days a master would better serve the owners by discharging the men and then hiring a new crew for the return run. Nor did sailors seem to mind this tactic; rather than mope about a ship in port they preferred to hit the bars on shore or find another ship. Yet this rapid turnover must have hurt the efficiency of a crew's performance in a crisis, and put a tiresome responsibility on the master of a ship ready to leave port.

In July 1881, Captain Timothy Kelley was ready to be towed out of the Chicago harbor when he discovered his cook had jumped ship. He made fast his schooner, the *Lottie Wolf*, near the Lake Street bridge and went ashore to hunt up a cook. When he came back the entire crew had deserted (perhaps they were thirsty). Leaving the new cook, Kelley set off in search of a crew. Failing to find a single man he returned to the *Lottie Wolf* only to find the new cook had also jumped ship!

Cooks were generally among the more steady members of a ship's crew. A ship between cargos still needed a cook; besides a good cook was such a morale asset that a smart captain would try to keep him or her aboard. The food aboard schooners was good as a rule. "The fare or living provided by the cook under the captain's orders was in most instances of good quality," recalled Arthur B. Strough. "Most captains provided liberally for the living of their crews and the men generally lived better than when at home." At the start of the season ships put up stores of dried fruit, cured or salted meats, bags of flour, coffee, and sugar. They also made occasional purchases of fresh meats, vegetables, and stove wood at ports along the way. "Salt Pork and Lob-Scow was a the main menu," Nels Palmer recalled. "Lob-Scow was sailor's dish, you could call it stew or hash. This was the leftovers with every-thing put in one pot and warmed for supper."

All meals were taken aft in the galley. The captain presided at the table, or if he was on deck, the mate. "In the galley the captain sat at the head of the table," remembered one sailor. "The mate was next at his right and the boy in the crew was at the lower end of the table." If a certain formality prevailed on some vessels regarding seating at the table, the very fact that the officers and men ate at the same table was a significant departure from the custom of ocean vessels and perhaps provides the reason why the crews ate better on the Great Lakes. A journalist in 1884 observed:

> You have only to go below into the cabin and listen to the conver-sation which passes around the table, to hear the sailor and the master discuss abstruse questions of politics and religion, science or social life, and the interjected comments of the remainder of the company, to know you are in the midst of a good-tempered family. Social distinctions, there are none at the table, but the meal over and the routine business of the vessel resumed, all is changed. The Captain is again the autocrat for six hours, the lapse of time between meals. Some captains would send the cook to take the helm so that all the officers could share in a meal togeth-er.

Both vessel owners and sailors sought collective action as a means to control wages. What ensued was a sort of tug-of-war that extended through the shipping season. Early in April masters and vessel owners in major ports like Chicago and Milwaukee would meet and try to establish uniform rates. Sailors, anxious for work at the start of the season, would accept the usually modest wages offered. In 1860, for example, masters of grain vessels from Buffalo, Cleveland, Oswego, Detroit and Chicago met in the latter city and resolved to pay seamen twenty-five dollars per month. To enforce this agreement, they also resolved that all hiring of sailors would be done through the port shipping office. These non-binding terms would be challenged during the course of the season. A rise in the price of wheat would encourage a captain anxious to get underway as soon as possible to offer a higher wage and to seek his crew at a waterfront saloon, not at the shipping office.

Nor were masters the only ones paying attention to the freight-rates. Savvy seamen responded to a jump in rates with a demand for higher wages. The dockside was the scene of numerous ad hoc negotiations and calculations based on the latest news. Nor were disputes always settled peacefully. In 1874, with a national depression slowing shipping to a trickle, a Lake Michigan bound schooner, the *Annie Vaught*, was stopped at a Buffalo wharf by a gang of fifty sailors who had heard that the captain had signed on his crew for $1.25 per day. The men contended that $1.50 had been the going rate in the port and would not allow a lower wage. A "parley" ensued after which the master of the *Annie Vaught* raised the pay of his crew and was allowed to make sail.

Wildcat strikes set in motion by mobs of sailors surging over the docks, stripping ships of their crews, were common in the 1860s and 1870s. The master of a schooner at a Cleveland wharf in 1874 defended at gun point his ship and loyal crew from a mob of wildcatters.

Captains were esteemed for their ability to get as much as possible out of their ships and crews. Along the docks of Lake Michigan the sailing qualities of masters and ships were fiercely debated. "Alver Swanson," for example, was known as a "Swede from the old school and a real sailorman." His 321 ton, three mast-

ed schooner, *Ellen Williams*, was known as "a heavy weather vessel." Which meant that it "seldom laid in for bad weather." The
master of the *Annie Peterson* named his ship after his daughter and
with a father's pride he never could bear any ship getting the best
of her. He permanently kept a broom tied to his mainmast to signal his willingness to challenge all comers to a test of speed.
According to the dockside scuttlebutt he too was "a good weather
man," meaning he could get the most speed out of any wind conditions.

Captain Peterson's aggressive spirit sometimes got the better of
his judgement. Once, just outside the Chicago River Peterson
raised the broom to the schooner *Gassliaf.* The ships were neck-
and-neck all the way down the lake. When they reached the
Sturgeon Bay channel both schooners were still clipping with all
sails set. Neither captain would "give way" for the other and as the
ships tried to maneuver in the confined space of the channel their
spars became entangled. To the sickening chorus of splintering
wood and ripping canvas the duel came to an inglorious end with
"much damage" done to each vessel. Such lapses of judgement,
however, were tolerated in a skipper whose regular devotion to
good sailing might mean one or two more runs per season.

A master's zeal for speed could also infect his crew and rally
them to extra exertion. William Houghton, helmsman of the
schooner *Mechanic*, remembered staying at the wheel for two
straight watches as his ship passed every down bound vessel "one
after the next." To encourage speed the shipping establishment
often awarded prizes to the first vessel to enter the harbor at the
start of the season. Silk hats or new suits frequently were garnered
by the winning masters.

Schooner captains were confident men who sought to control as
many facets of their trade as possible. Frequently they would seek
input in the building and fitting out of vessels. Most sought an
ownership share of the ships they commanded and looked for a
free hand in the management of the ship. A.P. Dutton, one of the

pioneer merchants of Racine, recalled a resolution passed by a council of schooner masters in the 1850s:

> The "court" held that when a man had once been appointed master of a craft the owner had nothing to do or say about the vessel until she laid up in the fall and that the master was the sole director of the vessel in and out of port. The masters declared that they had the right to insure, hold all funds, give no trip sheet, or send in any statements until they settled up after the vessel went into winter quarters.

While masters may have sought this type of complete authority, it was, generally, only achieved by men who owned their own vessels outright. More typically owners used telegraph or messenger services to convey to captains special instructions regarding what cargos to take and at what rates.

The business side of operating a schooner could be the most challenging aspect of command. The fixed costs of operating a vessel—wages, provisions, towing, insurance, unloading—constantly had to be balanced against the rates paid for bulk cargoes. The advent of grain elevators in the major grain ports of the lake meant that vessel masters needed to maintain an accurate knowledge of the fluctuating price for grain, lumber, and iron ore. Grain merchants used their elevator capacity to hold grain not only for its best wholesale price in the East but in order to obtain cheap freight rates from the schooner captains desperate for a cargo. Conversely, a good master might dock his vessel for several days and wait for an advance in rates. The key was to be able to properly anticipate a rate change. Among things a veteran skipper in the grain fleet might calculate would be the strength of the lumber and ore markets. Lumber hookers or ore boats might seek grain cargos if their normal trade was depressed and this would, of course, drive down grain freight rates. Another factor would be how close the elevators were to capacity. If the elevators were full and more crop was on its way merchants would grow anxious to move the grain and the rates would advance.

The strain on masters, managing their boats, crews, and trade, was often extreme. Captain Augustus Pickering, who in 1834 had been the toast of Chicago as the man who brought the first ship into the Chicago River, is an example of a master who broke under the pressure. In 1844, he supervised the building of a new schooner at Sackets Harbor, New York. In order for the *Columbia* to reach its Lake Michigan destination it needed to use the Welland Canal. With his new ship loaded with 130 western immigrants Pickering discovered to his mortification that he had built the vessel one inch too wide to fit in the canal locks. Amid a chorus of complaints from the west bound settlers Pickering set about the arduous process of planing an inch off the sides of the schooner. As the work dragged on and the complaints mounted, Pickering's nerve broke. Although he was the father of six children, the forty-year-old captain walked into the woods along the canal and fatally cut his throat.

In the fall of 1875, another Lake Michigan captain took his own life. William C. Rothwell was an English immigrant who rose through the ranks to the position of master. After years serving as a mate in the lumber fleet of Charles Hackley he was entrusted with the charge of the schooner *Rouse Simmons*. One week after taking the helm, Rothwell's ship collided with another schooner in heavy fog off Grand Haven. After a lengthy lay-up the *Rouse Simmons* was back to work, although due to heavy weather she suffered repeated damage to her rigging. Finally, after a stormy November passage from Muskegon to Chicago the ownership became exasperated with Rothwell's management. The *Simmons* had lost her mainsail off Manitowoc, collided with a pier and lost her anchor at the mouth of the Chicago River. When he was relieved of command Rothwell hit bottom. He checked into the Sherman House hotel, downed a bottle of morphine, turned on the gas in his room, and lay down in his bed with a brand-new revolver and a razor. The latter were unnecessary as he was found dead of an overdose the next morning. Even a dispirited master was careful and thorough.

Masters like the unfortunate Captain Rothwell did not last long on the quarter deck. The shipping season was too short for owners to long tolerate mishaps which kept schooners off the lake. Captain A.L. Huntley of the schooner *Merrill* learned this lesson in 1849. A Congregational minister, George Nelson Smith was a one-quarter owner of the *Merrill*. When Huntley reported a $100 debt at the end of the season, the Reverend felt impelled to investigate his conduct. Smith discovered "The hands say he is drunk in port, goes to the theater . . .

Great Lakes sailors often hung around on Chicago's docks until a schooner master was ready to sail and recruit a crew. In the winter, when lake shipping was minimal, they often worked cutting trees in the forests of Wisconsin and Michigan. (CMS Collection)

and cares not whether he sails or beaches or what, often sleeps during his watch." Huntley was sacked. While Rothwell may have simply been guilty of bad luck and Huntley the victim of sailors' gossip, such was the lot of the master who did not own at least a share of his vessel.

Captain Samuel Ward, who in 1825 took the first ship from Lake Michigan through the Erie Canal, would not have inspired most owners with confidence. He had a distinctly non-nautical bearing. "He might have been taken for a prosperous country merchant," a friend recalled. Nor did he relish life aboard ship. In port he preferred to stay in hotels. Nor was he a particularly attentive master. He once ordered his men to set all the sails only to discover that he had yet to order the crew to raise the anchor. Yet, Samuel Ward was a gifted manager of the business of chartering and marketing cargos and as master of his own ships he never had to brook criticism for his shortcomings as a sailor.

It was not uncommon for a master to be a business man first and a sailor second. Skippering a schooner was one means to the end of making a fortune on the Lake Michigan frontier. Leonard Noyes, who came in the 1840s to Grand Haven from Massachusetts with salt-water experience, disliked the life of a sailor but understood he could do quite well as a vessel master. "This is a wild Place to live," he wrote of Michigan in the 1840s, "but I can stand it [if] I can make Money." Noyes was constantly on the watch for other investment opportunities. For a time he thought about trying his hand at fur trading with the Indians or marketing grain. He did sell lumber, and salted shell fish from New England, before finally leaving schooners to operate a freighting business on the Chicago River. With a partner he bought a steamboat for $3,500. Each man put up $500 with the rest due in a year. Noyes went deeper into the hole to have a new canal boat built at a cost of $400. His timing, however, was excellent. The Illinois and Michigan Canal, after twelve years of on-and-off construction, opened that summer. Noyes' new canal boat was suddenly worth $1,000 and his passenger and freight business between Chicago and Bridgeport boomed.

Vessel ownership was the key to independence for the schooner master and it was a goal that was within the grasp of most captains. The cost of a new schooner was generally too high for anyone living on wages to afford. The schooner *Rouse Simmons*, a typical lumber hooker, cost $17,000 at the time it was built, in 1869.

Yet because wooden ships rapidly depreciated in value older schooners could be purchased at modest prices. William Callaway, a saltwater sailor who had been drawn to the lakes by the vision of meat three times a day, became a vessel owner in 1862. He was approached by the mate of a grain schooner on which he had just completed a run from Buffalo to Milwaukee:

"Bill, lets you and I buy a vessel of our own."

"I asked him how much money he had and he said: 'A hundred dollars.' I had the same amount. Our united resources did not seem a sum that would go far toward the purchase of a vessel, but 'where there's a will there's a way.' We started out, got as far as Division Street bridge, and there saw a smart little schooner called the *Mariner*. We asked the captain if he knew of a small vessel for sale, and he told us the *Mariner* was for sale . . . the next day we bought the vessel for $850, paying $200 down and giving our notes for the balance—$100 to be paid each month for five months and $150 in the following July."

The whole venture "looked rather risky" to Callaway, but he and his partner managed to pay all the notes as they came due and in less than a year were profiting from the venture. Callaway's $100 was his entry ticket to a new world of risk and opportunity. As owner of a schooner he rose to the rank of master. He was sought out by other men of business to participate in a variety of ventures. With that investment he moved from being a laborer to a capitalist. It was an entry into a world inviting in its prospect of profit yet with the potential of disaster looming with the approach of every weather front.

Vessels were frequently under insured by schooner men who wanted to reduce their fixed costs. Fortunes won over years of hard work and good luck were not infrequently blown away by a single gale. Asahel P. Lyman, one of Sheboygan's leading merchants, had his share of marine misfortunes. His first ship, the schooner *Morning Star*, into which he had invested years of savings, went to the bottom with its entire cargo of wheat on its maiden voyage. Within a few years Lyman recovered his fortune and again invested in the shipping business only to again meet with disaster. In June 1868, his clipper bark *Cortland* collided with a passenger steamer bearing the ill-fated name *Morning Star*. In the cold and confusion 300 lives were lost. Lyman paid $85,000 in damages and retired from all further involvement with sailing ships.

One way to lessen the risks inherent in Great Lakes sailing was to only own a partial share in a vessel. Even the master of a ship who could afford to own the ship outright might prefer to only own a half or quarter interest in the ship he commanded and invest a portion of his profits in a share of another ship. Many schooner masters may have persisted in their jobs out of pure love for sailing, but it did not hurt that the potential for considerable profit was ever present.

Samuel Ward's 1825 voyage from Green Bay through the Erie Canal to New York was said to have netted him $6,000 profit. That sort of windfall, however, was not typical. Captain Arthur N. Nelson, a Norwegian mariner based in Chicago, reported that during the prosperous years before the Panic of 1873 he was able to net earnings of $6,000 per year for his small schooner *White Mary*. In 1887, the *City of Grand Haven* grossed an estimated $4,281 for ten trips between Muskegon and Chicago during a two month period of time. At that rate a vessel could pay for itself within three years of being launched. In hard years vessel profits could dwindle to a few hundred dollars.

Although some dedicated mariners would operate their ships as tramps, hunting up a cargo whereever it could be found, smart owners understood it was not wise to risk a vessel when the rates did not pay, and they would lay up the ship for the season, or until the rates recovered. The low cost of maintaining a schooner in port as well as its modest operating costs gave sailing ships an edge over their steam competition. In his study of the schooner

Rouse Simmons, historian Theodore Charrney argued that due to the high cost of steamer personnel, insurance, and fuel, a $1,000 schooner often earned a higher profit margin, in proportion, than a $100,000 steamer.

Since most masters would at some point have had an opportunity to share in the profits of vessel ownership, the key to social and economic mobility for sailors was to rise through the ranks. Sailors who perceived and accepted this challenge were easily identified by their willingness to learn and their acceptance of responsibility. They tended to avoid the expense and emotional ties of marriage until they had at least obtained the rank of mate. Timothy Kelley did not marry until he was a mate, although his decision to help his sister at the time of the Great Fire in Chicago rather than stay with his ship cost him his job. But aside from that incident Kelley had made a good name for himself and within a year he attained his goal of being named captain, at the tender age of twenty-two.

The relationship between master and mate was a critical one in the management of the vessel and in the training of future captains. A good skipper was a role model and an invaluable employment reference. Timothy Kelley as mate of the *Annie Sherwood* in 1870 had a very cordial relationship with Captain Henry Reed. On one occasion when Reed was away from the ship visiting his wife, the vessel's owner suddenly visited the ship at Buffalo pier and ordered Kelley to immediately set sail. Kelley did so but doubled back and quietly picked up the captain unbeknown to the impatient owner. The young mate could have used the opportunity to try his hand as master, but either affection for the captain or desire for his approbation persuaded him to disobey the owner instead.

In his later years Kelley liked to tell the story of a master and mate who did not get along. One day, after relieving the mate, the Captain discovered the mate had made an entry in the log: "The

Captain's drunk today." Outraged the captain added his own entry: "Mate sober today." Some officers formed close bonds of trust and friendship and sailed together for years. The unfortunate William Rothwell, who later failed as a vessel master when finally given his chance, had served long and well as second in command to Captain Seth Lee on a number of Hackley lumber schooners.

The voyages of Lake Michigan captains were measured in days and weeks, not the months and years of the salt water marine; nonetheless they were plagued by a longing for home and loved ones. Port-bound by a gale in November 1872, Captain Timothy Kelley wrote in his diary "Awful lonesome." He was anxious to complete the last run of the season and get home, but the next morning the gale continued to blow across Georgian Bay causing the master to write: "Never so lonesome and Discouraged." Able seamen experienced the same sentiment. John Treiber, a German immigrant sailor on a Lake Michigan schooner, wrote his wife:

> Dear Darling and how ar you weall I hope and thinking of me I hope for I am thinking of you all the thime and the tim that I shall sea you.

Great Lakes sailors had more of an opportunity to visit family between voyages than saltwater sailors, but such reunions were made difficult due to the variable schedule and changing destination of schooners. With only a six to seven month sailing season Lake Michigan schooners were kept in constant motion. Even men who thrilled at commanding their own ship became demoralized by the time away from loved ones. New Englander Leonard Noyes constantly looked for opportunities to get out of sailing and home to Massachusetts. "I can do as well here at sailing as anywhere and Probably better," he wrote his brother in 1845, "but it kills me by inches, I can not stand it." In 1879 Timothy Kelley was able to make a brief stop at his home in Manitowoc during the middle of the season. After the overnight visit he wrote: "I am awful lonesome leaving Manitowoc this evening. I wish I could stay at home. I do hate this sailing business and hope I can give it up this fall." Kelley did not give up the sailor's life. Instead he spent sixty-one years sailing the freshwater sea.

Loneliness, like foul weather, was an occupational hazard. Lakemen weathered those depressions like they weathered autumn low-pressure systems, watch by watch, doing their duty, managing their ships, and earning their pay or profits. When the season finally came to an end, the captains and sailors alike would stuff their possessions into their white dunnage bags, join shipmates for a parting glass, and repair to family or friends. Only a month or two at home was enough for most captains to begin to itch for the tug of the wheel in their hands. Many sought out shipyards in the off-season where they helped to oversee the rebuilding of old ships or the rigging of new vessels. In spite of vows dutifully made to their spouses, most schooner captains could not resist the urge to return to the lakes when the ice went out. As one of their number later recalled, "We always went back the next season as long as the old schooners lasted."

PART IV

Some Maritime Institutions

Chapter Eighteen

Captain Streeter's District of Lake Michigan

Chicago has had its share of characters over the years—such politicians as Hinky Dink Kenna and Bathhouse John Coughlin, transit mogul Mike McDonald, and aviation pioneer Horace B. Wild, to name a few. However, none were more colorful than Captain Streeter. When his boat ran aground just off the shore in Lake Michigan, he stayed put, arranged for the shoreline to surround it, and declared a separate republic. Now one of Chicago's poshest neighborhoods, it was for decades the scene of pitched battles.

This story of Cap Streeter by K.C. Tessendorf, a freelance writer, originally appeared in the fall 1976 issue of Chicago History, *a publication of the Chicago Historical Society.*

by K.C. Tessendorf

Ask a Chicagoan about Streeterville and your attention will be directed to the Near North Side area bounded by Oak Street on the north, Michigan Avenue on the west, Grand Avenue on the south, and Lake Michigan on the east, the site of many of Chicago's fanciest shops, most expensive apartment buildings, and finest medical institutions. Your informant may even volunteer some bits of folklore about its eccentric founder, the legendary George Wellington "Cap" Streeter. Even in his lifetime, Cap Streeter made better newspaper copy than history.

George Wellington "Cap" Streeter, shown here with his wife "Ma," was one of Chicago's strangest characters in an era populated by such other characters as Hinky Dink Kenna and Bathhouse John Coughlin. (Chicago Historical Society)

Streeter was shipwrecked off what is now the Gold Coast in 1886, and he stayed put in the most positive sense until 1921. He was literally the man who made this choice slice of lakefront, but he gathered little gold over the years. Instead, he survived and even thrived upon derision, threats, abuse, mayhem, armed insurgency, and imprisonment before encountering defeat and death. His passing was marked neither by disgrace nor dishonor but, as we shall see, it was greeted by sighs of relief from the establishment. During his prime, he founded a comic-opera republic and for decades exercised effective, if improbable, sovereignty over the 186-acre territory he called the "Deestric of Lake Michigan." The pesky Cap Streeter never ducked a fight.

George Wellington Streeter was born on a farm in Flint, Michigan, in 1837. One of thirteen children, about all he inherited beside a sonorous name were the genes of fighting ancestors. One Streeter, a drummer boy in the War of 1812, died following a too-strenuous drumming display at a Fourth of July fete. He was 105. Streeter's mother proudly traced her descent from Francis Marion, the Revolutionary War hero known as the Swamp Fox.

Streeter was, in many ways, a typical pre-Civil War adventurer. He wandered the Great Lakes working as a logger and trapper, as an ice cutter on Saginaw Bay, a deck hand on a vessel plying Canada's island-studded Georgian Bay, and a miner in the iron and copper country.

Then he married Minnie, a saucy hometown girl—"a very charming young lady," by his own description—"but she later proved to be more of a charmer than a lady, as I found to my sorrow." With two friends, Streeter later traveled in a covered wagon as far as the Rockies and Texas, returning to Michigan on the eve of the Civil War. He entered the Union army as a private, quickly became Gen. John M. Oliver's aide, and was discharged as a captain after fighting in the Tennessee theater.

The Civil War veteran now indulged, perhaps at his wife's prompting, in a short career as a showman. He collected a menagerie of Michigan animals and birds and created a wagon-drawn road show, gradually adding bunco and exotic carnival acts. In its second year, the George S. Wellington Shows went bankrupt. After returning to the Michigan woods as a lumberjack, he recouped enough money to purchase the *Wolverine*, a small steamer in the service of the logging camps on the Saginaw River. Following its profitable sale, the Streeters migrated to St. Louis. Cap built the *Minnie E. Streeter* himself, but his wife was not sufficiently impressed. Fortified with the family's savings, she ran off with a vaudeville troupe.

The jilted mariner plied the central rivers of America for several years, sold out, bought a hotel in New Bedford, Iowa, and sold out again. He came to Chicago in the mid-1880s and used his stake to buy a half-interest in the tawdry Apollo Theatre. He was back in show business and destined to remain in a limelight of publicity for the rest of his days.

Cap Streeter quickly established himself as a raffish personality, circulating garrulously amid the bars and shows of the city's entertainment district. He was a rather small man, sporting a flowing red mane, shaggy eyebrows, and a mussy moustache which framed a face turned brick red by prolonged exposure to the outdoor elements and indoor spirits. The wiry Streeter was a memorable sartorial spectacle in his ever-present top hat and the "tobacco-stained, rusty-green frock coat several sizes too large" that dangled from his lean shoulders to his ankles.

It was in Chicago that Streeter met and soon married his second wife, Maria Mullholland, a tough, middle-aged Irishwoman who could sustain a bender for a week, and whose fierce loyalty and skill with weapons proved to be important assets to her husband in the battles to come.

Together they encountered a flamboyant adventurer standing drinks to an appreciative barroom audience—Captain Bowen, a soldier of fortune who had recently returned from the Banana Republic wars in Central America. Down in Honduras, he told the Streeters, there were always opportunities for mercenaries and those with the capital in hand to support them. A soldier who chose the winning side would be rewarded by the successful caudillo with land grants and a lucrative position. Meanwhile, paid in advance, the wily gun runner couldn't help but get rich, Bowen said. It was just the sort of alcohol-inflamed dream which appealed to the newlyweds.

Cap Streeter sold his theater and purchased a hulk which he repaired and furnished with a secondhand boiler. On the occasion of its launching on Lake Michigan, Maria crashed a champagne bottle upon the weathered prow and announced, "I christen thee *Reutan*." She was thinking Roatan, an island off the Honduras coast that was probably a lair of revolutionaries.

Before piloting the *Reutan* down the Mississippi and on to Honduras, Streeter decided to perform some shakedown cruises on Lake Michigan, excursions to Milwaukee with paying customers. A lake gale, the captain decided, was just what was needed to prove seaworthiness; if the *Reutan* couldn't weather Lake Michigan, it surely couldn't survive a gulf storm.

On July 10, 1886, a gray and blustery day, the *Reutan*, with the Streeters, an engineer, and a few passengers aboard, embarked on

The Streeters lived for a time in a tent after they were evicted from their independent "District of Lake Michigan." (Chicago Historical Society)

its maiden voyage. The trip was so distressful that all the passengers elected to take the train back from Milwaukee. At 3 P.M., the *Reutan* passed beyond Milwaukee's breakwater and chugged south. But the wind and waves only became increasingly violent, and the master realized he had his lake gale with a vengeance.

The unwieldy vessel arrived off Chicago at 10 P.M. and, at this critical juncture, its aged boiler failed. Narrowly missing the breakwater at the mouth of the Chicago River, the Reutan drifted northwest, a captive of the storm, and ran aground about four hundred fifty feet (451.42 feet, Cap's surveyors would later aver) from the beach. Tying himself by a length of rope to the wheelhouse, the dauntless commander spent the wild night on deck and sometimes overboard, as the boat was pounded to a sieve.

In the calmer days that followed, Cap Streeter pondered his cash reserve and his liabilities and decided to stay put. The storm had banked a soggy drift of sand around the sprung bulwarks of the *Reutan*. This promised a degree of temporary safety: the hulk might provide a rent-free shelter until something better turned up.

Chicago was then in a building boom, and Streeter found excavation contractors eager to pay a fee for the right to dump fill on the beach near the *Reutan* rather than make the customary long haul to the city's northwest fringes. With little difficulty, a causeway was constructed in the shallow water. From the *Reutan*, now cozy behind a rock breakwater, a sandy desert with a network of transient shacks gradually spread to the north, south, and west. In these early years, the Streeters subsisted on the contractors' fees, the sale of junk they found in the debris, and rents from their tenants.

A dreary marsh area called The Sands, once a lawless shack town, abutted the Streeter domain. In 1857, Mayor "Long John" Wentworth had led a crowd that burned down the community of bordellos and saloons while the residents were at a dog fight. The Sands was now vacant, and no one bothered about Streeter. Not until Potter Palmer began erecting the original Gold Coast residences was Streeter noticed by the rich and powerful: he was spoiling their lake view.

In the 1890s, Cap Streeter became both a formidable and objectionable presence on the lakefront. The old showman refloated the *Reutan*, renamed it the *Maria*, and used it as a sightseeing boat for the World's Columbian Exposition of 1893. He encouraged friends and visitors to buy lots in "my valuable proppity." He had consulted an 1821 government survey which showed Lake Michigan's shoreline to be much farther west than in later surveys. From this, Streeter determined that his manmade land lay beyond the certified boundaries of Chicago, Cook County and, indeed, Illinois. He claimed to have advised Washington that he was therefore exercising his riparian rights and that he was homesteading as a Civil War veteran.

At about the time the landfilling operation merged with the original shore, the owner of that property, millionaire N.K. Fairbank, hustled out in his buggy to evict the squatter from what he believed was his land. A shouting match over the property ensued, Streeter produced a shotgun, and Fairbank fled. The choleric tycoon went straight to his lawyer, who advised him that riparian rights were an ambiguous part of the law. Going to court might result in lengthy litigation, he counseled. That was the best legal forecast the anti-Streeter forces would receive for decades to come.

The embattled Cap Streeter then broadcast his own, freewheeling, cracker-barrel legalisms: "Ripairan' rights is the right to ripair yer shore where it's wore off by the water. Don't gi'en ye no more right to fill in the lake and own the fillin' 'an it does me to dig a hole in your front yard an' own th' hole." As for the oft-repeated charge that he was nothing but a squatter, the homesteader scoffed: "Shoot; when I come here ther warn't a particle of land for me to squat on!"

Sensing that his growing throng of enemies would conspire to muscle him out in extralegal fashion, Streeter replaced the *Maria*, when it was water-borne, with a homemade castle. He secured a high-sided old scow, beached it on his domain and, upon it, built a two-story structure. The scow was his castle's buttress, and it featured a retrievable ladder. The first story was Cap's war room, the second floor his residence.

The mettle of Streeter's castle and its defenders was often tested. In the beginning, the assailants were parties of private detectives and sluggers hired by real-estate men, armed with specious warrants. Cap and Maria responded with sawed-off muskets loaded with birdshot. Their aim—pretty good, as nearby doctors testified—was to repel, not kill. Such assaults were numerous in the 1890s. As Cap told E.G. Ballard, author of *Captain Streeter: Pioneer*, who probably "fixed up" the wording:

My wife could usually hold the fort in the upper story while I skirmished around on the outside and tried to protect the place from invasion.

One day they almost succeeded in ejecting us, being able three times to throw our furniture and piano from the house, but each time I managed with a little assistance to drive them off by the use of my guns and replace the furniture in the home. I was also obliged occasionally to make trips down town to buy provisions and ammunition, for these would run out. During these absences, which the detectives were always looking for, advantage would be taken to attempt ejection. My wife, however, was a brave woman, and able to handle a gun when necessary to keep them from the top story of the house, and they learned to respect her commands after receiving a few bird shot in places where they would have preferred more ease.

On one occasion, the doughty Maria unerringly doused three deputies with boiling water from a tea kettle. Cap, then in their clutches, later affirmed that nary a drop scalded him!

Unable to budge the Streeters by force, the establishment now turned to the courts to obtain a decree dispossessing the pair. But Streeter, who had his land professionally surveyed and platted and who paid his own lawyers with deeds of land, was protected by skills his adversaries consistently underestimated.

Streeter had occasionally written to Washington seeking government assistance. These letter had gone unanswered but, in 1899, the federal bureaucracy finally replied, reporting that it could find no basis for jurisdiction over his affairs. Cap was elated. He had already "proven" by federal surveys that his domain lay beyond the control of both Chicago and Illinois. Therefore, if the federal government claimed no jurisdiction, the land was indeed his own. He was sovereign! In April, he proclaimed a republic: the District—"Deestric" in Streeterese—of Lake Michigan. A "constitutional convention" was held although, according to Cap, it was no big deal:

We established our government in the District of Lake Michigan without any flourish of authority or blare of trumpets, and, in fact, without any undue demonstration. One of my outhouses was converted into a temple of justice, and a sign placed above its door proclaimed its august character. Our deliberations, elections, and other necessary assemblages were held in this building until the police authorities of Chicago regarded it with secret disfavor.

Tipped off to one of many police raids, Streeter once arranged to be alone when two hundred invaders, led by Inspector Max Heidelmeir, arrived. The inspector's English lapsed in time of stress, as the *Kansas City Star* reported:

> "In der name of der beeble of Illinois, I gommands beace!" Cap paid no attention, but continued to read his newspaper. "In der name of der beeble of Illinois," the inspector began again, "I gommand you to disperse." "Hold on, thar," Streeter interrupted. "I cain't disperse. They ain't but one 'o me. I'd do it if I could, Max, but I cain't. "Vell," the Inspector insisted, "you god to go oud mid here." The captain refused to except by force, so was lifted, rocking-chair and all, into the patrol-wagon. He was booked for refusing to disperse when ordered, but after hearing his very logical defense, that, being only one, he could not very well "disperse," the charge was dismissed.

The numerous assaults by police and thugs led Streeter to appoint William Niles, an adventurer, military governor of the district. Shortly thereafter, Captain of Police Barney Baer drove out to reconnoiter. Niles sent two solid bullets crashing through the buggy roof, each barely missing the occupant's skull. Baer retired gracefully.

On May 25, 1900, five hundred police were readied to attack Fort Streeter "to suppress anarchy." The police soon wavered and retreated with their wounded, forced back by the Captain's rag-tag militia armed mostly with stones and clubs. While the authorities pondered their next move, Cap's army melted away. That night, the police captured Streeter and Niles, took them to jail, and gave the military governor a severe beating. Both, however, were released without being charged — jurisdictional problems again.

Although a number of invaders were killed in attempts to storm the district — one allegedly by a pitchfork — the city found it difficult to put or keep Cap in jail. He was once acquitted on self-defense; another time he proved that the birdshot from his rifle couldn't possibly have killed the policeman found with a hunk of lead in his heart. In March 1902, John Kirk, an imported Western gunman, was killed in the district. Cap was convicted of murder and sentenced to life in prison in 1904. He claimed he was framed, and Gov. John Peter Altgeld agreed by pardoning him nine months later. But while he was away, Maria died — of a broken heart, said the newspapers.

Cap resumed control over his domain, now greatly shrunk by attorney's fees. He married again in 1906: Elma Rockwood — known as "Ma" — was as stalwart as Maria had been. The city built a lakeshore road which surrounded the "Deestric," but the fading potentate said he didn't care — it improved his "proppity." In 1918, the courts finally ruled that an 1895 government patent, signed by Pres. Grover Cleveland, giving him sole title to the land was an obvious forgery. Streeterville was now a small enclave of bars and dives: "This is a frontier town, and it's got to go through its red-blooded youth. A church and WCTU branch never growed a town big yet. Yuh got to start with entertainment," philosophized Cap.

Shortly after his arrest in 1918 for selling liquor without a license and assault on a police officer, agents of the Chicago Title and Trust Company, armed with real warrants, put the torch to Streeter's castle. Ma's final charge with a meat cleaver was unavailing. Cap and Ma retreated to a third vessel, the *Vamoose*, to wanly continue the fight. Docked on the Calumet River in East Chicago, Indiana, for legal shelter, the *Vamoose* became a floating hot dog stand, in seasonal weather, often hovering around Municipal Pier and the lakefront.

The last home of Cap and Ma was the derelict Vamoose, *which Ma inherited upon Cap's death and defended with a rifle. (Chicago Historical Society)*

The feisty Captain lost his final battle—to pneumonia—on January 24, 1921, at 84. The Grand Army of the Republic buried him, and he had a forty-car funeral attended by numerous dignitaries, including Mayor William Hale Thompson. Harrison B. Riley, president of the Chicago Guaranty & Trust Company, issued a honey-tongued accolade:

> The Cap'n's ideas of law were somewhat at variance with that of the preponderant legal opinion but he was a gallant and able antagonist nevertheless. We shall miss him more than might be imagined. He kept two lawyers and one vice-president busy for twenty-one years. . . . May he rest in peace and find his lost "deestrict" in some fairer land where law and courts cease from troubling and title companies are at rest.

The Captain's death failed to end the battle over Streeterville, however. Ma continued the fight in the courts when she wasn't fending off the police, who occasionally hauled her in for violating the city's harbor laws. In 1925, the federal district court in Chicago finally ruled that, because Cap never divorced Minnie, Ma was not legally married and thus not eligible to file claims for the property. She persisted until she died penniless in Cook County Hospital in 1936, and the last suit brought by alleged heirs was dismissed in 1940, tamely ending a half century of colorful struggle and litigation over the District of Lake Michigan.

Chapter Nineteen

Maritime Music

Music has been an important part of the lives of mariners since the dawn of history, perhaps before. Chants and drums were used on ancient galleys, and songs were developed to enable seafarers to pass the long, boring hours between ports. When commerce developed on the Great Lakes in the seventeenth century, the French voyageurs brought along their canoeing songs. There has been singing on the waters ever since. These days the music emanating from a vessel on the lakes, whether it be a thousand-foot ore boat or a little sailing yacht, is apt to be a rock-and-roll beat throbbing at a hundred decibels from a boom box.

Tom and Chris Kastle for this chapter, researched and wrote about a nostalgic time before Marconi when crews on ships and in port sang sea chanteys.

by Tom and Chris Kastle

The saltwater sailor who came to the Great Lakes brought his music with him. This music not only was maritime in character but reflected a diversity of ethnic and cultural backgrounds. The music of the shellbacks blended with the songs of the voyageur and Native American to create a wealth of unique stories and songs heard in Chicago and around the lakes.

It might be a good idea to look at the differences between a sailor's life on the inland seas and on the saltwater oceans. During the heyday of sail, many of the sailors on the Great Lakes had worked previously on salt water. In the language of lake sailors, they had come "from below." They came for a host of reasons: better pay, shorter runs, fresher and higher-quality food, seasonal work, and a chance to someday have a vessel of their own. In his 1995 dissertation, Jay C. Martin quotes an English sailor named William Hulme, who heard of the relatively kind conditions of working on the Great Lakes while serving aboard a full-rigged ship sailing from Australia to Boston in 1880. Hulme was so impressed with his shipmate's description of an easy life on the lakes that he went from Boston to Buffalo by rail and embarked on a career as a Great Lakes mariner. In contrast to the rough discipline, rationed provisions, long saltwater voyages, and abusive treatment both aboard and ashore, the lakes presented Hulme with a new world where there was "no allowance of provisions, no allowance for water, and the sailors eating in the cabin with the Captain and mates; what next?"

All of the reasons why seamen, like Hulme, came to the Great Lakes are perhaps best expressed in the first two verses of the forecastle song "Me for the Inland Lakes," as imparted to Professor Ivan Henry Walton in the summer of 1933 by Captain Walkingshaw of Port Colbourne, Ontario:

> Late gales may blow an' the seas run high,
> An' the lee's full of country jakes;
> But the quarters are warm an' the grub is great,
> It's me for the open lakes.
>
> Two dollars a day they often pay,
> Much better than ocean crates;
> An' when the season's done, all winter you bum;
> It's me for the inland lakes.

The skill and determination of sailors on the lakes should not, however, be underestimated. Navigation was mostly determined through a combination of local knowledge and the process of dead reckoning. Unfamiliar shorelines as well as quickly developing storms have claimed many a ship and crew on the lakes. Although some forecastle tunes, as well as a few shanties (work songs), about working conditions, life ashore, and historical events have survived, the vast majority of lake songs, per the observations of scholars like Edith Fowke and Walton, deal with fast passages and shipwrecks.

Many of the shanties evolved from previous saltwater versions. Popular songs that documented current events of the time, as well as old favorites, were also sung on the lakes. Such songs do not necessarily reference the lakes in any way.

The ethnic influences on the body of maritime music in the Great Lakes are almost as varied as the people who came to settle on the shores. In the season of 1869–70 there were approximately 21,000 sailors—12,300 on sailing ships alone—around the lakes. During that season Captain Thomas E. Murray remarked that crews "were principally English, Irish, Scotch, a few Welshmen, with a sprinkling of Scandinavians," although one Scandinavian author has attempted to prove that the "sprinkling" of Scandinavians amounted to 65 percent of all sailors on the lakes.

African-Americans were relatively well documented and represented in the naval fleets of the

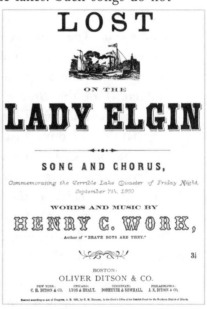

Besides traditional songs—sea shanties (chanteys) sung by mariners on the lakes, some commercially produced songs were written to commemorate specific events. This largely forgotten song was composed in 1861 by Henry C. Work about the Lady Elgin disaster the year before. (Collection of Tom and Chris Kastle)

Great Lakes, but little is known about them as far as the inland merchant fleets are concerned. Walton does mention that "Negro sailors had an excellent reputation as skilled seamen on ocean sailing vessels, particularly in the cotton trade, but very few of them ever shipped on the Great Lakes schooners."

African-American dockworkers, along with some of their singing, are mentioned later, but one of the most noteworthy references to black sailors comes to us in highly derogatory language in the ballad "Fayette Brown." The ballad, set during the 1880s, reflects the anger and resentment expressed by union sailors toward the scab, or nonunion, crews recruited by shipowners like the master of the schooner *Fayette Brown*. The tension between sailors and owners escalated into riots and frequent bloodshed as owners began to entice more sailors from the Atlantic Coast to come inland. This song was said to have been sung to the master and crews of the *Brown* whenever they were within earshot. Walton cites seaman William Head of Picton, Ontario, as reporting that the ballad was printed and distributed as a broadside during a sailors' strike in Cleveland. Though offering a negative depiction of African-American sailors in the crew, the song aims most of its malice at the *Brown*'s master, Captain Moffett, for shipping "a crew of Africans to immortalize his name" made of "waiters, aye, and bellhops too." The singer of "Fayette Brown" eventually warns the crew that in the autumn:

> They'll gather 'round the forecastle hatch
> A' wish that they were drown'd;
> They'll curse the day they sailed away
> On the schooner *Fayette Brown*.

Great Lakes Shanties

In general, shanties are work songs of the sea and, in this discussion, of the inland seas. Some mention specific places, such as

Chicago. Shanties may be considered a tool that helped to maximize effort and to make a job easier or adjust the pace of work. Additionally, shanties were sometimes used as a permissible means of expressing a grievance and were surely a way to boost morale and relieve boredom. They could be used for a variety of tasks on board a ship, perhaps best summarized by Captain Dan McDonald, of Port Huron, Ontario: "[We] usually shantied while making sail. [The] work was made easier by singing. At times [we] used any song that had the right time." The fact that shanties were used on the Great Lakes is supported by many of the interviews that Walton did with sailors at different locations. "Old Schooner crews would shanty and band at all work on the ropes or capstan. They would always sing on a hard pull. In Chicago and Buffalo Harbor they often had to kedge the old schooners. [They] would carry an anchor out with a line attached and then haul up to it [and] repeat," according to Captain James St. Young, age 84, retired 12 years, who had sailed on schooners during the 1880s. Of the sailors interviewed, many felt that shanties would most likely be done if there were saltwater hands on board. Henry G. Loher, age 65+, from Toledo, Ohio, who recalled singing "Ranzo Ray" and other shanties when warping sail or hauling in towline or anchor, said that shanties were always used when ocean men were in the crew.

Captain William Clark from Buffalo, New York, who considered himself a shantyman, learned the following shanties when he was "before the mast" on the old schooners: "Blow the Man Down," "Paddy Doyle's Boots," "Away Rio," "Rueben Ranzo," "Sally Brown," "Drunken Sailor," "Santa Anna," "Dreadnought," "Around Cape Horn," "Whiskey Johnny," "Homeward Bound," "Shenandoah," "Haul Away Joe," "Old Stormalong," "Leave Her, Johnny, Leave Her," and "Heave 'Er Up and Bust 'Er." Other specific shanties that were sung on the Great Lakes include "Sally Riley," according to Carl Joys, age 80, of Milwaukee, Wisconsin; "Lowlands," per Captain David McCloud of Port Colborne,

Ontario; and "High Barbaree," per Captain Charles Mullard of Sarnia, Ontario. Captain S.E. Leonard of Ashtabula, Ohio, who worked tugs for more than 55 years, recalled that there was much shantying aboard schooners while they were being towed out at the Chicago River. "Some crews would start making sail as far up as State Street. They always had a good shore audience, specially at the bridges!" Audiences were, apparently, not uncommon. Captain Timothy Kelley from Manitowoc, Wisconsin, told Walton that they used shanties to raise anchor and make sail and that people would "line the docks to hear them in Buffalo, New York."

Olaf Hansen of Arcadia, Michigan, said that "shanties were done when saltwater men were in the crew and especially when warping about a harbor with an audience on shore with women in it!" Dan Sterderson, the Cleveland Harbor master who began sailing as a boy, said that working old schooners was "a dog's life" but he always liked it. He enjoyed hearing sailors shanty when they made sail, which was a common practice on large vessels. Further, he said that good shantymen were often paid extra. From the preceding recollections we can see that shanties were used to raise sail, hoist anchor, and warp out of docks. They were also used to foot-load cargo, as discussed previously. And according to Harry and George Parnell of Waukegan, Illinois, shanties were used on fishing boats to row when there was no wind.

On the other hand, some Great Lakes sailors did not remember shantying as a common practice. A Norwegian sailor, Madr Anderson, recalled that when he first came to Chicago for the World's Fair and signed on his first Great Lakes vessel, he "sang out" on his first pull (on the halyard) and other sailors laughed at him, which ended his singing aboard ship.

There has been much research about and cataloging of the shanties that originated in salt water, by Stan Hugill, William Doerflinger, and Joanna Colcord, among others. To anyone who has read these texts, it is evident that the vast majority of shanties mentioned in the Walton interviews as having been sung on the

Great Lakes are of saltwater origin. Many of the shanties that were created on the lakes have been lost. Only a handful that are clearly Great Lakes in origin or that were adapted to the lakes have survived.

"Heave 'Er Up and Bust 'Er," is what would seem to be an anchor-raising shanty from the context of the song. No record of a tune is suggested in the Walton collection or in any other source that we can find. Stan Hugill once said that he had heard of the song but had never heard a definite melody associated with it.

> Come gather 'round, boys, now all hands—
>   Chorus: Heave 'er up, lads, heave 'er high.
> Lean and heave 'er all who can.
>   Chorus: Heave 'er up and bust her.
>
> Oh, we'll say farewell to this old town.
> We'll ship once more we're outward bound.
>
> If we ever get out and can let go
> We'll point her nose from Buffalo.

"Rolling Home" was originally written by journalist Charles MacKay in 1858 aboard the liner *Europa* while he was sailing home to London from New York, where he was the *London Times* correspondent. The singing of the seamen aboard the vessel inspired him to write a poem that was eventually published and picked up by sailors and reworked to become the classic sea song "Rolling Home." It was further adapted to be place specific, as in "rolling home to dear old England," ". . . to Nova Scotia," and, eventually, ". . . to old Chicago." The following is adapted from the Walton collection.

> Chorus:
> Rolling home, rolling home
> Rolling home across the sea

Rolling home to old Chicago
Rolling home, old town, to thee.

When the mate calls up all hands
Man the capstan walk 'er 'round
Heave 'er up, lads, with a will
For we are homeward bound

Up the length of old St. Clair
And at Port Huron we let go
We'll hoist the canvas forward
On the main and mizzen too

Through the straits our best to win'ard
Far astern the Isle Boblow
Then south'ard through Lake Mich'gan
To the town of Chicago.

And finally, "Leave Her, Laddies, Leave Her," also from the Walton collection, is the Great Lakes version of the saltwater shanty "Leave Her, Johnny, Leave Her," which was traditionally sung at the end of a voyage. The crew at this time, had a few grievances to air.

There was this ship that put to sea,
   Chorus: Leave her, laddies, leave her—
She was not the ship she ought to be,
   Chorus: And it's time for us to leave her!

And just before this ship did go,
The rats, they marched off in a row.

The mate was a shellback from below,
To cuss and swear he well did know.

The cook came from a lumber camp,
He'd made his livin' as a tramp.

Our hands were sore, and our backs were humped,
And half the lakes went through our pumps.

Although no specific halyard shanty, with Great Lakes references was cited by the sailors that Walton interviewed, and because the most popular boat was a gaffed rigged schooner, we can assume that the most commonly sung sail-raising shanties would be hand-over-hand shanties, such as "Drunken Sailor" or "Roll the Old Chariot," where the rhythm could be easily adjusted to fit the task. Many square-rigged vessels existed on the Great Lakes, and many schooners were square topsail rigged. This does not imply that shanties used on salt water for square-rigged applications were not used in like fashion on the lakes. Work songs were not confined to the decks of sailing ships. Occasionally sailors interviewed by Walton suggested that, in the Great Lakes, shanties as well as ballads were sung ashore, particularly in taverns; though among those interviewed, the terms *song, tune, shanty,* and the like were frequently used interchangeably.

Forecastle Tunes or Forebitters

Singing was a very common and important part of a sailor's life ashore. The songs spoke of fast passages, hard weather, good times as well as bad, and, quite often, shipwrecks. Walton interviewed many sailors who told of many lakeside bar sessions where the songs helped to document as well as fortify the sailor's life. Lakeside characters such as Sheets, Foghorn, Asa Trueblood, Beachie MacIvor, and Gasoline George were all known singers whose standing within their community, as well as their ability to garner free drinks, depended upon their singing and composing abilities. Robert "Brokenback" Collen, in a letter to Ivan Henry

Songs about some disasters that occurred before the United States entered World War II (such as railroad engineer Casey Jones's fatal train wreck in 1900 and the sinking of the U.S. destroyer Reuben James *by torpedo attack in October 1941) became legendary. This song about the* Lady Elgin *disaster, however, is largely forgotten. Obscure railroad engine wiper Wallace Saunders's "Ballad of Casey Jones," written a few days after the wreck, eventually caught the attention of vaudeville performers and became popular, and folksinger Woody Guthrie's song about the* Reuben James *is still in the folk-song repertoire. (Collection of Tom and Chris Kastle)*

Walton dated March 12, 1933, offers a glimpse of a sailors' saloon during the heyday of sail. In addition to drinking and card playing:

> We'll tell old yarns and talk of home
> As sailormen will do.
> We'll brag of girls in other ports
> And wonder if they're true.
> We'll split the old harmonica
> With all the tunes we know
> And then again unless
> We have a fight below.

Captain Jeremiah Cavanaugh of Port Dalhousie had spent most of his life on the lakes:

Whenever men forward (crewmen as distinct from officers) would gather ashore and at once make for a saloon and have a drink or two, someone would call for a song, and then each man had to sing a song, clog (dance), tell a good story, or buy a round of drinks. I always had to sing the Bently.

Some of these songs developed slowly, while others were composed during the duration of a single voyage. Captain Sylvester "Ves" Ray of Port Huron started sailing schooners as a boy in the late 1860s and retired as master in the 1880s. When Walton visited him in 1934, Ray (who was by then 80 years old) told him of a song about the schooner *Lavindy*—a song he had written and "fetched [his] own name to it." He had signed on the small Lake Michigan schooner as mate after two of the *Lavindy*'s crew left the vessel. He explained that he had a few good singers in the crew and they helped him make up the song. They put the verses to the tune of "Cumberland's Crew." After they tied up in the Chicago River, they went to a Clark Street bar, where they got free drinks for singing a new song. The verses that follow were sent to

Walton later in a letter from a former sailor named William J. Small, with a note saying that the song was from his friend Ves Ray, who had recited it to Small with the intention of sending the words to Walton. Walton edited the song into a more legible form. The following version of "A Trip on the Lavindy" includes, one assumes, a short introduction, or come-ye-all.

> Come all you young sailors and landlubbers too,
> An' listen to a song that I'll sing to you;
> It's about the Lavindy, the schooner of fame,
> Likewise her bold captain, Billy Parker's his (by) name.
>
> We set sail on a Saturday from Port Huron dock,
> All hands to the halyards they quickly did flock;
> "Yo-hee" and "Hi-ho" the mate he did bawl.
> An' we soon spread our wings, gaff tops'ls an' all.
>
> All murky and red the sun did arise,
> The wind backed to sou'west, and stormy the skies;
> We soon doused our tops'ls, oh Lord, how it blew!
> So we dropped our big hook under South Manitou.
>
> We made fast in Hamlin at a harbor dock,
> An' Pelton's whole crew around us did flock;
> They cursed and they swore an' the rough boards did fly;
> They soon filled our hold and the deck piled high.
>
> Now we're again on the big lake in a record time,
> So I will conclude and finish my rhyme.
> This song it was made while we was under way
> By a curly headed sailor by the name of Ves Ray.

One of the best-known singer-sailors was Billy Clark of Buffalo, New York, "who [made] up songs and sang them in shore saloons for free drinks all about the lakes." He is also mentioned as the author of the ballad "E.C. Roberts" or "Red Iron Ore" (or at least one version of that song). "Red Iron Ore," which follows, takes its melody from a British song about the Liverpool liner called the *Dreadnought*, also a very well known and often sung ballad around the lakes.

Come all you bold sailors who follow the lakes
On an iron ore freighter your living to make.
We shipped from Chicago, bid goodby to the shore,
All the way to Escanaba and the red iron ore.

Chorus: Derry down, down. Down derry down.

Some sailors took shovels while others took spades
Some took wheel barrels each man to his trade.
We looked like red devils, our fingers were sore,
And we cursed Escanaba and the damned iron ore.

Now the Roberts' in Cleveland made fast stem and stern
And over a bottle we'll spin a good yarn
But Captain Harvey Shannon had ought to stand treat
For to getting to Cleveland ahead of the fleet.

Another song that celebrates a fast passage is "Bigler." The *John Bigler* was a timber drogher built in Detroit in 1866. She sank off Marquette, Michigan, in September 1884. In the tongue-in-cheek version collected by Walton from Robert "Brokenback" Collen in Chicago, *John Bigler* may have danced across the "foam." In reality she was a boxy, slow vessel designed to fit through the canals while hauling coal and timber—a characteristic suggested by a line in the song: "We might have passed the fleet had they hoved-to and wait."

The numbers of Great Lakes shipwreck ballads are many, going beyond the scope of this piece; however, worth mentioning is "The Antelope," one example of such a ballad where the story begins in Chicago. Several vessels in the Great Lakes were called the *Antelope*, but none can be specifically traced to the following song; there was, however, a 350-ton schooner built in Buffalo in 1855 that may be the one. It is possible that the song, which follows, was originally written by Thomas Peckman, perhaps the only survivor of the crew, but this is not certain as several other vessels that bore the same name also sank during the same period.

> You all may bless your happy hearts that dwell safe on the shore
> Free from the billows and the blasts that 'round poor sailors roar
> Little think of hardships nor do they understand
> Of the stormy night we did endure on the Lake of Michigan.
>
> On the 17th of November from Chicago we did sail
> The sun shone bright the breezes light with no sign of a gale
> On canvas set unto the wind our hearts as light as air
> We left Chicago far behind our colors flying fair.
>
> On the 18th of November a storm it did arise
> The billows raged around us and dismal were the skies
> We reefed her down made all things fast and then contrived a plan
> To try and save the *Antelope* from the Lake of Michigan.
>
> On the very next morning and what I say is true
> Our cook in the fore rigging froze by the fiercest wind that blew
> Our ship she spring a leak me boys to the pumps went every man
> To try and save the *Antelope* from the Lake of Michigan.
>
> On the very same evening as we on deck did stand
> Our Captain says to his brother John I think I see the land
> Oh yes I see the land says John, I see the people stand
> But there's only One can save us now from the shore of Michigan.

On the very next morning our ship she struck stem on
The mainmast at the deck was broke and the mizzen it was gone
Our Captain tried to swim ashore his brother's life to save
But for his bold and manful task he met a watery grave.

Final Thoughts

It is apparent that shanties and forecastle tunes were in common usage among sailors in Chicago and around the Great Lakes as a shared body of knowledge. It is also clear that, although many of the songs may have originated elsewhere, they were altered via the "folk process" to become reflective of the lives of those who worked in the maritime trades in the Great Lakes region. In the songs, sailors described the places they traveled on the lakes and cited them by name. They recorded occupational information that was important to them, such as wind, water and shore conditions, navigational markers, ship rigs, and ports of origin. Socioeconomic conditions and attitudes were also part of the songs as sailors recorded wages, cited treatment of themselves and their vessels, and referenced attitudes about the political and administrative structure.

Sailors also sang of shared customs of celebration, such as the camaraderie of working together on board ship or gathering in saloons at the end of a trip to drink, exchange stories, and sing. They sang in the vernacular of the larger worldwide maritime culture (with some Chicago and Great Lakes nuances) using a terminology that helped to solidify their group identity. They also sang songs that documented events important to their community, such as fast passages and disasters.

As we read, recite, sing, and reflect upon this body of music, we become aware that, as a group and as individuals, these inland mariners also disclosed many of their intimate personal feelings, concerns, and needs. We become aware of recurrent themes—themes of occasional joy but more commonly of homesickness, missed loved ones, trial and tribulation, and, indeed, basic survival as they are reflected in the shanties and forecastle tunes of the Great Lakes. Such reflections also suggest an emotional bond between those who worked in the trades, their loved ones, and the towns they called home. That Chicago was one of those many homes is self-evident. These songs of the freshwater mariners can still be heard on the decks of a modern Great Lakes schooner, in the cockpit of a Mackinac racing sloop, or in a shoreside saloon. They are sung alongside contemporary variations of older shanties and a new generation of forecastle tunes that have arisen as part of the dynamic culture and living maritime tradition of the Great Lakes.

Chapter Twenty

A Steamboat Named Chicago

Perhaps the most famous ship named Chicago *was the heavy cruiser* USS Chicago, *which performed so poorly in the battle of Savo Island on August 9, 1942, that her captain committed suicide in embarrassment. She was later sunk by Japanese planes (in 1943). Long before that happened, a succession of merchant ships on the Great Lakes bore the name of the Windy City. One—a side-wheel wooden packet— performed credibly, albeit largely anonymously, during a long, 44-year career that spanned the transformation from wood to steel in ship construction.*

CMS member John Heinz tells the story of the Chicago *and the sometimes dangerous days in which she plied her trade on the lakes.*

by John Heinz

"Can it be possible that . . . I have in less than a week traveled from Ohio to Wisconsin and met with no accident . . . ?"
—Annie Henderson, 1849

Annie Henderson's letter home epitomizes travel in the settlement era on the Great Lakes. As a teacher, she would have read about the boiler explosions, fires, and storms that filled the newspapers of that innocent time. In fact, the wooden paddle steamer *Niagara*—on which she happily traveled in 1849—later burned on upper Lake Michigan with the loss of 60 lives. Its scorched timbers are now along the shore, north of Port Washington, Wisconsin.

In November of 1847, just two years before Henderson's voyage on the *Niagara*, the propeller-powered passenger liner *Phoenix* burned on her way to Chicago in what remains the deadliest ship fire in Great Lakes history. The vessel had been hired by the Society of Christians to carry Netherlands immigrants from Buffalo to the western shore of Lake Michigan, but in the early morning, a ship's crewman discovered fire in the woodwork above an overheated boiler. The pumps were manned and passengers worked a bucket brigade as the vessel was steered toward Sheboygan, Wisconsin.

As the fire spread, two lifeboats were lowered, but they had the capacity for only a fraction of the estimated 300 people aboard. Of the 46 survivors, 43 had found places in the lifeboats and three had clung to the floating wreck. A wealthy merchant turned down a place in the boats and made a little raft, which he clung to with two small children. Two sisters held hands and jumped, only to sink like stones. Most of those who survived the flames tried to save themselves by clinging to the wreckage—doors, planks, and cargo—but quickly froze in the icy water.

Most of the ships of the era were little more than floating tinderboxes. Plentiful white oak was the basic element in boat construction on the Great Lakes in the era before iron and steel. The sturdy timber resisted the penetration of water and rot but not fire. The keel of a ship in those days was built up of sections of white oak linked with what were called scarfs, or lock joints. This sectional keel might be topped with an upper timber called a keelson, and this even further topped with a rider keelson. The ribs—or frames, as they were called—also were built up in sections, called futtocks, cut from curved branches called compass timbers. The hull had caulked planking outside and inside to make two shells with these frames locked between them. To avoid rot, all of the surfaces where these interlocking timbers touched were covered with tar or paint.

However, it was the superstructure of the ships that was most vulnerable to conflagration. Passengers like Henderson typically slept on an upper deck in a cabin built of lighter timber and perhaps topped with painted canvas for waterproofing. The cabin usually received one coat of paint for every year of the vessel's career. At night crewmen prowled the upper decks with fire buckets to empty on sparks smoldering from the stacks. If a cabin roof leaked, the bunk might get an overhead canopy of canvas and the deck above might get a coat of hot tallow. An added hazard was the many coats of varnish applied to the interiors of the cabins—and the small wood stoves strategically placed for heating.

The bow of the ship was the strongest place, with almost solid assemblies of timber for strength against the waves and ice. These massive head timbers, the stem and the stemson, and many other interlocking wooden shapes gave the ship an almost solid ice-resisting front end, which would be slow to reach the combustion point. Sailors and knowledgeable travelers knew this and clung to that mighty bow during a fire.

Aside from fire at sea, wooden ships were also vulnerable to heavy seas. Caulking in the seams between planks on older boats often came loose under the constant pounding of waves. The ship's pumps could keep this seepage under control in normal conditions, but a plank might spring open in a storm or if struck by a rock or another vessel. The big wooden paddler *Lady Elgin*, owned by early insurance man Gurdon S. Hubbard, was en route from Chicago to Milwaukee one night in 1860 when it was rammed by a small wooden schooner and broke up off suburban Winnetka, Illinois. Apparently, the long bowsprit of the schooner hit the *Lady Elgin* like a battering ram, and the superstructure's intricate timber scarfing and fine interior joinery came apart while the ship was still moving. Many people aboard the *Elgin* rode for a while on the separated main cabin, but 279 people died before rescue efforts could be mounted from shore.

Such disasters were an accepted risk of travel in the nineteenth century—even after the arrival of the railroads. The high toll in ships did not seem to be a deterrent to the men who owned and

manned them or to the passengers who rode on them. Chicago
Captain Albert E. Goodrich, who founded the steamboat line
bearing his name in 1856, lost the wooden paddler *Sunbeam*, and
98 people, in a storm in 1863, and his *Seabird* burned in 1868,
killing 28 aboard, after an untrained porter threw stove ashes into
the wind and set the vessel on fire. The Goodrich line not only
survived those disasters but continued to expand. The replacement for the *Seabird* was the wooden paddler *Alpena*, which vanished in a storm in 1880 with the loss of 73 people.

Also in 1868 Captain Goodrich had built the wooden side-
wheeler *Manitowoc* with engines salvaged from an older vessel.
But he judged the *Manitowoc* to be a dangerously unstable ship,
took her out of service, and ordered a new passenger steamer to be
built with its cabins and engines. This vessel was the wooden pad-
dle-wheeler *Chicago*. Despite the hazards of the wooden ship era,
it served for 44 years without a serious incident. By the time it was
retired in 1916 (because of obsolescence—it had survived into the
era when steel replaced wood in ship construction), the *Chicago*
had steamed in all weather and seasons for thousands of miles
between growing Manitowoc and booming Chicago. Perhaps
because its long career was so uneventful—lacking any disasters—it has been largely forgotten even by maritime historians.

This namesake ship of the largest city on the Great Lakes was
205 feet in length on her oaken keel and 30 feet in beam, or hull
width, but across those domelike guards that protected the paddle
wheels she was 55 feet wide. The wheels themselves were 26 feet
in diameter by 5 feet in width. The wooden paddles, called buckets, were flat planks that dipped into the water at each revolution.
These wheels were enclosed in semicircular boxes that were ven-
tilated by fan-shaped side vents to keep air pressure from creating
drag on the buckets, according to the *Chicago*'s hull plans recorded in the 1930s by the Works Progress Administration and published as part of the Historic American Merchant Marine Survey.
The plans show a long, narrow, and shallow hull that needed those
arched trusses.

The paddle-wheel steamer Chicago *was one of nearly 30 vessels to have borne the name of the Windy City. It had a long, 44-year career that spanned the transformation from wood to steel in ship construction. The apparatus that transferred power from the engines to the paddle wheels can be seen here behind the smokestack. The distinctive curved beam, called a truss, was to prevent the hull from hogging (sagging in the middle). (Collection of John Heinz)*

Nothing will ever be seen again like those great white paddle-wheel lake boats! The *Chicago* had Victorian gingerbread on the bow and on the octagonal pilothouse, where a careful Captain Barney Sweeney reigned supreme. Her paddle-wheel boxes had the ship's name printed alongside in ornate red letters with painted black shadows. The smokestacks were red—the trademark of the Goodrich fleet. Seven flagpoles displayed the American flag, the naval jack, four Goodrich Company flags, and a flag with the ship's name in two-foot high letters. Holidays called for appropriate decoration, such as many Christmas trees on deck. The walking beam might sport the figure of a running deer. At night the engineer could hang lanterns behind the paddle wheels to give a stroboscopic effect to the vents.

All this for $3 to go from Chicago to Manitowoc in second class—no berths, no meals. First class was a half dollar more.

Like many passenger ships of the time, the *Chicago* had a dance band on board. And as Annie Henderson wrote of the boats: "The fun we used to have, you better believe it was a sin!"

Nineteenth-century Great Lakes steamers were described as boats and classed either as propellers or side-wheelers. There were few, if any, stern-wheeled boats on the lakes. Propellers used screw propellers, efficiently hidden below the waterline, while side-wheelers or paddle steamers were moved by big paddle wheels mounted in boxes on each side. Side-wheelers were perhaps more stable and were widely used in the passenger trade, but propellers were favored in the freight business because their operating gear required less space, leaving more room for cargo, and they could tie up flush with the docks for easier loading and unloading. On the Great Lakes in 1856 there were 118 propellers and 120 paddlers, according to Lloyd's Register.

The larger propellers were one of the grand sights of the old lakes because they also carried sails and often used them. They were among the largest sailing vessels in the world. For instance, the *Helena*, at 275 feet in length, was rigged as a four-masted schooner. By the turn of the century, propellers were simply known as steamboats, or steamers, and all lakers were known respectfully as boats.

Like most Great Lakes steamers that plodded on regular schedules between two ports, the Chicago *carried passengers on the upper decks and freight on the lower levels. (Collection of John Heinz)*

The *Chicago* was like many Great Lakes boats in that it had full-length curved arches called trusses, running from bow to stern, which were needed to keep their long hulls from sagging, or hogging. Big wooden boats and oceangoing ships did not need trusses, because their deeper draft hulls allowed internal trusses. This was a Great Lakes characteristic, because the shallow river ports did not allow for deep draft ships.

Paddlers also had extra timber amidships to deal with the stress of the walking beam, or working beam, that linked the vertical boiler to the paddle crank. They were diamond-shaped linkages, usually painted red and sometimes decorated with figures out of the imagination of the ship's carpenter. An average walking beam might be 20 feet long with a height above the engine bed of 35 or 45 feet. They joined at one end by a crank linkage to the paddle-wheel axle and at the other end to the large single-piston engine of perhaps 38 inches in diameter. All of this was quite heavy and the weight was high up, unlike that of propeller-driven vessels.

One of the worst Lake Michigan disasters was that of the pro-peller *Vernon*, which sank in 1887 in view of passing ships that could not give aid in the storm. This wooden Chicago-built ves-sel had a reputation for being top-heavy, somewhat like the later *Eastland*. On the rough night of October 29 she was traveling with cargo ports open to allow more room for cargo when she cap-sized with the loss of all aboard but one survivor, a new immigrant crewman, Axel Stone, whose testimony about the open cargo ports was confirmed by modern divers. The *Vernon* crewman went public with the tale of his ordeal in this maelstrom of our lakes— and also of the captain's alcohol abuse problem—and then he dis-appeared.

The advent of the iron and steel boats not long after the *Chicago* went into service began to change shipbuilding radically. Although the first iron ship on the lakes was the government's paddle frigate *Michigan*, built in 1844, the first successful iron-hulled freighter, the *Onoko*, did not appear until 1882. A wooden boat's lofting, or drafting, could be in error by as much as one-eighth of an inch, but metal boats needed precise lofting to get exactly the right size of plate cut together with the exact locations of the rivet holes. Metal frames could not be sawn out on a rolling bevel band saw but had to be hammered into exact curves from red-hot angle stock.

Metal ship building was pioneered on the lakes due to the proximity of Midwestern mines and mills. Metal lake ships had great savings in weight and space. For one important thing, these revolutionary ships did not need a keel to tie their frames together. Most steamer keels became simply keel plates that allowed them to better slide on their launching ways or to even run aground without plowing deep. Sometimes there was a vestigial flange keel of a few inches, but most steel lake steamers became nearly flat-bottomed boats. Few people of the traveling public were aware of these details, but metal ships generally had a reputation for safety.

For aging wooden ships like the *Chicago*, a compromise was available. In about 1890 the *Chicago* was sheathed all over with metal plates, giving the vessel some protection from both fire and ice and perhaps making it look to the public like a steel ship. At about this time the young Goodrich heir decided to use more funereal black paint on his fleet, perhaps for cosmetic reasons related to the ships' aging process.

By the time the *Chicago* received her iron plating, the Goodrich line had already begun its conversion to steel ships. The steel whaleback steamer *Christopher Columbus* brought multitudes to both the World's Columbian Exposition in 1893 and the Century of Progress Exposition three decades later. The *Christopher Columbus* was a futuristic design of a cigar hull topped by turrets supporting flying decks. After the 1893 fair closed she ran from Chicago to Milwaukee for nearly 40 years—mostly safe years, except for somehow ramming a water tower in downtown Milwaukee. But her safety record was exceeded in longevity by that of the *Chicago*.

Steel hulls were not a perfect insurance against disaster. In 1915 the steel-hulled *Eastland* capsized in the Chicago River, drowning more than 800 people in a few minutes within a few feet of dry

The Goodrich Transportation Company, the Windy City's largest ship operator, used a painting of the Chicago *to promote the Goodrich line of side-wheel passenger steamers in this advertisement. (Collection of John Heinz)*

land. The disaster attracted a confidence man named Devereaux York, who claimed to be a naval architect. York was promoting his own design for an uncapsizable ship with a deep keel like a sailboat. He took advantage of the Chicago public's sudden awareness that *Eastland* had no keel.

But old age, not the *Eastland* disaster, doomed the *Chicago*, and it was retired. The next year (1916), the *Chicago*'s captain, Barney Sweeney, said, "Finished with engines," and those 63-year-old steam fixtures finally got a rest. The *Chicago*'s lifeboats had never been needed. Its 44-year-old wooden hull was not worn out; it was only superannuated in favor of her young steel sisters. The old hull became a floating hotel for Manitowoc Shipbuilding and Dry Dock Company. The interior was equipped with two large dining rooms, a smoking room, a bakery, a kitchen, showers, and lunch counters on the main deck. On the upper deck were staterooms for 110   men, another dining room (for office workers), pool tables, and a reading room. The fate of this vessel was not noted by Manitowoc chroniclers, but it was likely burned for its metal after World War I.

Steel paddle steamers kept on serving the city's lakefront. One of them, the *Florida*, was retired to serve as the Columbia Yacht Club. Still another steel sister was the big paddler *City of Chicago*, which ran from 1890 to 1935, first for the Graham and Morton line and later for the Goodrich line. The *City of Chicago* was larger than the *Chicago*, being lengthened twice, up to 254 feet. Mostly she ran in the passenger and fruit trade between the city and St. Joseph, Michigan. Her luxurious interior was used for a silent film that seems to have been lost.

In the 1960s I was working at the Art Institute of Chicago with Dora Goodrich of the Goodrich family. She lured me away from modern art with her stories and photos of floating works of art. She wanted me to make a model of the steamboat *Chicago*. Her refrain was, "Build *Chicago*, John." So I did. I built a 1:48 scale model of it that was displayed at Manitowoc until it was purchased by a private collector.

This writer once traveled by a steel paddle steamer, the *Greater Detroit*, in the late 1940s. The cruise was not eventful, but I never thought of fire. Modern lake passengers miss all the drama of the settlement era thanks to the Coast Guard—and to insurance regulators.

Chicago is a good name for a ship, and 30 known vessels have proudly borne the name, including five Navy warships. The first was a sailing schooner built in Buffalo in 1836 when the Windy City was a frontier hamlet. Since then tugs, towboats, dredges, ore boats, tankers, and freighters have carried the name. Like an old ship, the city itself thrives upon challenges and keeps going with pumps and bucket brigades.

Chapter Twenty-One

The Rise of the Goodrich Line

The largest and most successful steamship company in Chicago was the Goodrich line, which was in many ways a microcosm of maritime traffic on Lake Michigan. The line operated from antebellum times until it succumbed to competition from railroads and motor vehicles and the Great Depression. In their heyday, Goodrich packets carried people and goods across and up and down Lake Michigan on regular schedules, and the company name was synonymous with steamer travel on the lake. In all, more than 60 vessels sailed under the Goodrich flag. Among them were the Huron, *with which Goodrich began operations; the ill-fated* Alpena; *and the hermaphroditic whaleback* Christopher Columbus, *perhaps the strangest flagship ever to sail the Great Lakes.*

This chapter, on the rise of the Goodrich line until the second generation of the family took over, has been excerpted by John Holton from James Lee Elliott's book Red Stacks over the Horizon: The History of the Goodrich Steamboat Line, *originally published in 1967 and reissued in 1995. The following chapter deals with the decline of the packet lines on Lake Michigan—and with them, the demise of the Goodrich line.*

by James Lee Elliott

After the formation of the partnership between George C. Drew and Captain A.E. Goodrich [1826–85], they turned to the task of securing a suitable ship with which they could enter the steamboat business. Captain Goodrich appealed to his former employer and old friend, Captain E.B. Ward, owner of the Ward Line. An agreement was reached whereby the new partners would charter the side-wheel steamer *Huron* from Captain Ward. Since the discontinuance of the cross-lake service by the Ward Line, *Huron* had been on charter to the Clement Steamboat Line of Chicago.

Huron was a wooden side-wheel steamer rated at 348 tons burden. She had been built in the Ward Yard at Newport, Michigan, in 1852. This sturdy ship was not large, even by the standards of her day. She was 165 feet in length, had a beam of 23 feet 6 inches and a draft of a little over 9 feet. Her low-pressure boilers used cordwood as fuel and she carried the walking beam, so familiar with vessels equipped with the vertical beam engine, on her hurricane deck.

In general appearance she had a single mast forward, a single black stack, and her hull was painted entirely white. Her name appeared in large black letters on her paddle-wheel boxes. Arched trusses, to add longitudinal strength to her hull, appeared topsides. By all standards, *Huron* was a staunch and pretty ship in her day. Under the very capable command of Captain Goodrich, they made a most dependable and popular combination.

After the leasing of the *Huron*, Captain Goodrich began to make plans for routes, docks, and port arrangements for his new steamboat service. In 1856 property on the south bank of the Chicago River, just east of Michigan Avenue, was secured. This location was on land now occupied by the Michigan Avenue link [bascule] bridge and extended eastward along the river for about a block and a half.

On this site's dock, some small sheds and a small office were constructed. From here, the *Huron* sailed on August 10, 1856, carrying the first Goodrich excursion from Chicago to Milwaukee. Strangely enough, this same dock location was to serve the Goodrich interests for the next seventy-odd years!

At the outset *Huron* did not attempt to keep any regular schedule of sailings. At her normal rate of speed she required about ten hours to make a trip from Chicago to Milwaukee. Trips between the west-shore ports were made whenever the traffic warranted it.

At the time Captain Goodrich began service with the *Huron*, steamers were the only means of transportation between Chicago, Milwaukee, and the west-shore lake ports of Port Washington, Sheboygan, Manitowoc, Two Rivers, and those located on Green Bay. The railroad did not enter Manitowoc, for example, until about 1873. [ed. A rail line between Chicago and Milwaukee was completed in the early 1850s.]

The early steamboat cargoes consisted of livestock, both for the farms and the market, dried peas, beer, merchandise for the stores, specie for the banks, machinery, and many other items required to sustain the life or comfort of the early settlers in rapidly expanding Wisconsin. New settlers, German, Polish, Bohemian, and Scandinavian, were landed at Milwaukee and points north by the boatload. As early as 1855 there is a record of a boatload of the new Bohemian settlers being landed at Manitowoc by the steamer *Huron*, then under charter to the Clement Line.

In the spring of 1857, Drew and Goodrich purchased the *Huron* outright from Captain Ward for $16,000.

Travel on *Huron* was a true test of a passenger's patience and durability. Whatever food was consumed was brought aboard by the passengers themselves. Like all vessels of her day, the only cabin space available on *Huron* was for use only as a shelter from rain and winds. Sleeping, if any, was done in the deck chairs or on the deck itself and passenger comfort was a term that had not yet been coined!

On May 1, 1958, only two years after the beginning of *Huron*'s service, the wooden propeller *Ogontz* was purchased.

Even as far back as when he commanded *Comet*, his third ship, Captain Goodrich was striving to make his steamers better, safer, and more attractive. In February of 1861, *Comet* was sent to the shipyard for extensive overhaul. Her hull was divided into four watertight compartments and her interior repainted and refitted throughout. On April 4 of the same year, Captain Goodrich announced that *Comet* would make four trips north each week. Her days of departure from Milwaukee were Tuesday, Thursday, Friday, and Saturday. Her new route was to include Kewaunee, Wisconsin, and this marked the first time that regular service was offered from Milwaukee to points north of Two Rivers.

Sunday night, July 1, 1865, found Lake Michigan lashed to a fury by a big storm. *Comet*, en route to Green Bay, was driven ashore on the rocks at Washington Island. The vessel was in grave danger from the pounding seas so her commander, Captain Gaylord, ordered her scuttled. She sank in about thirteen feet of water. Except for the loss of cargo, valued at $10,000 and covered by the Home Insurance Company, she suffered no great damage. After the storm subsided, she was pumped out and taken to Manitowoc for repairs.

Comet continued her colorful and very successful career as a Goodrich steamer until the close of the 1869 season. In November of that year the sturdy old side-wheeler was dismantled. Her engine, boilers, most of her machinery, and some of her cabin fittings were utilized in the construction of the new steamer *Corona*. The stripped-down hull was sold to Captain Cobb for conversion into a tow barge. Sale price was $1,000. None of the early Goodrich steamers contributed more to the company's reputation for dependability than did *Comet*. Throughout her life she was also a good money-maker for Captain Goodrich.

The year 1864 was an important one in the life of Captain Goodrich. In the previous year he had met and since then courted a very beautiful and lovely young lady from Milwaukee by the name of Rosamond Francis Whaling. During the late summer of this significant year Rosamond gave her consent and the couple announced their engagement. The beautiful wedding, a social highlight in Milwaukee, took place in the Episcopal Church on November 30, 1864.

After the honeymoon, Captain Goodrich took his charming bride to Chicago to live. He carried her over the threshold at 1474

Albert E. Goodrich founded his Chicago-based shipping line in 1856 with a leased vessel. He made enough money that four years later he was able to buy (for $32,000) the 168-foot paddle-wheeled Comet. *(CMS Collection)*

South Michigan Avenue, and this address became the Captain's home as long as he lived.

During the winter of 1867–1868 Captain Goodrich took time to reflect on his progress and to contemplate the problems that lay ahead. Up to this point he had operated alone and had built up Goodrich's Steamboat Line to a very secure position in the Lake Michigan trade. While the total numbers of steamers actually in operation was eight, he had purchased, constructed, sold, and scrapped the amazing total of sixteen steamships in the past twelve years!

His steamboat line had survived the recession of 1857, the slump in passenger travel following the loss of the *Lady Elgin* in 1860 [ed. The *Lady Elgin* was a non-Goodrich ship that sank after a collision with the schooner *Augusta* about seven miles off of Winnetka, Illinois, with the loss of 279 persons.], the ravages of the war between the states, and the sinkings of *Sunbeam* [ed. The *Sunbeam* sank in a storm off Copper Harbor on Lake Superior in 1863, with the loss of life estimated at 30.] and *Seabird* [ed. The *Seabird* burned off Lake Forest, Illinois, in 1868, with the loss of life estimated at 67.] with their combined loss of well over one hundred lives. In spite of these many and serious setbacks, Goodrich's Steamboat Line was, in 1867, in a good financial position.

Business throughout the country was good. Travel and shipping on the Lakes was booming after the Civil War. Lake steamers were now being built larger, more palatial, and of course more expensively. After considering all the angles, Captain Goodrich reached the conclusion that the formation of a formal corporation (Goodrich Transportation Company) would be the most logical way to secure stable management and to give his loyal staff an opportunity of sharing in some of the profits as shareholders.

Sunday evening, October 8, 1871, was unusually warm for the time of year. Chicago, like most of the Midwest, was tinder dry, the result of a prolonged summer drought. About 8:30 P.M. fire broke out in the small barn of an Irish family by the name of O'Leary. The O'Learys lived at 137 DeKoven Street in the Bohemian quarter of the sprawling wooden city. This location is, today, just east of Taylor and Halsted Streets.

Fanned by a strong southwest wind that grew in velocity as the fire spread, the wall of destruction moved from the southwest section of the city in a northeasterly direction. When the fire reached, and then finally leaped across, the Chicago River, it took with it the bridges and ignited the ships in the river itself.

The harbor tugs did brave and yeoman service in towing all shipping free of the river and out into the safety of Lake Michigan. After the bridges failed, the tugs served as ferryboats to transport panic-stricken persons to the north bank of the river, as they fled ahead of the inferno.

As the fire moved eastward, toward morning on Monday, Captain Goodrich became concerned about the company records and the families of his Chicago staff. There were two Goodrich steamers in the river at the Goodrich dock as the rising sun dimly made its appearance through a wall of smoke, highlighted by large, flying, burning embers. One was *Navarino*, under the command of Captain Clark, and the other vessel was *Skylark*.

The harbor tug *Magnolia*, under command of twenty-five-year-old Captain Joseph Gilson, had worked like a beaver through the long night of holocaust and terror. As the fire threatened elevators A and B on the south bank of the river just east of the Michigan Central Depot [the train station also served the Illinois Central Railroad], the tug and her fearless captain had succeeded in towing two freighters from their berths in the slips at the elevators and out into the Lake.

Magnolia then proceeded to the *Navarino* which was now in the direct path of the flames. A line was passed to her, and the tow downstream to the lake was begun. In trying to tow *Navarino* as rapidly as possible, she ran aground on the north side of the channel, directly in front of Rathbone's Stove Works, which was the next structure east of Kirk's Soap Factory. Try as he might, Captain Gilson could not dislodge *Navarino*. Later she was scuttled to prevent her from floating free and becoming a blazing torch as the current carried her toward the Lake. Shortly thereafter she caught fire and burned to the water's edge.

Captain Goodrich ordered all company records, the families of his staff, office furniture, and many unscheduled passengers aboard *Skylark*. Captain Gilson and his somewhat charred *Magnolia* then managed to tow her safely into the open Lake.

The Michigan Central Depot, Elevator A, the Goodrich wooden office building, the freight sheds, and the docks were all consumed by the flames. Only a small part of the loss of the office, sheds, and dock was covered by insurance. The insurance claim on the loss of *Navarino* amounted to $16,112.

Like so many Chicagoans that were faced with the complete destruction of their property and the loss of their businesses that had gone up in smoke and flame, Captain Goodrich refused to be discouraged by his losses. Compared with many firms in Chicago, he felt that Goodrich Company was not too bad off.

The office and freight sheds were soon rebuilt from the shipload after shipload of Michigan pine that poured into the stricken city. The boilers, engine, and machinery from the burned and sunken *Navarino* were salvaged. The hull was raised and sold for use as a barge. As a replacement for the burned *Navarino*, Captain Goodrich ordered another wooden propeller of 796 tons burden. Named *Menominee*, she was built at Manitowoc in the winter of 1872–1873 and cost Goodrich $60,600. She was powered by the machinery from the unfortunate *Navarino* and was almost identical in size and appearance to her, having only a thirty-ton greater burden rating. Both vessels had a single stack located well aft. Each carried a tall single mast forward with the familiar gaff boom. Both steamers had arched trusses that added strength to the hull.

By 1872, the experiment with the *Truesdell* and *Ottawa* had been in effect long enough for the results to be carefully evaluated. The popularity and good earnings of these two small propellers left no doubt as to the wisdom of Captain Goodrich's decision to build steamers that catered to the comfort and convenience of the overnight passenger. This policy of offering an overnight service on year-around basis wherever the traffic justified was maintained until the very end of the company's existence.

De Pere, a wooden propeller of 736 tons, followed *Menominee* just a year later. Built at a cost of $57,200 by Rand, she was almost identical in size and appearance to both *Navarino* and *Menominee*. Upon completion she was placed on the west-shore routes.

Operating as much as possible on a year-around schedule, *De Pere* was a real pioneer in winter operation. At the time she was built, special emphasis was placed on her bow and hull construction to combat the ice. During her career she proved to be a most capable winter steamer. Her regular schedule included ports north of Manitowoc and she became a very familiar sight in the Green Bay area.

When *De Pere* would find a harbor frozen solid, as she often did on her winter travels, she would approach as close as possible and then discharge her cargo into horse drawn-sleighs that would come out from shore. A large wood-burning stove heated the main cabin but many parts of the sturdy little steamer were without heat of any kind. Life aboard the early steamers engaged in winter service was certainly not for the timid or the weak. One of the most bothersome aspects of winter service were harbors that became frozen solid and thus prevented the steamers from getting to their docks to discharge freight and passengers.

Captain Goodrich specifically built *Ludington* for the cross-lake route to handle package freight for the Flint & Pere Marquette Railroad from their western terminal at Ludington to Milwaukee and other Wisconsin ports. It was for this reason that she was named in honor of Ludington, Michigan. The first winter *Ludington* was in service proved to be a most severe one. By all standards of comparison the winter of 1881–1882 was a tough one and the ability of the new steamer to withstand the crushing ice of Lake Michigan was put to many tests. On one occasion, while on an eastbound crossing, *Ludington* became entrapped in a huge ice floe as she approached the Michigan shore. Unable to work free she had no choice but to move up and down Lake Michigan in the relentless grip of the huge floe. After a week the sturdy steamer found herself at the southern end of the lake just off of St. Joseph one morning, and a few days later the next recognizable bearing found her off Manistee. In that length of time she had traveled over a hundred and fifty miles without her shaft turning a single revolution!

At one point in her long imprisonment of over a month, some of her crew actually made their way ashore to make contact with Goodrich officials and pick up badly needed supplies. Finally a warming spell and a sudden shift in wind caused the floe to break up and release its unwilling prisoner. Examination revealed no hull damage from this long and trying experience and *City of Ludington* returned to her regular run.

The cold winter days and long, windy winter nights spent in unheated pilothouses and cold cabins began to take their toll. The captain had been a victim of frequent attacks of neuralgia for quite some time. As time went on, these attacks became more frequent and more severe. The lake winds seemed to affect him the most in fall and spring. In 1884 this situation became so serious that he rode from his residence on Michigan Avenue to his office in a closed carriage to avoid exposure to the chill winds that blew in from the Lake.

On Monday morning, September 14, 1885, at 9:25 A.M., the beloved Captain Albert Edgar Goodrich passed away. He was survived by his wife Rosamond and his only son Albert Whaling Goodrich, who was attending school in Germany when his father passed away.

On December 1, 1889, Albert W. Goodrich was installed as President of the Goodrich Transportation Company. Young Albert (born in 1868) had been a good student of the affairs of the company since his father's death, and very little time elapsed before all those around him were convinced that he would make a fine and capable replacement for Captain Goodrich. The years that followed certainly justified this conviction.

Chapter Twenty-Two

The Decline of the Lake Packets

Sometime after the turn of the century, the once flourishing packet lines on Lake Michigan went into a precipitous decline. When aviation pioneer Octave Chanute in 1898 was hurriedly summoned to St. Joseph, Michigan, by colleague Augustus Herring to witness a flight (unsuccessful, as it turned out) of his powered airplane, Chanute took an overnight packet across the lake. The railroads had driven most of the Great Lakes passenger ships out of business in the 1850s but could not make a dent in the packet traffic.

Automobiles and motor trucks that began appearing in greater numbers in the early twentieth century were another matter. Especially after hard roads were built following World War I, a truck could pick up a western Michigan produce crop at a farm and have it in Chicago by the time the markets opened the next morning. Windy City residents found they could drive the family car to Michigan vacation resorts as fast as a packet could take them and had touring transportation available when they got there. The lake packets, like the ill-fated Eastland, *increasingly were relegated to group excursions, which couldn't cover their high overhead. Passage of the LaFollette's Seaman's Act by Congress in 1915 also imposed additional safety costs on ship operators and is blamed for much of the Great Lakes shipping industry troubles. Like all failing industries, a wave of consolidations swept the packet business; then it failed.*

This chapter was also excerpted by John Holton from James Lee Elliott's book Red Stacks over the Horizon.

by James Lee Elliott

As a youth, Albert W. Goodrich [1868–1938] had crossed the Atlantic to Europe and he had a strong feeling that at least one of the several new ships being planned for building should be built of steel, should have twin screws, and be fast like the liners he had crossed the ocean on and had observed in the world ports he had visited. He also hoped that in general appearance the new steel steamer could look more like an ocean going craft than the new wooden propellers like *Indiana*, etc. did. The Lehigh Railroad had a new package freighter, the *Cuyuga*, that he cited as an example.

To bolster his reasoning that an unusual steamer was necessary at this time, he quoted the fact that the word was out regarding the proposed construction of the world's first whaleback passenger vessel, *Christopher Columbus*. With the World's Fair [ed. Columbian Exposition of 1893] in the offing, it seemed important to Albert Goodrich that the Goodrich Line also have something equally as large and as fast if the prestige of the Red-Stack Line was to be maintained.

Launched on May 2, 1891, the beautiful steamship was christened *Virginia* and immediately designated as the flagship of the Goodrich fleet. *Virginia* had two steel pole masts and one stack located amidship. All three were sharply raked and gave a very sleek look to the new boat. Finished in the standard Goodrich colors of black hull, white cabins, topped with the bright red stack, she was truly a beautiful steamer. There are many who claim that *Virginia* was the most handsome ship in all Goodrich history.

After four years at the helm of the Goodrich Line, Albert W. Goodrich had demonstrated, to everyone's complete satisfaction, that he possessed many of the qualities of leadership so capably demonstrated by his father. Like his father, he was keenly interested in all aspects of the Goodrich Company and its operation.

Possibly the most unusual passenger ship to steam the lakes was the Christopher Columbus. *It was the only passenger version of a succession of ore boats and barges that were built on unusually shaped hulls and commonly called whalebacks. (CMS Collection)*

In addition, he had a very definite flair for the publicity and public relations department of the steamboat business. He even found the time to take an interest, and later an active, behind-the-scenes part, in Chicago politics.

After the tragic accident of the *Eastland* [ed. As many as 844 persons were drowned when the ship capsized.] in the Chicago River on July 24, 1915, the lake passenger business took a terrific beating. The traveling public lost all confidence in the stability and safety of the lake steamers. As a result their normal passenger patronage came to a standstill. The ships remained tied to their docks, idle, because no Chicagoan in his right mind would board them to go anywhere. All kinds of wild statements, rumors, and accusations continued unabated. Because of her unusual design and different appearance, *Columbus* [ed. renamed from *Virginia*] was the victim of some very vicious and wholly ungrounded rumors regarding her stability and passenger safety.

Things were so serious that a special meeting of the Goodrich Transit Company board of directors was called for the purpose of determining what could and should be done to restore the passenger traffic to a degree of normalcy. The board session had all the earmarks of a coroner's inquest into the sudden demise of a public idol. Every board member realized the seriousness of the situation but none, including the operating officers of the line, could offer a solution to the problem.

Finally one director, Mr. Charles Hermann, asked a pointed question that could only be answered by Messrs. Goodrich and Thorp [ed. Harry W. Thorp, general manager of the company]: "If the whaleback were fully loaded with passengers and all of them went to one side of the ship at the same time, would it tip?" Both Goodrich and Thorp replied quickly and emphatically, "No!" "Well," replied Mr. Hermann, "then we must, without delay, but with plenty of publicity, make such a demonstration."

All present agreed that it would not be possible to assemble a sufficiently large crowd brave enough to make the test. It was agreed to secure as many as possible, including a band and some prominent city officials. On the basis of an average weight of 150 pounds per passenger, sandbags would be used to make up for the missing passengers.

On a cloudy warm Saturday afternoon, August 24, 1915, the test was made just off the entrance to Chicago harbor. Among the passengers aboard were many gentlemen of the press and a few of the braver city officials. Five hundred tons of sandbags were placed aboard to compensate for the missing passengers who would not even avail themselves of an opportunity for a free boat ride.

When all was in readiness and the shore was lined with thousands of the morbid and curious, the sandbags were shifted to the extreme starboard side of the ship. Then all aboard took places along her starboard rails so that all on shore could see that all weight was on one side of the pigboat! With this tremendous load off-center and concentrated on her starboard side the big ship listed but a few scant degrees in that direction.

With much whistle blowing and accompanied by tugs, Coast Guard craft, and many sight seeing vessels, *Columbus* triumphantly cruised about the harbor area for all to see that she was a safe and stable steamship!

Right through World War 1, and on into the roaring twenties, *Columbus* continued her daily round-trip service between Chicago and Milwaukee. Each year she operated she set new records for the total number of passengers handled by any American flag vessel. Other steamers were acquired and still others were sold or retired from service with the Goodrich fleet, but Old Reliable continued to operate, thereby justifying the faith of Captain McDougall, her designer and builder [ed. Alexander McDougall, beginning in 1888 in Superior, Wisconsin, built 50 steel whaleback

The Goodrich line later bought the Christopher Columbus, *which saw service at the Columbian Exposition of 1893, for shuttle use on its heavily traveled Chicago–Milwaukee route. At one time it was rated to carry as many as 4,000 passengers. (CMS Collection)*

barges and steamers with their distinctive rounded decks for various Great Lakes shipping companies.], by her continuous and very efficient performance year after year. No steamer in Goodrich history earned the total profit produced by *Christopher Columbus*. As a result, she remained in Goodrich service until the bitter end.

The city of Manitowoc continued to be the operating base for the Goodrich line. A large storage yard, shops, and coal bunkers were maintained there. This was also the winter lay-up port. The port-of-hail continued to be shown on the stern of all Goodrich boats as Kenosha.

Passenger and freight traffic on the Great Lakes in general, and on Lake Michigan in particular, was setting new records each season. With the exception of the Chicago-Mackinac Island route, Goodrich had pretty well outdistanced its competitors on the routes they had concentrated on these many years. Goodrich by now was not only the largest steamboat operator on Lake Michigan, but did a larger volume annually than any other passenger line on any of the Lakes.

After the purchase of *Carolina* in 1906, there were no further acquisitions or changes in the Goodrich fleet until the year 1910. It was in this year that the most photographed Goodrich steamer of all times [the *Alabama*] was launched.

The beautiful steel steamer *Virginia* had been a fantastic success for the Goodrich Company. Inspired by the experience with *Virginia*, the Goodrich management wisely decided to construct another steel, combination freight and passenger ship to replace the aging *Sheboygan* and *Chicago*.

Designed for year-around operation on the cross-lake route, much care was given to her bow construction as ice-breaking would be an important part of her winter duties. Over her five-eighths-inch steel hull plates was placed a one-inch steel doubling plate. This doubling plate extended for about six feet on either side of her water line to give additional strength when breaking heavy ice. In addition, her sixteen-inch frames were placed on ten-inch centers which made for a very stiff and sturdy ship. Her exciting record over the years is mute testimony to her ability as an ice-breaker. During her career, she rescued many ships caught in the frustrating Lake Michigan ice.

1928 was the beginning of the twilight for the Red-Stack fleet. The automobile was making deep inroads in the summer tourist traffic from Chicago to west Michigan and Wisconsin. Highways were being rapidly improved and the automobile was looked upon as a reliable and fashionable means of travel. The railroads were also making a concentrated effort to attract business. Patronage, especially on the overnight boats, fell off drastically.

The merger of the Graham and Morton Line with Goodrich in 1924–25 brought several G & M officials into the Goodrich family. As profits fell and things began to look glum, internal strife developed between the old G & M officers and some of the Goodrich officials. The company finished in the red in 1928 and hard times ahead for the old Lake Michigan line seemed a certainty.

Robert M. LaFollette, known for many years in political circles as "Battling Bob," was United States senator from the state of Wisconsin from 1905 to 1925. As far back as 1885, when he was elected a United States congressman, he was known as a liberal and was outstandingly progressive. Upon his election to the Senate he advocated strict railroad regulations, lower tariffs, and better working conditions for American seamen.

Senator LaFollette wrote, sponsored, and succeeded in having passed a law known as the LaFollette Act. This law in its original concept was very far-reaching and its enactment struck a serious blow to the steamship business on the Lakes. The Seaman's Act was passed in 1912. [ed. The sinking of the *Titanic* on April 14, 1912, after striking an iceberg in the Atlantic Ocean with the resulting deaths of 1,523 persons because there were insufficient lifeboats for all persons and crew was considered the precipitating factor in passage of the Seaman's Act, which for technical reasons had to be passed again by both houses of Congress in 1914 and

1915, after which it was signed into law by President Wilson on March 15, 1915.]

The operation of the excursion steamer *Columbus* is a good illustration on the added operating expense brought about by the restrictions imposed by the LaFollette Act. While the *Columbus* was always operated as strictly a day-excursion ship and carried no overnight passengers, a large duplication of officers and crew was necessary to comply with the new law. Her normal rated capacity of approximately four thousand day passengers was reduced to about 2,200.

The normal summer season for *Columbus* was from June 15 until Labor Day. It was customary to hire a crew at the beginning of each season and lay them off right after Labor Day. The best of the crew were often retained for service on those ships used on the year-around routes. Under the stipulations of the LaFollette Seaman's Act, a man had to have four years' experience to qualify as an able bodied seaman. This rule forced the line to carry a larger payroll through the winter months, thereby greatly increasing operating costs.

After weighing all the factors involved, Mr. Goodrich decided that he would sell his majority interest in the Goodrich Transit

The Goodrich line in 1891 bought the sleek propeller steamer Virginia. *It was requisitioned by the Navy for use in World War 1. (Great Lakes Historical Society, Vermillion, Ohio)*

Company and step down from the presidency. He also decided to retain as his personal holdings some of the dock properties and real estate held in various locations by the company.

Near the end of 1920, a group of local investors known as the Maritime Securities Company of Manitowoc Mr. Harry Thorp, and a small group of key personnel and their friends—purchased most of the Goodrich Transit Company from Mr. Goodrich.

After World War I, passenger travel on the lakes began to decline. The railroads began to offer attractive rates to vacationers, but more important, the automobile really began to come into its own at this time. It became quite fashionable to "motor" to the summer home or vacation spot selected. "Touring" became a common word and this contributed to a lower passenger traffic volume. Most of those connected with the lake passenger business thought that the loss could be offset by larger freight volume and the trend in lower passenger volume was only temporary. In view of A.W. Goodrich's keen insight in business affairs and the later developments, one cannot wonder whether or not he felt he saw the handwriting on the wall at the time of his selling his holdings.

The fall of 1929 was stormy on Lake Michigan. On October 27 the Grand Trunk car ferry *Milwaukee* sailed from Milwaukee harbor about 1:00 P.M. bound out for Grand Haven. Caught in a ferocious gale, the ship disappeared from the face of the Lake, carrying with it to a watery grave all fifty-two souls aboard. That same evening the *Wisconsin* was making her regular trip from Chicago to Milwaukee and took a terrific beating. She passed her normal stop at Racine and arrived in Milwaukee with her cargo shifted with a bad list to port.

On the evening of October 29, just two days after the tragic and unbelievable loss of *Milwaukee*, *Wisconsin*, with four passengers and a crew of sixty-four men aboard, departed Chicago on her regular run to Milwaukee. A northeasterly gale was beginning to make itself felt as she rounded the Chicago harbor pier heads and started north on her regular course. Captain D.H. Morrison was in command.

As the wild night progressed the winds shifted to east-northeast and increased to gale force. The huge seas began to pound the ship unmercifully on her starboard bow. Holding her head up was a difficult task and the old ship was taking a terrible beating as she fought her way in the mountainous seas.

The engine room crew became aware of the presence of large quantities of water in the aft end of the ship. This information was quickly relayed to Captain Morrison on the bridge. When the pumps failed to handle the incoming water properly it was apparent to her master that the ship was in serious trouble.

At 4:30 A.M. Captain Morrison gave the order to "abandon ship." The crew, aided by some of the passengers, began the perilous task of launching the port lifeboats. Due to the heavy list of the steamer to port, the starboard lifeboats were rendered useless. After two and one-half hours of dangerous and difficult effort, two boats pulled away from the sinking steamer with forty-nine persons aboard. Ten swimmers were plucked from the storm tossed waters, making a total of fifty-nine that owed their lives to the brave men on the tug *Search* and the members of the Coast Guard that manned the little surfboats. It was now 7:00 A.M. and the waves were mountainous.

At 7:10 A.M. *Wisconsin* began her final plunge. As the ship sank beneath the waves her entire superstructure lifted clear off the hull and scattered wreckage over a large area. The gallant old steamer was gone and she carried Chief Engineer Julius Buschman, from Manitowoc, age seventy, and three or four others with her. Captain Morrison was rescued but he died shortly thereafter from shock and exposure. A total of nine lives were lost in the sinking.

The tragic loss of the *Wisconsin* did nothing to help the financial picture for 1929.

The year 1930 found the depression setting like a pall of gloom all over our great country. The lake steamers were no exception and traffic began to fall off at an alarming rate. Gross revenues for Goodrich fell approximately 30%, to $1,820,000. The number of employees dropped from 760 in 1928 to just over four hundred in 1930. This plunge in gross revenue signaled the beginning of serious troubles for the Goodrich Transit Company.

The death blow to the Goodrich Transit Company came on December 20, 1932! On that fateful day E.W. Sims of Chicago, attorney for the receivers, filed a voluntary petition in bankruptcy.

Following the demise of Lake Michigan's oldest steamship company, other lines tried to operate some of the former Goodrich steamers in their attempt to stay in business. Eventually, each fell by the wayside in the attempt and one by one they sailed away over the horizon of progress and changing times, until today, the lake passenger steamer is, with only a very few exceptions, a thing of the past. An exciting, challenging and wonderful era is now gone forever. But fortunately, for some, the memory still strongly lingers on!

PART V

Safety on the Seas

The second worst disaster on the Great Lakes involved a collision between the paddle-wheel steamer Lady Elgin *and a schooner during a storm in 1860, about seven miles off the north shore suburb of Winnetka. The lumber schooner, having sustained little damage, continued on to Chicago, but the* Lady Elgin *broke apart and 279 persons drowned. (CMS Collection)*

Grosse Point Light Station

The development of the skyscraper in the late nineteenth century had the unintended effect of displacing the lighthouse as a navigation beacon for Great Lakes mariners. The 100-story John Hancock Center, with its ring of light on top, is visible from the bridges of ships north of the Illinois-Wisconsin state line, and the Allen-Bradley clock tower on Milwaukee's near south side can be seen far out into the lake. Nevertheless, lighthouses continued to play an important, though somewhat diminished, role in navigation into the twenty-first century. In some cases decommissioned lighthouses were preserved as public attractions even though they no longer had any navigational function.

The Grosse Point lighthouse (in Evanston), 13 miles north of the Loop, was for many years perhaps the most important navigational beacon on southern Lake Michigan, guiding ships to the busy Chicago port. Terry Pepper wrote the article on the Grosse Point light station reprinted here for the fall 2004 issue of the Chicago Maritime Society's newsletter. The name of the lighthouse over the years has been variously spelled Grossepoint, Gross Point, and Grosse Point in government documents and history books.

by Terry Pepper

Chicago of 1870 was in a state of tremendous industrial growth, and with that growth a pall of thick smoke from the industries around the city enveloped the foot of the lake, making it increasingly difficult for mariners to locate the harbor through the gloom. As part of ongoing harbor improvements, the Army Corps of Engineers had extended the protective piers at the river mouth to a length of over 2,000 feet, exacerbating the task of locating the narrow channel between the piers.

Evaluating the situation in the spring of 1870, newly appointed Eleventh Lighthouse District Engineer Brevet Brigadier General Orlando M. Poe recommended the establishment of a coast light to the north of the city to serve as a leading light to guide mariners towards the harbor entrance. After conducting a survey of the area, the decision was made to locate this new coast light on Grosse Point, a major promontory which lay 13 miles to the north of the harbor in what is today the suburb of Evanston, and Poe requested that funding be provided for the station's establishment in his annual report for that year. Congress evidently concurred with the need for the new light station, as it appropriated $35,000 for its construction in March 1871.

With funding in hand, Poe supervised the drafting of plans and specifications for the new station at the Detroit depot, and bids for furnishing the construction and iron work were opened on August 13, 1872. In accordance with federal policy, the lowest bids were accepted, and contracts were entered into with the appropriate parties immediately. Work at Grosse Point began in September of 1872 with the excavation for the foundations of the tower and dwelling. When weather caused the end of work for the season in November, all of the stonework had been completed to grade level and the necessary drainage tile installed. Work at the site resumed in the beginning of May 1873, with the driving of a tight cluster of 30-foot long oak piles into the earth to serve as a base on which the tower's concrete and stone foundation would be laid. By the end of June, work on the exterior of the dwelling and a 41-foot long covered way leading to the tower were virtually complete, and plastering of the interior walls and ceilings was well underway. Finding costs of construction to be greater than originally projected, an additional $15,000 was appropriated on March 3, 1873.

As work drew to a close towards the end of 1873, the double-walled Cream City–brick tower stood 113 feet in height, with its 8-inch thick cylindrical inner wall serving as a support for the 141-step cast iron spiral stairway, which wound its way from ground level to the lantern scuttle. The outer wall stood 22 feet in diameter at the foundation, gracefully tapering to a diameter of 13 feet, 3 inches at the cast iron gallery, which was supported by 18 gracefully formed cast iron corbels. A circular watch room was centered on the gallery, and topped by a lantern with vertical astragals and outfitted with a huge second order Fresnel lens. The lens was manufactured by the Henry-Lepaute Company of Paris.

Outfitted with a red flash panel, the lens rotated around a three-wick lamp. Power for the rotating mechanism was provided by a clockwork mechanism with a steel cable that was suspended within the air space between the inner and outer tower walls. The clockwork was carefully monitored on a daily basis to ensure that the station's prescribed characteristic fixed white light with a red flash every three minutes was maintained. Work at the station continued through the winter of 1873–1874 and it was completed on March 1, 1874, in readiness for the opening of the navigation season a few weeks later.

The following year it was found that the sandy shoreline in front of the station was eroding significantly, and $5,000 was requested to abate the problem. With funding finally available in early 1875, two large protective timber cribs were erected in front of the station in May. Sometime later, it was determined that a fog signal would have to be installed to aid maritime commerce during periods of fog or thick weather. To this end, a pair of buildings, 15 by 12 feet and 20 by 12 feet, were erected to the east of the tower in 1880. Standing 15 feet in height, both buildings were outfitted with identical horizontal steam boilers piped to steam-operated sirens located on the lakeward gable end. While only one of the signals would operate at any given time, the second was available to serve as a back up in the event of failure of the primary signal.

After the arrival of a work crew to replace the deteriorating water supply line from the Evanston municipal water works in 1882, the following decade was relatively uneventful at Grosse Point, with only routine maintenance and repairs recorded at the station. As witness to the important role played by the station, the decision was made to upgrade the fog signal apparatus to 10-inch locomotive-style team whistles, whose blast was considerably louder than originally installed sirens. Work on the north signal was completed and the new whistle placed into operation on March 30, 1892, and the south signal activated a month later on April 23. Prior to this time, lamp oil had been stored in the service room, which was incorporated in the covered way between the dwelling and tower. In order to lessen the likelihood of fire spreading throughout the station, the work crew also erected a prefabricated circular iron oil storage building to the east of the signal buildings. While the new steam whistles were a remarked improvement over the smaller sirens, it took hours to get sufficient steam raised within the boilers to activate them. To solve this problem, water heaters were installed in 1898, allowing the keepers to build a head of steam much more quickly, and thereby getting the whistles screaming in less than an hour when conditions changed quickly.

In 1900 a work crew arrived to erect an iron fence and gate on the Sheridan Drive property line and build a second oil house of brick, standing 8 feet by 10 feet and 12 feet in height. The work crew also raised a flag pole and poured concrete walks connecting the front doors of the duplex dwelling to the new Sheridan Drive gate.

By the turn of the twentieth century, the area around the light station had undergone a metamorphosis. At the time of the station's establishment 30 years earlier, the area was somewhat open, with but few houses scattered around the area. With Chicago's commercial success and expansion, an increasing number of moneyed businessmen had built mansions along the lakeshore around the light station in order to escape the turmoil of the big city. A conflict between the need to sound the fog signals and the peace and quiet desired by the area's gentry was inevitable. Learning from previous experiments undertaken in Duluth in 1895 and Marquette in 1897, the Lighthouse Board installed reflectors behind the whistles in 1901. Built on a framework of pine and sheathed in iron, the reflectors were packed with sawdust to simultaneously absorb sound landward, while successfully deflecting the majority of the sound to sea. With a semblance of peace restored to the area, life again settled into a relatively uneventful ten year period at the station. The boat landing was re-planked in 1904, the north fog signal building remodeled in 1905, and the illumination apparatus in the light was upgraded from the triple-wick kerosene lamp to an incandescent oil vapor system in 1910 with an increase in output to 10,000 candlepower for the fixed white light and 32,000 candlepower for the red flash.

Evidently the Cream City brick used in building the Grosse Point tower was of an inferior consistency, as Twelfth District Inspector Lewis M. Stoddard noted the deteriorating condition of the brick during his inspection of the station in 1913. While similar conditions had been rectified with the installation of steel casings over the brick at Big Sable Point in 1900 and at Cana Island in 1902, Stoddard proposed a less expensive remedy at Grosse Point. The following spring, a work crew from the General Cement Gun Company arrived at the station, and after erecting a wooden scaffolding around the tower, applied a protective coating of cement to the entire tower exterior from ground to gallery. The work was completed on May 20 at a total cost of only $2,678.52.

In 1935, the decision was made to automate the station, and a work crew was dispatched to Grosse Point to undertake the work. Electricity from the municipal utility was brought to the building, and the light automated with the installation of an incandescent electric bulb with automatic twin bulb changer. As part of this new installation, the lamp was also outfitted with an automatic flash mechanism and the characteristic of the light changed to exhibit a pair of 68,000 candlepower white flashes every 15 seconds. While the automation work crew was on site, a large gap was found between the assistant keeper's wing and the main dwelling. With the station's automation eliminating the need for live-in keepers, the decision was made to demolish both this wing and the covered way connecting the tower and dwelling.

After the placement of the Grosse Point outer lighted bell buoy offshore in 1939, it became clear that the Grosse Point light was obsolete, and the station was decommissioned in 1941 and turned over to the City of Evanston. The building sat empty until 1944, when the tower was used by two physicists from Northwestern University to conduct experiments in the U.S. of infrared transmission as a form of enhanced radar. After creation of the historic Lighthouse Park District, the City of Evanston managed to obtain permission to have the light reestablished as a private aid to navigation in 1946.

With Evanston's conversion of the station into a museum, a major $100,000 improvement project was undertaken during the early 1990s to restore the buildings to their turn of the century appearance. To this end, the Assistant's Wing and cover way which had been removed during the station's automation in 1935 were both reconstructed to allow full interpretation of the station during the height of its operation. The majestic light station continues to serve as a museum and is open to the public for a small admission fee during limited hours during the summer months.

Lighthouses

Lighthouses, those lonely sentinels posted along coastlines the world over to guide ships to safety, are perhaps the most nostalgic artifact remaining from our maritime past—the subject of innumerable painters and photographers, and a favorite sight of many tourists down for a day at the beach. The galleons, clipper ships, and schooners are long gone from the seven seas, as well as the five Great Lakes, but the lighthouses remain.

They have been around since the ancient world. The Pharos lighthouse of Alexandria, built by the first two Ptolemaic kings of Egypt, ca. 290 B.C., was probably the most famous such structure, and The Colossus of Rhodes (282–226 B.C.) may also have served as a navigation light.

A former Chicago lighthouse that guarded the entrance to the Chicago River was relocated and reconstructed at Rawley Point, Wisconsin, just north of Manitowoc. (David M. Young)

America's first lighthouse dates from 1716 in colonial Boston and a replacement of the original is still in operation. The first on the Great Lakes was opened in 1782 by the British on the banks of the Niagara River near Lake Ontario. The first U.S. lighthouse was on lakes opened near Buffalo, New York, in 1819.

The completion of the Erie Canal in 1825 opened the upper Great Lakes to navigation, and as commerce increased, so did the demand for lighthouses to protect shipping. At the height of its operation in the 1920s, the U.S. Bureau of Lighthouses maintained some 536 lights on fixed structures along the U.S. shoreline of the Great Lakes. According to a National Park Service survey in 1994, a total of 196 such structures still survive.

Despite the widespread use of radar, sonar, and global positioning systems, lighthouses are still in operation in the twenty-first century—several in the Chicago area—to show the mariners the way into harbors and to warn them of obstructions

The existing Chicago harbor lighthouse, ca. 1893, sits at the end of a breakwater just off Navy Pier and is familiar to thousands of visitors to that facility. (Collection of Donald Terras)

This rather modest lighthouse stands at the north end of Beaver Island, Michigan. (David M. Young)

This classic stone lighthouse, ca. 1872, sits at Fort Niagara, New York, near the point where the Niagara River downstream from the falls flows into Lake Ontario. (National Archives)

One of the strangest lighthouses in the Great Lakes region sits more than 17 miles inland near Lemont, Illinois, at a junction of two canals—the Sanitary and Ship Canal (right) and the Cal Sag Channel (left). A towboat pushing two barges of limestone can be seen upstream on the canal. (David M. Young)

The Sand Island light-house was built ca. 1882 to guide ships on Lake Superior. It sits on one of the Apostle Islands off the northern tip of Wisconsin. (National Park Service)

*The upper works
of the Grosse Point
lighthouse loom above
the foliage at north
suburban Evanston.
It is the first of a long
string of lighthouses
between Chicago and
the northern end of
Lake Michigan.
(Terry Pepper)*

*Like most nineteenth-century lighthouses, Grosse Point had an attached house
used as the keeper's residence. (Terry Pepper)*

A considerable amount of scaffolding was needed to build or rebuild lighthouses, like the Grosse Point lighthouse, shown here. (Terry Pepper)

Chapter Twenty-Four

The Coast Guard in Chicago

The existence of some sort of government aquatic presence on the Great Lakes predates the American Republic. The French never had a fleet-in-being on the lakes, but the British established one, and so did the United States after it was founded. The first American fleet, oddly enough, was operated by the Army as a way to resupply forts, but the Navy came in during the War of 1812 and stayed until the Coast Guard was formed in the early twentieth century. The Coast Guard was in fact an amalgamation for a variety of government agencies that had a presence on the Great Lakes in the nineteenth century: the Cutter Service, the Life-Saving Service, the Lighthouse Service, and the Steamship Inspection Service.

Retired Coast Guard Boatswain Mate Chief (BMC) J.A. Wall, a CMS member, wrote this history of his agency's presence in Chicago expressly for this book.

by BMC J.A. Wall (Ret.)

Although the modern Coast Guard was not organized until January 28, 1915, its predecessor, the U.S. Life-Saving Service, was well-established in the area, but it, too, was predated by another group—several volunteer students from Evanston's Northwestern University. The annals of lifesaving began on a windswept Lake Michigan in the middle of the nineteenth century. It was on the morning of September 8, 1860, when the passenger steamer *Lady*

Elgin, en route to Milwaukee, collided in the dark with the cargo schooner *Augusta*, off Winnetka, Illinois.

At first light, cries for help were heard below the bluffs at Winnetka and Glencoe, as survivors struggled in the surf amidst the wreckage of the ill-fated ship. Some of the first to respond to their cries were several students from the Garrett Biblical Institute (Northwestern University), among them Edward Spencer and Charles Fowler, who were able to save 17 lives. Lying on the beach in exhaustion that afternoon, Spencer questioned, "Did we do our best?" The *Augusta*, having sailed on in the dark, was not aware of the sinking until she arrived in the Chicago River that morning.

The students never forgot the *Lady Elgin* and on subsequent lifesaving missions rescued the entire crews from the schooner *Storm* (in 1864) and the *Sea Bird* and *Arrow* (both in 1869) off the Northwestern University campus. In 1870 Commodore Murray, of the Navy, gave the university a 26-foot lifeboat to assist the students in their rescue operations.

With the industrial development of the Great Lakes after the Civil War, the federal government, under the Revenue Marine Bureau of the Treasury Department, began an energetic program of building surf stations throughout the country to be manned by local volunteers. Knowing that the students at Northwestern were already operating a boat, the bureau built a boathouse on the university's campus in 1875. Congress, with the passage of the Organic Act on June 11, 1878, created the U.S. Life-Saving Service independent of the Revenue Marine Bureau, putting an end to the all-volunteer status of the surf stations. The surf station on the south bank of the Chicago River, which had opened on May 25, 1877, was also taken over by the Life-Saving Service. It would thereafter be known as the Chicago Life-Saving Station, and the University Station was renamed the Evanston Life-Saving Station.

With the industrialization of the Greater Chicago area in the last quarter of the nineteenth century, Chicago became the gateway to the Midwest and thus saw an increase of waterborne commerce. It was soon apparent that the two existing stations were inadequate to handle the load. Two new stations were planned south of the Old Chicago Station, and on May 3, 1890, the South Chicago Station became operational at the mouth of the Calumet River. With the increase of pleasure boating, the second station, at Jackson Park, became operational on July 1, 1892. During the open water season all four stations were manned by eight to ten surfmen including the captain.

The records show that prior to 1884, most of these stations were operating 26-foot Whitehall dinghies or Higgins & Gifford pulling surfboats of six oars. In 1884 the stations received a Long Branch, and in 1890 they were reequipped with 25-foot Monomoy surfboats. These craft could all be rigged for sail, which was done as often as possible. However, the surfboats weren't motorized until the turn of the century, when Lieutenant C.H. McLellan, of the Revenue Cutter Service, and Henry Cleary, of the Life-Saving Service, installed internal combustion engines.

For almost four decades the Life-Saving Service kept vigilant watch along Chicagoland's lakefront from Waukegan to Gary. Most of their search and rescues were routine, with a minimum loss of life, considering the volume of vessel traffic. Some of the rescues, however, were anything but routine. Captain Lawrence O. Lawson and his crew of volunteer students were awarded the Gold Life Saving Medal for saving the entire crew of 18 of the steamer *Calumet* when it foundered on November 28, 1889, off Highland Park.

History was to repeat itself almost six years to the day after the daring rescue of the *Calumet* complement when Lawson and his crew were called upon to perform a feat of equal daring. The steamer *J. Emory Owen*, with the schooners *Michigan* and *Elizabeth A. Owen* in tow, ran aground off Glencoe on November

29, 1895. Captain Lawson and his crew had to cross the angry surf line 12 times to get all 36 crew members safely to shore. Today Lawrence O. Lawson, surfman extraordinaire, is regarded as the father of lifesaving in the Chicago area.

In 1912 the Taft administration began to investigate how they might reorganize government in an effort to eliminate duplication and waste in the various bureaus. A commission was appointed to make recommendations on how this could be best achieved. Secretary of the Treasury Franklin McVeigh's recommendation to merge the Life-Saving Service and the Revenue Cutter Service, two agencies that had worked closely together for many years, was finally accepted. On January 28, 1915, President Wilson signed into law the bill creating the U.S. Coast Guard.

The term *Coast Guard* was not new. It had been used during the War with Mexico in 1846 and again during the Civil War, when referring to the Revenue Cutter Service. The motto of the Life-Saving Service, *Remis Velisqui* (by means of oar and sail), no longer seemed appropriate in the twentieth century, so the new Coast Guard adopted the Revenue Cutter Service's Latin motto of *Semper Paratus* (always prepared).

The transition was not immediate, particularly in personnel. The Coast Guard could not maintain a volunteer membership and retain its credibility as a military organization. Although the Life-Saving Service had been a quasi-military establishment, it was not an armed force capable of repelling or containing an aggressor and enforcing federal law. The Coast Guard had to replace the volunteers with qualified men from other units or enlist and train new men.

On all shore units, signs were put up that read "U.S. Coast Guard," and the term *lifesaving station* was changed to *lifeboat station*. It was an indication of the influence that the Revenue Cutter Service had on the newly formed Coast Guard.

Soon after the formation of the U.S. Coast Guard, tragedy struck. On the morning of July 24, 1915, the excursion vessel *Eastland* capsized in the Chicago River between LaSalle and

Clark Streets. More than 800 men, women, and children lost their lives in what was the largest maritime disaster suffered in Chicago. The grim task for the crew of the Old Chicago Lifeboat (Lifesaving) Station was to recover the bodies from the river.

Although the Coast Guard had been taken over by the Navy during World War I, it had virtually no impact in the Chicago area, with the exception of an occasional parade to sell victory bonds. However, from the Great War came wireless communications, and by the 1920s the first Coast Guard radio station was installed at the Evanston station.

With the end to the war, the various branches were reduced in manpower, and so it was with the Coast Guard. On May 14, 1920, the Evanston station was reported to be down to two men. The South Chicago and Jackson Park stations had only their officers in charge on board, and the Old Chicago station was down to five men. A shortage of personnel seemed to plague the Coast Guard from its inception, and the 1920s and 1930s were no exception.

In the late teens and early 1920s the Coast Guard began replacing their traditional pulling boats with motor surfboats that were

For much of its history, the Evanston Life-Saving Station was operated by Northwestern University students. The lifeboats were carted to the water aboard carriages. (U.S. Coast Guard)

25 feet, 10 inches in length and had a four-cylinder Buda diesel engine that propelled the craft at 7.6 knots. At the same time, the

36-foot motor lifeboat capable of rescues in heavy weather was introduced. It was powered by a six-cylinder Buda diesel engine and had a maximum speed of 9 knots. Although over the years the Coast Guard's Buda engines were replaced by General Motors diesels, many of the rescue vessels continued in service to the late 1960s.

The Evanston crew was photographed launching their boat from a carriage in 1908. (U.S. Coast Guard)

In July 1927 the excursion vessel *Favorite* capsized about a half mile off North Avenue during a sudden squall. More than 50 men, women, and children were rescued through the efforts of the Coast Guard, local yachtsmen, and lifeguards from North Avenue Beach. The Chicago City Council presented the Chicago Lifeboat Station with a citation for their efficiency and professionalism in saving so many lives.

In the mid-1920s the South Chicago station, which had been built at the mouth of the Calumet River, was moved to Calumet Park when the sea wall was extended. Thereafter it was referred to as the Calumet Harbor Lifeboat Station. Beach erosion and a March 1929 storm that caused severe damage to the Evanston station caused the Coast Guard to abandon it. A replacement, which was built in Washington Park in Wilmette, became operational on June 1, 1931.

Prohibition had no direct effect on any of the Chicago's lifeboat stations [ed. unlike those on the Detroit, Niagara, and St. Lawrence rivers used by rumrunners from Canada], but its repeal in 1934 was to enhance their operational capabilities. The Coast Guard began distributing 38-foot single-screw motorboats to all the stations on the Great Lakes, including Chicago. The vessels—dubbed picket boats because of their role in chasing down rum-runners during Prohibition—were fast for their day, with six-cylinder gasoline engines capable of turning out 14 knots. They became the standard crash boat for search-and-rescue missions well into the late 1940s.

The Coast Guard was quite active in the Chicago area in 1939. With rumors of war spreading across Europe, the U.S. military was expanding to meet the inevitable challenge of another world war. On June 23 the Reserve and Auxiliary Act was passed in anticipation of mobilization, and on July 1 President Franklin D. Roosevelt signed his Reorganization Order #11, which transferred the U.S. Lighthouse Service to the Coast Guard. On November 5, 1940, Chicago was designated for a captain of the port, and the Coast Guard opened an office a short time later in the U.S. Custom House at 610 S. Canal Street.

The Motorboat Act of 1940 increased the Coast Guard's role beyond assisting vessels in distress by giving the agency the power to inspect both private and commercial vessels to ensure they had proper safety equipment on board and their crews knew how to use it. The Marine Safety Office was created to do that job, and at the same time, the rest of the Coast Guard was organized into clusters called groups. The Chicago Group, under the captain of that port, included a territory that ranged from Waukegan to Gary and to Peoria. It consisted of stations at Wilmette harbor, Chicago, Jackson Park, and Calumet harbor as well as at the Chicago light off Navy Pier and the Indiana harbor light at the bottom of the lake.

With World War II raging in Europe in 1941, Congress created (on February 19) the Coast Guard Reserve and Coast Guard Auxiliary, two groups that would play a very important role in Chicago over the next four years. On November 1—slightly more than a month before the United States entered the war—the president signed Executive Order #8929, transferring the Coast Guard to the Navy. For all practical purposes the 9th, 10th, and 11th Coast Guard districts ceased to exist and were replaced by the 9th Naval District, which was headquartered at Great Lakes, Illinois. The Coast Guard subdivided this vast region into two parts for administrative purposes, with offices in Chicago and Cleveland.

The nation was stunned by Japan's surprise attack on Pearl Harbor, but with the declaration of war on December 8, 1941, the Coast Guard's Chicago Group swung into action. The captain of the port issued orders for the security of all waterfront facilities under his authority. The responsibility to implement these orders fell upon the group commander, whose standing orders were to maintain complete port security of the Greater Chicago lakefront and inland waterways.

There was much to be done. All boats were painted navy gray, small arms were issued, billets were changed, and personnel were transferred. In anticipation of being transferred to sea, a great number of enlisted never unpacked their sea bags. In mid-1942 the Bureau of Marine Inspection and Navigation was temporarily transferred to the Coast Guard for the duration, and it would become a permanent part of the Coast Guard in 1946. The Chicago Group was now not only responsible for its traditional duties of search and rescue and its wartime duties of guarding docks, bridges, locks, and vessels, as well as promoting fire prevention, warehousing, and lakefront and inland water patrols; they would also maintain all aids to navigation.

In late 1942 it became apparent that complete security could not be accomplished with the manpower and equipment available. To alleviate the situation, 18 privately owned yachts were commandeered for the duration, and the Coast Guard's ranks swelled with civilians, auxiliaries, and reservists in addition to regular personnel. The Chicago area had become the arsenal for LCIs (landing craft infantry), LCMS, (landing craft mechanized), minesweepers, submarines, and auxiliary type vessels from the shipyards in Michigan, Wisconsin, and Illinois, all of which passed through the Chicago River and the inland waterway to get to the Gulf of Mexico. Lake carriers and barges from Lake Superior came with the raw materials for the blast furnaces, and ships of every size and shape arrived with the essential elements for total war.

At this time the Navy acquired two coal-burning side-wheel excursion ships and converted them into aircraft carriers at Detroit and Buffalo. They were used to train future carrier pilots from the Glenview Naval Air Station in the techniques of takeoffs and landings as well as flight deck crews destined for the Pacific Theater. (See Chapter 29.) The USS *Sable* (IX-81) and the *Wolverine* (IX-64) arrived in Chicago, at Navy Pier, in August 1942, and operations began immediately. To assist in these operations, the Coast Guard brought in four 83-foot patrol craft—the CG 83477, 83478, 83479, and 83480—to escort the carriers and rescue pilots when they crashed into the lake. A maintenance and repair base to service the patrol craft was established on board an 80-foot, 57-ton pleasure craft moored on the north branch of the Chicago River at North Avenue. During the open water season the patrol craft were berthed at the Chicago station.

With the steady expansion of the war effort by late 1942, it became apparent that the communication system at Wilmette station was inadequate to handle the volume of radio traffic generated by units on Lakes Michigan, Huron, and Superior. That same year a site for a new facility was chosen along Dundee Road in Northbrook. Construction began immediately, and the station became operational by early 1943. (This station was closed on March 1, 1969.)

By early 1944 men assigned to the Chicago Group performed every sort of job imaginable, from putting out brush and rubbish fires along the banks of the Chicago River to removing logs and debris (that might prove a menace to navigation) from the water. Chasing suspicious-looking individuals and spectators from restricted areas around industrial plants also became their responsibility, as did checking or issuing identification cards. In all kinds of weather, they provided security watches for loading explosives and other cargoes on vessels and other facilities engaged in the war effort. A Coast Guard fireboat, the CG-7300, patrolled from Gary to South Chicago and the Pullman Standard Shipyard in conjunction with the Chicago Fire Department.

As might be expected because of the strain and anxiety imposed on everyone during the war, some imaginations ran rampant. Among the more preposterous sightings reported on the Great Lakes was that of a German U-boat off the steel mills. There was no truth to the rumor, but it served its purpose in that boat crews became more alert on their patrols.

With the capitulation of Japan in August 1945, the Chicago Group again resumed its peacetime role, but for the next ten months it also served as a depot to muster out of the service guardsmen returning from overseas. At the same time, the Navy relinquished its authority over the Coast Guard, and it was returned to its prewar status. The Coast Guard, like all the other branches of the service, underwent congressional economy cuts in personnel and equipment after the war. To save money, several stations in the group became seasonal and remained open during the open water season and closed during the winter months.

At the end of the 1947 season, the Chicago Group was reduced from an authorized complement of 75 men to 47. Even with this reduced number, the group turned in an impressive record of 411 cases [ed. incidents involving rescues of both life and property]. The Chicago station answered 179, Jackson Park 78, Wilmette 73, Michigan City (which had become part of the Chicago Group during the war) 43, and Calumet harbor 38.

Tragedy was to strike the North Shore in late October 1951, when Wilmette's CG-30315 and her crew, EN 1 Max Wage and

BM3 Robert Sawyer, disappeared on a routine search-and-rescue mission somewhere off Waukegan. They had gone in response to a report that some duck hunters out on the lake were overdue. At first light Chicago's captain of the port, William P. Hawley, sent the following message:

TO ALL UNITS - SOUTHERN LAKE MICHIGAN - SITUATION IMMEDIATE - COMMENCE SEARCHING FOR CG-30315 - DEPARTED WILMETTE HARBOR LIFEBOAT STATION 27 OCTOBER 1951 - SITUATION - OVER DUE.

Every available Coast Guard boat from Milwaukee to Muskegon got under way, as did CG auxiliary boats and private yachts. Joining the search were aircraft from the Glenview Naval Air Station and Traverse City Coast Guard Air Station, along with small boats from the Great Lakes Training Center and the destroyer escort *Daniel A. Joy* (DE 585) from Chicago.

The duck hunters' boat was found partly submerged a half mile off Waukegan Harbor; of the three hunters, only one body was recovered, on November 8. What happened to CG-30315 is unknown to this day. The only things ever recovered were the wooden lid to the battery box and a side panel to the engine compartment found 20 miles off Wilmette on November 1.

On June 26, 1954, a seiche, or rapid rise in water level, slammed into the Chicago lakefront, causing repercussions from Milwaukee to Grand Haven, Michigan. The wave reached a height of ten feet, the highest on record, and left seven dead in its wake. It raised havoc with pleasure boats moored in harbors and damaged breakwalls. The entire Coast Guard group responded to the situation, assisting the vessels that were affected.

The decade of the 1950s saw many changes. The Coast Guard began to phase out their prewar and war surplus equipment with more efficient and faster rescue boats to replace their gasoline-driven 30- to 38-foot wooden hulls. The new boats would be powered by diesel and built of steel. The first to be delivered was the 30-foot Mark I, a single screw with a top speed of 21.8 knots. It was shortly followed by a 40-foot, twin screw boat with a speed of 20.3 knots. This version was improved with the Mark IV class, which was capable of 23 knots.

At the close of the decade, the Coast Guard transferred the yard tug CGC *Arundel* (WYT-90) to the Chicago Group from Boston. Her duties were law enforcement, search and rescue, and ice breaking along the Chicago lakefront and southern Lake Michigan. A *Rartan*-class cutter at 110 feet, displacing 328 tons, and carrying a crew of 16, the *Arundel* was commissioned on July 6, 1939, and saw service on the Greenland patrol during World War II. After the war, Chicago (Ogden Slip at the head of Navy Pier) was her house port for 20 years until she departed in June 1979.

With the phenomenal growth of pleasure boating along the lakefront, the Chicago Police Department in the early 1960s created a marine division to assist boaters in distress. This alleviated some of the Coast Guard's workload, primarily at its Chicago and Jackson Park stations. A few years later the Coast Guard reevaluated these stations. Because both had been in existence for more than 70 years and both required rehabilitation, it was decided to close them as an economy move. The CPD marine division took over their task of patrolling the city's lakefront.

Tragedy again struck the North Shore. On a quiet August evening in 1965, United Flight #380 from LaGuardia to O'Hare disappeared from radar on its final approach over the lake somewhere between Waukegan and Fort Sheridan. The first to respond was the Wilmette harbor station. They were quickly joined by the CPD's marine division, Kenosha station, the Chicago Fire Department, CGC *Arundel*, and CGC *Woodbine* from Grand Haven. There was no one to rescue, however, and the aftermath became a grueling search operation. In all, 24 passengers and 8 crew members on board the Boeing 727 lost their lives.

After 177 years under the Treasury Department, the Coast Guard was transferred to the newly formed Department of Transportation in 1967. At the same time, the middy, navy blue uniform was replaced by a single-breasted lighter blue uniform, similar to the type worn by the surfmen. The whole image of the Coast Guard was changing with the introduction of the racing stripe and the words "U.S. COAST GUARD" painted on the agency's small boats, ships, and planes.

In March 1969 the Coast Guard established an air station at the Naval Air Station in Glenview. This enhanced the area stations' response time to search-and-rescue missions throughout the southern Lake Michigan area, and the helicopters stationed there proved their value time and time again with some daring rescues. Unfortunately, the air station came with a high price. On January 20, 1977, an HH 52A helicopter, #1448, crashed into the Illinois River on a routine ice patrol flight. It had accidentally struck some electrical transmission wires. Those who perished were LTJG W. Caeser, USN; LTJG J.F. Taylor, USCG; Aviation Technician Second Class J.B. Johnson, USCG; and W.S. Simpson, a civilian. The Coast Guard air station was closed in the 1990s after the Navy shut down its Glenview base for economic reasons; the government subsequently sold off the land to private developers.

In the early 1970s the Coast Guard's group system was again reorganized, this time with a central command base at Milwaukee and encompassing the entire western shore of Lake Michigan from Green Bay to Gary. Chicago was downgraded to a subgroup consisting only of the Wilmette harbor and Calumet harbor stations. The Great Lakes were under the command of the Coast Guard 9th District headquarters at Cleveland. Today under the new system, Wilmette is a Coast Guard auxiliary station but continues to maintain a regular Coast Guard and reserve crew under the direct command of Calumet harbor station.

By the mid-1970s the Coast Guard's 40-foot utility boats and the 36-foot motor lifeboats were showing their age and were fazed out and replaced by 41-foot utility boats and 44-foot motor lifeboats. Wilmette received a 41-footer with a speed of 26 knots, and Calumet received a 44-footer capable of 14 knots. The other miscellaneous boats at these stations were overtaken by old age and replaced with inflatable rigid hull boats for quick response. At this time the term *lifeboat* was dropped from the stations' official names and replaced by *SAR* (search and rescue).

During the late 1970s and early 1980s both the Wilmette harbor and Calumet harbor stations were completely renovated. Although they maintained much of their original facades, they were enlarged and modernized with state-of-the-art equipment. Wilmette station cost $39,791 to build in 1931, but 50 years later the 20-foot, two-story addition and remodeling of the interior of the original building ran in excess of $100,000.

During the 1980s the three Coast Guard Reserve units in the area were merged into a single survivor, the Great Lakes unit. The reservists continued in their role of augmenting the two SAR stations and the Marine Safety Office, and in September 1990 a third of this unit was called up for active duty to serve in the Persian Gulf War to provide port security unit for several Saudi Arabian cities.

In the early 1990s the Chicago marine safety office (as the captain of the port's office was by then called) moved from 610 S. Canal Street to west suburban Burr Ridge. In 1994 all reserve units were dissolved and their members were integrated with the regular Coast Guard personnel at the agency's three surviving Chicago-area facilities: Wilmette, Calumet, and Burr Ridge.

Over the years the Coast Guard has been heavily involved on Chicago's lakefront and inland waterways not only in the areas of search and rescue and boating safety but also in regard to law enforcement, water pollution, and all aids to navigation. Their annual involvement also includes the Chicago to Mackinac Island Race, the Chicago Air and Water Show, the Venetian Night festival, and the Christmas tree ship, to name a few.

Chapter Twenty-Five

The Globe *Explosion*

The Chicago River, a sluggish stream navigable for only a few miles, somewhat surprisingly has been the site of a number of disasters. There was the flood of 1849 (see Chapter 4), the Eastland *capsizing of* 1915 *(see Chapter 28), and the Loop tunnel flood of 1992. One of the forgotten disasters was the boiler explosion aboard the steamship* Globe *in 1860 — an event like the* Sultana *explosion of 1865 that was overshadowed by the Civil War.*

CMS member David M. Young adapted this from an article he wrote for the Inland Seas, *Vol. 58, No. 1 (spring 2002), and from his book* Chicago Maritime: An Illustrated History *(2001).*

by David M. Young

By most standards the Chicago River does not rank as one of the world's great waterways. It is a sluggish stream navigable for only a few miles. But it has been the site of a number of disasters.

The 12-year-old steam propeller *Globe*, a once-proud passenger ship relegated to the cargo trade although she was still technically a packet, chugged into the Chicago River in the early morning hours of November 8, 1860, and moored at a dock on the north bank just below the Wells Street bridge in the heart of the city's mercantile district. The *Globe*'s handful of passengers disembarked at 4 A.M., as did some of the crew whose duties required them to be ashore. Over the next five hours while the *Globe*'s engines methodically hissed and chugged at idle, stevedores began unloading some of the cargo and representatives from various commercial houses to whom it was consigned came aboard to check their shipments.

The mercantile district was just beginning to come to life. Workers had begun dribbling in to the offices along the river, a few stopping to eye the new arrival, and some gleaners had shown up at the dock to see what they could salvage from spilled cargo. It was nearly 9 A.M. when the routinely tranquil scene was disrupted by an explosion that destroyed the ship and hurled debris and shrapnel over the area, some of it with enough force to poke holes in the walls of nearby buildings, which fortuitously still were only partially occupied because of the time.

The explosion claimed probably 15 or 16 lives, but it could have been much worse. Had it occurred an hour later, the mercantile district would have been jammed with people. Because it wasn't, the *Globe* disaster has been relegated to relative obscurity despite the bizarre but tenuous relationship the vessel had to Abraham Lincoln. He had traveled on the *Globe* in 1848 and was elected president within days of its destruction.

By the time of the explosion, the Chicago River had, in the space of 30 years, been transformed from a sluggish little stream useful only for voyageurs seeking the shortest canoe portage between the St. Lawrence and Mississippi rivers' watersheds to one of the busiest ports in the world, even though the main stem of the river and its two branches combined were commercially navigable by big ships for only about a dozen miles. Yet the river was jammed with shipping schooners and steamers off the lake, canal boats, and the array of tugs and auxiliaries necessary to maintain traffic in a port that by 1870 exceeded in numbers of arriving vessels the nation's six busiest saltwater ports combined.

The *Globe* explosion has been largely forgotten over the years to a large extent because Chicago, with its status as the nation's mid-continental transportation center, has had a number of disasters with even greater death tolls. (The *Titanic* disaster in 1912, for example, obscured the earlier tragic loss of all aboard the *Pacific*, which in 1856 became impaled on an iceberg in the North Atlantic not far from the spot where the *Titanic* met its demise.)

In Chicago on July 24, 1915, the capsizing of the *Eastland* at its dock on the Chicago River dwarfed all other disasters: As many as 844 people aboard the *Eastland* drowned within a few feet of the bank in an accident that still ranks as the worst disaster on the Great Lakes in terms of loss of life. About 250 people died in the Great Chicago Fire of October 8–9, 1871, but the toll in damage to the city's buildings, docks, warehouses, and ships made it one of the single most destructive events in the history of the Great Lakes.

The Chicago area has had several train wrecks with casualty lists dwarfing that of the *Globe*, including rear-end collisions of Chicago, Burlington & Quincy Railroad trains in suburban Naperville in 1946 and of Illinois Central Gulf Railroad commuter trains on the South Side of Chicago in 1972 — each of which claimed 45 lives. The 1918 circus train wreck in south suburban Hammond, Indiana, killed 68.

No fewer than eight air crashes in the immediate vicinity of Chicago in the second half of the twentieth century had greater death tolls than the *Globe*. The worst was the American Airlines DC-10 that crashed on May 25, 1979, at O'Hare International Airport, killing 273 — a toll approximating that of the *Lady Elgin*, the Great Lakes' second worst disaster.

It was probably the loss of the *Lady Elgin* and the impending Civil War that did the most to obscure the *Globe*. At the time of the explosion, the nation was staggering toward the War Between the States, and the city was still in shock from the sinking of the *Lady Elgin* in a collision with a schooner on Lake Michigan off north suburban Winnetka during a storm two months earlier. Two hundred seventy-nine people lost their lives in the *Lady Elgin* disaster on September 8, 1860; the toll resulting from the *Globe* explosion was but a mere fraction of that.

In retrospect the *Globe* was probably best known as the vessel that carried then congressman and future president Abraham Lincoln and his family to Chicago from Buffalo, New York, in 1848. Lincoln, like most travelers of his day, preferred the comforts of a journey by water to the rigors of being bounced about in a drafty, dusty stagecoach. Whenever possible he used a combination of Illinois River steamboats and Illinois and Michigan Canal boats to travel between his home in Springfield and Chicago, at least until the Chicago & Alton Railroad was built (in 1858), offering a faster and more direct route.

In fact, Lincoln in 1852 added 100 miles to the length of his trip between Springfield and Chicago to avoid a long stagecoach ride. He traveled 53 miles the wrong way (west) from Springfield to Naples on the Illinois River to catch a steamboat and avoid the more direct but grueling stagecoach ride from Springfield to Peoria. The steamboats connected with the I&M Canal at the river's head of navigation at La Salle, Illinois. The 97-mile canal bypassed nonnavigable sections of the Illinois and Des Plaines rivers between there and Chicago and linked the Great Lakes with the Mississippi River system.

When Lincoln, his wife, and their two young sons boarded the *Globe* in Buffalo on September 26, 1848, to begin their return home after some politicking on behalf of the Whigs, they discovered they were to sail on one of the newest side-wheel steamers on the lakes. The 251-foot, 1,300-ton (burden) vessel had been built along the Detroit River by D.C.M. Goodsell and had entered service only two months earlier.

At the time, sail was the preferred method of propulsion on the lakes, and the 548 schooners registered on the lakes outnumbered the steamships by more than four to one. The 95 paddle wheelers in service were favored for passenger travel, and the 45 propeller-driven ships were used mainly for freight. There was also a safety factor: deepwater side-wheelers with their low-pressure steam engines were inherently safer than the high-pressure engines used to develop sufficient revolutions per minute to drive screw propellers.

Steam engines had evolved from Thomas Newcomen's device to pump water from mines and James Watt's refinements later to provide superior performance to the point that, by the end of the eighteenth century, a variety of American inventors began developing engines to power vessels. The advantage of steam was obvious: it freed ships from the vagaries of winds, tides, and currents. The problem was to build an engine with sufficient power to propel a vessel upstream against a strong current. The early steamboats of John Fitch (1790), Robert Fulton (1807), and John Stevens (1809) were designed to operate on the tidewaters of the East. Their early engines often consisted of square copper boiler capable of developing 10 to 12 pounds of pressure, a single large vertical cylinder, and a condenser.

Oliver Evans in 1801 developed the high-pressure engine by eliminating the condenser and venting the spent steam into air, permitting triple the pressure in the early engines. By the mid-nineteenth century marine engines routinely developed pressures of 100 pounds of more, contrasted to less than 20 pounds on a low-pressure engine of the time. This gave vessels sufficient power to move upstream in swift currents, as well as the power to be maneuvered off snags and bars when they became stranded. The problem given the metallurgical technology of the day was that high-pressure engines were vulnerable to boiler explosions, especially during idling or low power when the excess pressure was not properly vented.

The risks of boiler explosions on high-pressure engines was a well-known phenomenon in 1848. English author Charles Dickens in *American Notes* had complained of the risks of such explosions during his 1842 voyage up and down the Ohio and Mississippi rivers between Pittsburgh and St. Louis. From 1816 to

1853, when the federal government was forced to take action and established the Steamboat Inspection Service, a forerunner of the U.S. Coast Guard, boiler explosions accounted for some 7,000 fatalities on river steamboats and almost a third of the total accidents. Even after federal regulations required the licensing of pilots and engineers as well as periodic boiler inspections, explosions still occurred, albeit at a reduced rate.

The explosion of a high-pressure boiler on the steamboat *Sultana* above Memphis on April 22, 1865, caused the worst maritime disaster in U.S. history. Although the exact toll will never be known, more than 1,600 people, many of them repatriated Union prisoners of war, are believed to have died in the disaster. Death tolls in those days (when ship manifests were not reliable and before the development of adequate forensic techniques) were always tentative — and even the toll on the *Globe* is an estimate.

Although high-pressure engines were a necessity on non-tidewater, low-pressure engines at least initially were favored on the lakes and oceans because they were quite capable of driving side-wheel steamships in modest currents. High-pressure engines began appearing on the lakes after John Ericcson's screw propeller was introduced because they developed sufficient revolutions per minute to drive that apparatus.

As the number of high-pressure engines increased, so did the frequency of boiler explosions, though they were by no means as common on the Great Lakes as they were on the rivers. The steam tug *Seneca* blew up at the Randolph Street bridge on the Chicago River on October 16, 1855. The death toll included only her pilot and engineer. Then five years later the *Globe* blew up a few blocks upstream.

She had begun her existence powered by a low-pressure engine. The Lincoln family voyage aboard the *Globe* in 1848 — then a low-pressure side-wheeler — was mechanically uneventful, although a stop to help the steamer *Canada*, which was grounded in the Detroit River, and stormy weather on Lake Huron caused the scheduled seven-day voyage to take ten days. But like many other

Great Lakes ships, the *Globe* was later modified in the 1850s to give her a new role.

The railroads in the 1850s began to take away the passenger trade on the lakes, causing many of the big passenger steamers to be laid up for lack of business, so the *Globe*'s owners decided to rebuild her for the freight trade. Side wheels and the bulky apparatus necessary to transfer power to them from the engines made it difficult to moor ships flush with the dock for efficient side loading of cargo. The power plant for a propeller ship occupied a fraction of the space of the apparatus necessary for a side-wheeler, meaning a propeller could carry relatively more cargo than a side-wheeler of comparable size. The engine for a propeller-driven vessel could fit in six square feet and consumed only 10 cords of wood a day, contrasted to 50 cords on a big side-wheeler.

By 1860 the Great Lakes maritime industry was well aware of the advantages of the propeller. Propellers, which in 1848 had been outnumbered two to one by side-wheelers, outnumbered side-wheelers on the lakes 197 to 138 by 1860. However, Great Lakes shipowners were a pragmatic lot, reluctant to scrap a perfectly good hull even after it had become technologically obsolete. Therefore, many side-wheelers were sent back to the shipyards to be rebuilt and refitted as propellers, which included the addition of high-pressure engines. That is what happened to the *Globe* in 1856.

Thereafter she sailed the lakes primarily as a freighter with room to haul whatever passengers were available, mainly from towns with infrequent rail service. On her final voyage, with a crew of 25, the *Globe* apparently stopped at several ports between Buffalo and Chicago to pick up cargo—3,000 barrels of apples, a shipment of stoves, and assorted miscellaneous freight—consigned to various parties. Her passengers included some crewmen heading home from the wreck of their brig, the *Clarion*, a couple of young ladies from Port Washington, Wisconsin, and two women who had boarded at Milwaukee.

All of the passengers had disembarked after the ship docked in Chicago, and the *Globe*'s master, Amos Pratt, was ashore. Perhaps the most telling description of what happened then came from George Bartholomew, second officer of the propeller *Prairie State*, which was docked nearby. According to his later testimony to a Cook County coroner's jury, he boarded the *Globe* two hours after she docked to eyeball her engine room, and because none of the crew was present to give him a courtesy tour, he looked around on his own. He found that one gauge registered 80 pounds of pressure in the boiler—about 20 pounds greater than a high-pressure engine idling at the dock should have had. (A low-pressure engine of that time would have idled at 18 to 20 pounds.)

Bartholomew left the *Globe* without mentioning the problem to anyone, and three hours later (9 A.M.) the starboard engine exploded with such force that the middle section of the hull was destroyed. The blast smashed the stern of the canal boat *Alonzo*, which was docked nearby. It also hurled large chunks of debris into the Board of Trade building across the river; a 200-pound section of hog chain into the nearby offices of Stewart & Youle, produce and commission dealers; and a 300-pound oak hull fender through the fourth-story wall of a nearby office on South Water Street. The Board of Trade was unoccupied at the time of the blast, and the other offices had only skeleton crews on duty, none of whom were injured.

But 15-year-old Mary Golding, who was on the dock gleaning apples that had fallen out of the barrels already unloaded, was only ten feet from the aft gangway of the *Globe* and was fatally mangled by the blast, although her ten-year-old sister survived unhurt. David Gibbons, an unemployed laborer, was wandering the dock looking for work when the explosion hurled him through the roof, and Patrick Donahue, who was standing outside a saloon on North Wells Street, had his head smashed by a ying timber.

Most of the rest of the dead on that fateful morning, some of whom were never found, were crewmen. Like most disasters of the time, the death toll was uncertain—perhaps 15 or 16.

Abraham Lincoln had been elected president on November 6, 1860 — two days before the *Globe* disaster. Newspapers around the country as late as November 9 still were filled with speculation of what his election portended for a nation on the verge of a civil war. But in Chicago, the headlines dealt with the latest in what was to be a long series of maritime disasters.

Chapter Twenty-Six

The Fleet Is In

Although assorted vessels had been pressed into temporary service on an impromptu basis to fight marine fires since the mid-eighteenth century in London, and New York City as early as 1809 placed manually pumped fire wagons on small boats, boats modified or built specifically to fight fires date only from the last half of the nineteenth century, when steam engines were adapted to pump high volumes of water. The first land steam fire engine in the New World appeared in 1853 in Cincinnati, and within two decades American port cities were converting tugboats to fight fires. It wasn't long after the Great Fire of 1871 that Chicago took an interest in acquiring fireboats.

The late Chicago firefighter Robert A. Freeman researched and wrote this history of Chicago's fireboats for the winter 1968 Chicago Fire Fighter. *An adaptation of that article edited for the general reader is reprinted here with the assistance of James E. McNally, president of Chicago Fire Fighters Union—Local No. 2.*

by Robert A. Freeman, Engine 44

The "paid" organization of the Chicago Fire Department took place as far back as August 2, 1858, however, the institution of a "fireboat" did not occur until some years later. In 1877, there were three tugboats that serviced the rivers, and they were equipped with fire fighting appliances. They were located in Mason's Slip, the 22nd Street Bridge, and at the foot of Franklin Street.

The city's original fireboats were strictly a private enterprise. The tugboats were established by a need for better fire protection of properties along and near the waterfront where the Fire Department's land-based companies (steamers, hose wagons, ladder trucks) had only limited access. Many industries were effective in acquiring the new system, but most prominent and influential were the lumber interests that flanked the south branch of the Chicago River in what became known as the "lumber district" around Robey Street (Damen) and Blue Island Avenue.

On May 8, 1877, a fire occurred in the lumber district on the south branch of the river that caused an estimated $421,000 damage. It was then that the lumber merchants demanded better protection by the city, and through the efforts of the Lumbermen's Association (many of whom owned yards along the riverfront) the fireboat service was introduced.

The city's first river fireboat, *Alpha*, was put into service on September 5, 1885, under the jurisdiction of the Chicago Fire Department as Engine 37 at Allen's Slip near 24th Street. The *Alpha*, like all subsequent fireboats, carried a name as well as a number. [ed. The term *engine* in fire department parlance designates what the general public calls a *pumper*.]

This coal-burning boat was owned by the lumber interests who furnished the fuel, while the City paid the salaries for those who manned her. Only a brief description is available of her as she was not commissioned long in the department. She weighed 87 tons and had two double acting duplex pumps built by Charles F. Elmes Machinery Company of Chicago, with a capacity of 3,000 gpm (gallons per minute). The hull was wood with plating added later. Her length was 77.1 feet, beam 19.4, and depth 13 feet. This boat had no turrets, as when she was built in 1881, it was for Fire Department use.

Although the *Alpha* was poorly designed for her intended purpose, the great need for a fireboat was shown when another large fire swept the lumber district on September 25, 1885. Definite plans were put forth then to incorporate a fireboat system within the Chicago Fire Department. In January 1886, the Common Council [ed. term for the City Council at the time] passed an order that authorized the construction of a completely new craft designed specifically for the fire service.

Officials of the Fire Department, including Brigade Chief Denis J. Swenie and his repair shop superintendent, visited New York, Brooklyn, and Boston to gain information, about fireboats in those cities. Upon their return, plans were made to construct a new craft; however, general labor troubles that year delayed the launching of the boat until July 29, 1886. The vessel was commissioned the *Geyser* and replaced the *Alpha* as Engine 37.

Meanwhile, the pumps from the *Alpha* were transferred to a newly acquired craft, a powerful towing tug called the *W.H. Alley*. She was designated as Engine 41 and went into service on December 31, 1886, at Sampson's Slip west of Throop Street at 23rd Street. At this time, the *Geyser* was moved to the north branch of the river at the Lake Street Bridge in the Fifth Battalion.

Chicago's earliest fireboats were little more than tugboats equipped with water pumps, and the earliest fireboats designed as such continued to exhibit many tuglike characteristics. The W.H. Alley, *shown here after she was renamed* Chicago, *was in fact a converted towing tug, which was bought by the city in 1886 for $8,800. (Chicago Historical Society)*

The Geyser *(later renamed the* Denis J. Swenie *after a Chicago Fire Department official who oversaw her design and construction in 1886) was Chicago's first fireboat designed expressly for that purpose. Note the water cannon mounted ahead of the pilothouse in this 1903 photo. (Chicago Historical Society, DN-0000485)*

The cost of the *Geyser* was over $39,000 — including $8,800 paid for the *W.H. Alley*. Some considered this a costly item for its worth, but later in 1887 she proved herself worth every penny.

Considerable ice formations blocked the rivers and Chicagoans feared a repetition of the Great Flood of 1849 [ed. see Chapter 4] where the river's flow was paralyzed and flooding ensued. The *Geyser* was sent up the south branch and was able to cut through at least four blocks of ice. This was repeated several times until the great mass started for Lake Michigan. The *W.H. Alley* had been unsuccessful in the same attempt.

Two two-wheel hose reels were added to the *Geyser,* and on July 1, 1887, when she was moved to the foot of Dearborn Street and assigned to the First Battalion. In the autumn of 1887, the *W.H. Alley* was renamed the *Chicago.*

Another new boat was placed in service on May 31, 1890. She was known as the *Yosemite* (Engine 58) and was used as a "spare" to take the place of other boats that needed repairs. At the time, all the city's fireboats were reshuffled and given new numbers, and the *Chicago*, on December 3, 1891, was shipped to the Calumet River on the South Side at the 95th Street bridge in response to the rapid industrialization of that area.

At this time all three of Chicago's fireboats had wooden hulls and coal-burning steam engines. The city's fourth fireboat, a conversion done in time for the Columbian Exposition of 1893, had the same characteristics. *Fire Queen*, as she was named (Engine 71 was her fire department designation), was privately owned by Exposition Enterprises but staffed by Fire Department personnel when she went into service on December 31, 1892, in the Jackson Park Lagoon near the Electricity Building. Acting Lieutenant John Payne was her first commander but he was soon succeeded by Lieutenant Thomas Barry.

The huge exposition required a considerable reorganization within the Fire Department. The new Fourteenth Battalion was organized on December 1, 1892, under the command of Battalion Marshal Edward Murphy exclusively to cover the fairgrounds. The battalion had six engine companies—including the CFD's engines number 63 and 71—and two hook and ladder companies operated by exposition employees.

The *Fire Queen* had been built about 1870 and was not in the best condition; however, she could pump 2100 gallons per minute from her old pumps that had been cannibalized from horse-drawn steamer engines withdrawn from service. She had no turrets but eight connections for 3.5-inch hose. In 1895, the *Fire Queen* went into dry dock to have iron plating put on her bottom.

During the year the *Fire Queen* served at the Columbian Explosion she helped fight the great fire that destroyed the Cold Storage building. The blaze took the lives of four city firemen and eight exposition firemen when the tower of the building collapsed.

After the fair closed and most of its buildings were razed, the exposition corporation transferred title to the *Fire Queen* to the city. The Fire Department made several modifications to her, gave her the designation of Engine 71, and on August 11, 1894, reassigned her to Goose Island on the north branch of the Chicago River under the command of the Third Battalion.

At about the same time, the city's fireboat fleet suffered its first fatality in action. A fire in the "lumber district" at Lincoln Street (Wolcott) and Blue Island Avenue on August 1, 1894, claimed the life of Lieutenant John McGuire, who died when he was thrown from the *Geyser* onto a hot bed of coals. Both the *Geyser* and *Yosemite* fought this fire.

Slightly more than a month later (September 12, 1894), disaster hit the *Yosemite* although luckily there were no fatalities. The boat was steaming to a fire in South Chicago at the Beck Lumber Company when she struck the Hyde Park Reef off 75th Street and went down in Lake Michigan. A contract for raising the boat was awarded to the Barry Brothers and after considerable work and unforeseen difficulties, the *Yosemite* was raised, brought onto Miller's Dry Dock (North Branch at Halsted Street) on Goose Island, thoroughly overhauled, and painted at a cost of $10,000.

Also in 1894, the city decided to augment its maritime capability by equipping ten private-owned tugboats with fire pumps to aid the Fire Department boats on an emergency basis. Although the existence of fire-capable tugs predated 1877, the city got involved in 1885 when the lumber industry offered the city an auxiliary force of such vessels to assist the *Alpha*. It cost the industry about $6,000 at the time, but the fire tug system was embraced by the Fire Department. Each tug had a water pumping capacity equal to five ordinary land steam pumpers.

The Fire Department began its conversion to steel vessels just before the turn of the century. The new steel-hulled *Illinois*—with a pumping capacity of 10,000 gallons per minute, or three times that of the old *W.H. Alley*—was put into service on January 14, 1899, at Engine 37's station and the *Yosemite* based there was shipped to a new berth alongside the 92nd Street Bridge on the Calumet River.

The Illinois *(right), a steel-hulled vessel put into service in 1899 and shown here with the* Chicago, *was the only Windy City fireboat lost at a fire. In 1908, while fighting a huge fire that had enveloped a grain elevator and warehouses along the south branch of the river at 12th Street, the* Illinois *was sunk when the wall of an elevator fell on her. She was later raised, repaired, and put back into service. (Chicago Historical Society? Check Disk..CMS Collection?)*

The arrival of the additional capacity in the form of the *Illinois* precipitated another reorganization of the fireboat fleet. The *Chicago* was reactivated from reserve status in late 1902, and the *Fire Queen* was reassigned to a new station on the north branch of the Chicago River near Fullerton Avenue and opposite the yards of the Deering Meat Packing Plant. The *Yosemite* was renamed *Protector* in 1903 and a month later the *Geyser* was rechristened *Denis J. Swenie*, after the late Chief of Brigade who had contributed so much to the design of the city's first fireboat built as such.

That began a city policy of naming fireboats after people. Under a new Chief of Brigade, James Horan, the fireboat *Protector* was renamed the *Michael W. Conway* on January 15, 1907.

Chicago lost its second fireboat in action in 1908. The *Illinois* the year before had been relocated to the foot of Franklin Street and the Chicago River with crew quarters nearby in a leased one-story brick building at 232 W. South Water Street. Then on August 3, 1908, while fighting a 3-11 alarm fire at 12th Street (Roosevelt Road) the walls of the Armour & Company elevator collapsed on the *Illinois*, sinking her in the river. The fire had consumed the entire elevator and scores of warehouses of the Chicago, Burlington & Quincy Railroad. Fortunately, the Fire Department was able to salvage the vessel by raising and rebuilding that same year.

She was soon joined by two new steel vessels built expressly as fireboats. They were the *Graeme Stewart* (1908), which had a pumping capacity of 9,000 gallons per minute, and the *Joseph Medill* (1909), named after Chicago's mayor [1871–73]. Their arrival precipitated yet another reshuffling of boat assignments with the Fire Queen going on reserve status.

Maintaining the city's fleet of fireboats required considerable attention besides simply polishing brass fixtures and checking engine oil. The *Illinois* was rehabbed in 1919 with a new second stack and with new deck railing, hull plating, and fresh paint. The *Medill* was completely painted inside and out in 1921, and the following year underwent extensive repairs. On March 15, 1922, while operating at a railroad building fire, the *Swenie* burned out a bearing and had to be taken out of service. As luck would have it, the *Stewart* broke a propeller shaft that same year, forcing her overhaul and her boiler being repaired. Some old boats were beyond repair, however. On December 29, 1927, the fireboat *Swenie* was dismantled, towed into the lake, and scuttled. The *Illinois* was retired in 1934.

As a practical matter, the department had only three full-time fireboats in service in 1930—the *Stewart* (Engine 37), the *Illinois* (Engine 41), and the *Medill* (Engine 58). The fleet remained at that size through most of the Depression until a new craft, the *Fred Busse*, was commissioned and placed into service on May 1,

1937. Named after another former Chicago mayor [ed. Busse's term ran from 1907 to 1911.], she was the first diesel with an all-steel hull. The *Busse* was built with a low profile to enable her to clear at normal water levels the city's many bascule bridges without waiting for them to be opened.

Although the *Medill* was disbanded on February 9, 1941, the city that same year was able to put into service three auxiliary boats donated to the Fire Department by the Sea Scouts of America. Originally commissioned by the Coast Guard, they were small in design, resembling a "whaler." For example, Auxiliary Boat No. 1 was 36 feet in length, had a 9-foot beam, and drew only 32 inches of water. Equipped with two 1.5-inch turret pipes and one 1-inch turret pipe, she had a modest fire fighting or pumping capability. The largest pipe could deliver only 105 gallons of water per minute. No. 1 was assigned to assist the *Busse* at the Franklin Street bridge.

Completion of the remodeling of the Chicago Fire Department fleet had to await the end to World War II. In 1949, the depart-

The Victor L. Schlaeger *(shown here) and the* Joseph Medill II, *both built in 1949, are the two newest fireboats in Chicago's fleet. Note the low profile, a design feature to enable the boats to get below Chicago's numerous bascule bridges without waiting to have them opened. (CMS Collection)*

ment got two new boats—the *Joseph Medill II* and the *Victor Schlaeger*. They were both diesels built in Sturgeon Bay, Wisconsin, by the Christie Corporation. Both were alike in design with steel hulls, a pumping capacity of 12,000 gallons per minute, tower turrets that would attain 35 feet when raised above the water line, and three other deck turrets each.

The *Medill II* was based at the Franklin Street bridge opposite Wolf Point on December 2, 1949, and the *Schlaeger* moored on the west shore of Lake Calumet at the foot of 128th Street. Both have crew quarters on board. The *Busse* in December, 1949, was reassigned as the new Engine 41 at the 23rd Street bridge east of Throop Street. Its crew is housed in a building adjacent to its moorings. In the past decade, the *Medill II* has been relocated to Navy Pier during the summer months as an added protection for ocean vessels using the St. Lawrence Seaway to get to and from Chicago. Also during the winter, the *Busse* replaced the *Medill II* at Franklin Street.

Four small jet powered boats were introduced to Chicago in the past several years to combat the problem of fighting fires in small craft and for rescue work during the boating season. A fifth boat was put into service later. All are able to travel at high speed in limited amounts of water and are useful in many respects.

Chapter Twenty-Seven

Fireboats in Action

Chicago didn't have any fireboats to battle the massive fires of 1871 a blaze on October 7 and 8 that leveled four square blocks of the city just west of the river where Union Station now stands, or the more famous blaze that began five and a half hours after the first one was extinguished and devastated 3.32 square miles and has since been known as the infamous Great Chicago Fire. The city's fireboat fleet, created soon after and in response to those conflagrations, was instrumental in preventing other large blazes from getting out of control and spreading through the city.

One such potentially disastrous fire occurred in 1908 in an industrial area south of the Loop and was fought by the fireboat fleet. Although no one was killed and the number of injuries was minimal, the now almost forgotten blaze claimed the fireboat Illinois. *CMS member John Heinz wrote this account of the incident. Fellow CMS member Kurt Van Dahm, a retired firefighter, reports that the* Illinois, *which was raised and salvaged after the incident, still survives in private ownership on the South Side.*

by John Heinz

On the hot days of August 3–4, 1908, a "Great Blaze," as the *Aurora Beacon* described it, raged along the Chicago River's banks from 12th to 16th streets between Canal and State streets. The conflagration, the cause of which was never determined but that may have been due to spontaneous combustion, a common factor in grain elevator fires, claimed five grain elevators, a Burlington freight house, a refrigerator plant, and 100 loaded railcars. Lloyd's of London got a bill for $1.5 million.

Fortunately, nobody was killed, and the inferno was stopped before it spread to the Loop or nearby homes. Its containment was largely due to the efforts of 40 companies of firemen, who suffered scores of burns and other injuries for their efforts, as well as civilian volunteers. There were no paramedics in those days, so firemen who collapsed from the heat got rough therapy—hoses were trained on them until they could get up.

As might be expected, the proximity of the fire to the Loop aroused great interest there from office workers who still had the Iroquois Theater fire of 1903 (603 dead) fresh in their minds. A *Tribune* photo shows men in suits and ties bucking the hoses. Only one spectator was hurt—in a fall from a boxcar.

One of the roles of fireboats is to furnish water from rivers (or lakes) to fire engines working closer to a blaze. One of the city's fireboats performed that function at this 1961 fire at Blue Island and Leavitt. (Chicago Historical Society)

The blaze was a tough one to fight. Because the fire occurred in a warehouse and rail yard area without hydrants, firemen had to lay miles of hose to get water to the blaze, and horse-drawn fire engines could only slowly cross the rail tracks. Those old steam pumper engines needed coal to get up pressure, and coal had to be carried in men's arms.

This is where the fireboats proved their worth. The adjacent river gave them mobility and an almost limitless source of water that they could shoot onto the burning buildings or pump to the land-based engines. However, once in action they had to tie up to the bank to buck against the reaction of their water cannons to drive them upstream. A dark photo in the *Chicago Tribune* of August 4 shows three fireboats shooting water into a mass of smoke.

Near the end of the battle, the *Illinois* tied up at the bank between two ruined grain elevators to hose down the ruins with

Grain elevator fires have been among Chicago's most spectacular, and because the elevators were located along waterways, fireboats were often involved in fighting them. The Fred Busse *and* Joseph Medill *both fought this elevator fire at 103rd Street and the Calumet River. (Chicago Historical Society)*

her capacity of 10,000 gallons per minute. Then at 3:30 A.M. an unexpected explosion blew out a granary wall and buried the bow of the boat. The mooring ropes held the hull above water for a few moments, just long enough for the crew to escape with their injured members. The worst hit was 30-year-old pipeman Hans Hanson, who was knocked unconscious by a brick. He was taken to County Hospital, where he eventually recovered.

The incident proved that the city's earlier decision to replace its old wooden-hulled fireboats with sturdy, steel-hulled fireboats was a good one. After the fire the *Illinois* was raised, salvaged, and rebuilt. It continued to serve the Fire Department until 1934.

Chapter Twenty-Eight

Investigating the Eastland Accident

The most incredible disaster in Chicago history, and the worst in terms of loss of life, occurred on a ship docked on the south bank of the Chicago River between LaSalle and Clark Streets in the city's central business district. There was no storm, fire, or explosion: the heavily loaded Eastland *simply rolled over at her dock. Most of the deaths occurred among the throngs trapped below deck. They drowned within a few feet of the safety of land. The death toll has always been disputed. The author of this chapter puts it at 812, but some estimates are as high as 844.*

This chapter is reprinted from an article by Ann D. Gordon published by the Chicago Historical Society in its Chicago History *magazine, Vol. X, No. 2 (summer 1981). She is research professor of history at Rutgers University, New Brunswick, New Jersey, and editor of the* Selected Papers of Elizabeth Cady Stanton and Susan B. Anthony. *This article is based on research she began when she was an assistant editor of the papers of Woodrow Wilson.*

by Ann D. Gordon

"The *Eastland* was all ready to pull out, when suddenly she went over on her side, and then there were horrible things happening. I heard women screaming and shrieking and children crying out and everybody seemed mad. It seemed to take the big boat only a few seconds to turn over on its side."

— Survivor Mildred Anderson as quoted
in the *Chicago Daily News*, July 25, 1915.

"On account of unseemly effort of labor and vessel interests to make capital out of *Eastland* catastrophe, this Department subjected to gross misrepresentation."
—Telegram to President Woodrow Wilson from Assistant Secretary of Commerce Edwin F. Sweet, July 26, 1915.

The 1903 steamship Eastland, *shown here when she operated out of Cleveland, exhibited some stability problems from the beginning. Her stability was the central issue in her disastrous capsizing in the Chicago River in 1915. (Collection of John Heinz)*

When the steamship *Eastland* capsized in Chicago in 1915 leaving a death toll of 812, an outraged public blamed not only the owners of the boat but also the federal Steamboat-Inspection Service. Since this agency was responsible for enforcing the government's safety regulations, it is not surprising that questions should have been raised about its effectiveness in carrying out its task. Shock and anguish fueled hopes of reforming the Inspection Service and pressure mounted to ensure that investigations of the accident achieved that result. For a few days it seemed that the effort might succeed, that President Woodrow Wilson might appoint a special commission of investigation. Instead he decided to back up his Secretary of Commerce, who intended to contain the protest in Chicago. Within a year emotions had subsided, and all avenues for responding to the tragedy with reform had been blocked.

Western Electric Company workers and their families arrived at the Chicago River early on July 24 to board excursion boats for their annual outing. The *Eastland* loaded first. She was a steel vessel, 265 feet long, narrow in the beam, and tall, built for fuel-efficiency and speed as a lake freighter. In the summer months she carried only passengers—as many as her decks would hold. Sailors considered her a cranky ship with a greater tendency to list than other ships, but to this day some navigators claim she was seaworthy when handled properly. When she listed sharply toward the dock with only half of her load of Western Electric workers, the chief engineer simply trimmed her up by letting water into the ballast tanks, and passengers continued to stream on board. With 2,500 passengers counted, gang planks were drawn up, lines thrown to a tugboat, and the order given to start engines. The *Eastland* suddenly tilted toward the river and, after a brief pause at a precarious angle, rolled over until her starboard side hit the river bottom. Bodies were thrown from the upper decks into the river where bystanders rescued many, though not before the current and the panic took hundreds of lives. Below deck, more passengers died as water rushed into the hull and as the downward slide of people and objects crushed them.

At a distance of sixty-five years it is difficult to recapture the horror that this accident evoked among Chicagoans. Newspapers announced it under banner headlines and remarkable photographs; sightseers gathered on the bridges and river banks to see the fallen queen of lake traffic and the heroes of rescue work. But the impact was greatest on Western Electric employees and the

section of Cicero where most of them lived. The Red Cross counted twenty-eight nationalities among the victims, with Germans,
Bohemians, and Poles the most heavily afflicted. Seventy percent
of those killed were between
the ages of fifteen and thirty,
and twenty-four of the victims were children under
five. A journalist found, on
one block in Hawthorne,
that every household had
lost someone and one house
stood empty because all of its
inhabitants had drowned.
Twenty-two families were
wiped out, and 660 families
lost at least one member.

*Most of the victims of what remains the worst mar-
itime disaster on the Great Lakes were passengers
trapped below decks, unable to get out before they
drowned. (CMS Collection)*

Relief and rescue work
involved hundreds of people
during the following week,
including police, firefighters,
and sailors. Survivors wandered through emergency morgues scattered in empty warehouses around the Loop until central facilities
opened at the Second Regiment Armory. A nursery there kept
children while their parents looked for the bodies of family members and friends. Office staff from Western Electric operated a
registry at the dock to find out who and how many were missing,
and the Red Cross opened relief offices at the Hawthorne plant to
be near those who would make claims. Philanthropist Julius
Rosenwald headed a mayor's committee to raise money for relief.
Settlement house workers and clubwomen fed rescue workers
from a tugboat in the river, and doctors gave free inoculations
against typhoid to anyone touched by the filthy Chicago River.
Clergymen and choirs from all parts of the city volunteered their
services for funerals. Mayor Thompson joined 1,000 people in a
funeral procession for a seven-year-old boy whose body had lain

unclaimed at the morgue because there were no survivors in his family. As Graham Taylor of the Chicago Commons settlement house mused, if federal inspection of steamboats had been as efficient as Chicago's management of rescue and relief work, the accident would have been prevented.

Steamboats were regulated by a patchwork, decentralized agency within the Department of Commerce, known as the Steamboat-Inspection Service. The Service divided the nation into regions, each with its own supervising inspector appointed with presidential approval, and hired two local inspectors by civil service examination for each port—one to inspect hulls and the other to inspect boilers. In addition, local inspectors counted and tested life-saving equipment, licensed captains and engineers, and determined the number of passengers a ship might carry. When an accident occurred involving a boat regulated by the Service, local inspectors routinely held the only legally constituted inquiry. They could revoke whatever certificates and licenses they had issued and impose fines if faulty equipment or incompetent sailing had contributed to the accident.

Within hours of the *Eastland* accident this investigative procedure came under attack from the Chicago Federation of Labor (CFL). The CFL had questioned the quality of federal inspection, particularly on excursion boats, one year earlier in a heated exchange of letters with officials of the Department of Commerce, and as soon as the *Eastland* went over, CFL Secretary Edward Nockels sent a telegram of protest to Woodrow Wilson referring him to those letters. The CFL had the advantage of the prophet, for it had warned in 1914 that the excursions leaving Chicago were so overcrowded that inevitably one would turn over before it left the dock. With the prophecy fulfilled, the CFL asked whether the nation could afford to let the inspectors investigate themselves. In a second telegram to Wilson on the same day, Nockels accused the inspectors of acting "more like shipping agents than public officials" and called for outside investigators.

Other labor organizations took the same stand. The Women's Trade Union League of Chicago prepared a message to Wilson, charging the federal government with criminal negligence and blaming the Inspection Service for "the dangerous overcrowding of excursion steamers." Over the next ten days, firemen, teamsters, garment workers, musicians, sailors, and American Federation of Labor President Samuel Gompers joined in urging Wilson to take action.

The Inspection Service was vulnerable to attack. Its inspectors worked independently and often without adequate directives. Precise guidelines governed their decisions with regard to ships' boilers, for instance, but the Service depended on the discretion of each inspector in such sensitive decisions as the limit on the number of passengers to be carried. Over the years the *Eastland* had been accorded very uneven treatment. An aggressive inspector in Cleveland had once lowered her passenger limit because he thought the existing figure too high for a ship dependent on water ballast. No regulations directed him to evaluate stability in ships,

A factor in the capsizing of the Eastland *was probably the ship's metacentric height—a naval architect's term for what landlubbers might describe as a high center of gravity. The ship shown in this postcard steaming on the Chicago River looks a little tall and narrow. (Collection of John Heinz)*

and his colleagues thought his action somewhat willful. The ship did lose money for her owners subsequently, though the reasons for that were more numerous than just the limit on ticket sales. Inspector Robert Reid had examined the *Eastland* in 1915 for its new owners in Michigan and had raised the limit simply by counting the number of life jackets. When the owners telephoned him to say that they had placed even more life jackets on board, he increased the limit again without visiting the ship. Where the rules of inspection were clear, Reid had a reputation for toughness. No regulations prohibited what he had done for the *Eastland*'s owners.

There were reasons to question whether the routine inquiry of the Inspection Service was adequate to investigate an accident of such magnitude. Though used on occasion to rid the Service of incompetent inspectors, the inquiry needed first to guarantee and protect agency operations. It was not a means to reform federal regulations. If it were true, as critics charged, that the *Eastland* turned over because she carried too many passengers, and yet the number of passengers on board matched the limit allowed by local inspectors, an investigation by the Service could only conclude that no one was at fault. But critics pointed out that unless investigators were free to step outside the bureaucratic circuit, their conclusions might only compound weaknesses in federal inspection standards.

The attack on inspectors following the accident was further compounded by a long and bitter conflict over sailors' safety. It had pitted the Lake Seamen's Union against the Lake Carriers' Association, a powerful group of ship owners, and caught the federal regulators in between. Sailors had sought federal legislation which would raise the minimum safety standards on all ships using American ports and guarantee employment of certified able seamen. Specifications about the number of lifeboats and the number of able seamen needed to man those lifeboats were included in the Seamen's (LaFollette) Act, which had finally passed early in 1915. Nockels of the CFL had served as labor's chief lobbyist in the House of Representatives during the last intense campaign for the bill in 1914 and another local labor leader, Victor Olander, vice-president of the Lake Seamen's Union, had lobbied in the Senate. Sailors had gained support for the safety legislation from social reformers nationally and locally through organizations like the National Consumer's League.

The Lake Carriers' Association had warred against the Lake Seamen's Union since at least 1908 when it blacklisted all union sailors in an effort to break the union. It had delayed passage of the Seamen's Act and fought to exempt inland shipping from its requirements. Provisions of the act were not yet in force on the Great Lakes in the summer of 1915, and the Association was using that respite to agitate for repeal. The *Eastland's* owners, the St. Joseph-Chicago Steamship Company, had complained to Secretary of Commerce William Redfield as recently as June 30, 1915. The company's vice-president insisted he could not make a profit if he were required to place lifeboats and life rafts on valuable deck space. The new law would require that he provide boats for only half of his passenger load during the summer season of lake excursions.

The Inspection Service, at its top levels, had lost credibility as an impartial regulator of the industry during the fight. Career men in the agency had taken positions which jeopardized the bill in its last stages, and union men were in no mood to trust them. Labor leaders were confident, however, that the Inspection Service was an exception in the federal government. Their appeals to President Wilson showed consistent faith that government could be neutral in a conflict between profits and safety. Because President Wilson had supported passage of the Seamen's Act against strong opposition, people counted on him to lay a heavy hand on the shipping interests if public welfare required it. Labor's demand that the President intercede spread to other sectors of Chicago. The national magazine of social reformers, *The*

Survey, featured reports of the accident and investigations to stir interest outside Chicago. Margaret Dreier Robins, president of the Women's Trade Union League, spoke for many reformers as well as labor when she suggested to President Wilson that he appoint a commission "on which labor and [the] travelling public are properly represented." The same message went to the President from the Chicago Common Council, some women's clubs, and Polish-American organizations.

At the Department of Commerce, the outcry against inspectors investigating themselves prompted an improvisational approach to the accident. Secretary Redfield, who was on vacation, and his acting secretary, Edwin Sweet, wanted to distinguish the inquiry "as far as practicable under the law from a purely departmental proceeding," as Redfield explained to President Wilson. He sent the acting Supervising Inspector General to take charge in Chicago on Sunday, July 25; when criticism of the Inspection Service continued to mount, the departmental Solicitor and Redfield himself took trains to Chicago on Monday; and on Wednesday, Redfield announced the appointment of extra, unofficial members to the board of inquiry. Nonetheless, when Redfield arrived in Chicago on July 27, he damned critics who drew conclusions before hearing the case, dared Victor Olander to make good his charges under oath, and taunted the city for reacting too strongly. According to the *Evening Post*, he failed to "invite public confidence" in the inquiry and concerned himself too much with finding "justification for his department and its officials." The *Daily News* said that he made an "unpleasant spectacle of himself" and took "a mild technical view of the situation."

Redfield maintained that his principal problem was to determine whether there were facts injurious to any government service. He was well aware of damage done to the Inspection Service after an accident in 1904 which killed 1,000 people in New York Harbor. [ed. This refers to the June 15, 1904, fire aboard the excursion steamer *General Slocum* in the East River.] After a presidential commission investigated that disaster, local inspectors and the supervising inspector lost their jobs. But in 1915 even the agency's critics detected weakness in that "solution," recognizing that it placed too much blame on inspectors without addressing questions about the quality of regulation. International Seamen's Union president, Andrew Furuseth, warned against a repetition of the 1904 response in 1915 and recommended instead that the Service be reformed. Eliminate "mere discretion" from the inspectors' work and tell them how to calculate a safe load of passengers, he urged. Figure out how to make safety the owner's self-interest and how to regulate an insurance industry that put "a premium on taking risks" with ships and lives.

Although a considerable part of the Eastland's *hull remained above water, divers had to be used to recover bodies of people trapped below decks. In the days before scuba gear, divers wore heavy suits and steel helmets and got their air through hoses attached to pumps at the surface. (CMS Collection)*

Redfield wanted no part of such extensive investigations. Carl Sandburg, then a journalist for the *Socialist Day Book*, pursued Furuseth's point in a conversation with Redfield and then published his notes of what was said. Sandburg reported that when he asked whether the Secretary had located the report on the *Eastland* by the American Bureau of Shipping, the insurance group which tested the ship's stability, Redfield replied: "That bureau does not enter into [the] affair. It is a private concern operated, I believe, by insurance companies." Sandburg persisted: "But the local inspector of hulls . . . told newspaper men . . . that all standards and tests with regard to stability of hulls are fixed by the American Bureau of Shipping." At that point Redfield laughed heartily and broke off the conversation.

Redfield and Edwin Sweet had defined the issues for head-on collision with the people who perceived the accident as the culmination of years of business risks and federal collusion. Even Redfield's appointments to the board of inquiry further showed his refusal to take seriously the terms of conflict that his critics had defined. Besides two experts in naval technology, whose impartiality no one doubted, Redfield chose businessmen: banker Harry A. Wheeler and merchant Marvin B. Pool from Chicago, and, from St. Louis, Philip B. Fouke, a man clearly identified with the campaign to repeal the Seamen's Act. Fouke was chairman of a Chamber of Commerce committee studying how to make the Steamboat-Inspection Service more responsive to shipowners' needs. No labor representative received an invitation. None was available who had not "expressed [his] views publicly in advance of the hearing," Redfield explained to Wilson. When Illinois Lieutenant-Governor Barrett O'Hara complained about this decision, Redfield appointed him to the board. O'Hara did succeed in pushing Redfield to consider questions which were a little broader than the most recent inspection of the *Eastland*.

Once Redfield's hearings opened, his handling of sensitive questions brought more criticism upon him. His cross-examination of hull inspector Robert Reid became notorious. Journalists had discovered that Reid's decision to increase the 's passenger limit coincided with the company's decision to hire Reid's son-in-law as the ship's chief engineer. Redfield questioned Reid on the first day of hearings:

Q.: Captain Reid, I understand from the vigilant safeguard and vigilant watchman [sic] of the press that you have been guilty of a crime which I myself have committed, in fact [m]any of us have, namely, that of having a son-in-law.

A.: I have. . . .

Q.: Is that son-in-law the chief engineer of the steamer *Eastland*?

A.: One of them, Mr. James Erickson. . . .

Q.: Did you make that arrangement for him to become your son- in-law?

A.: No, sir.

Q.: Was that a matter you fixed up?

A.: No, sir.

Q.: Did you prepare a scheme whereby he should become your son-in-law and then get that job on that boat so that you might increase the rating of the passengers in that boat?

A.: No, sir.

Redfield may have thought only to protect the men in his department from what he called the "unequalled carnival mendacity" in Chicago, but in effect he sneered at local efforts to answer all questions associated with the accident. The *Journal*, Chicago's only pro-Wilson paper, reminded Redfield that this was "a poor time for cheap sarcasm." With his "tone of sneering superiority," Redfield insulted the dead and cast an "unfair reflection on President Wilson." Among the many letters which Wilson received regarding the incident, one counseled, "You would drive a Bull out of a china shop, Well get Redfield out of Chicago." President Wilson, on vacation in New Hampshire, began to take the suggestion seriously, especially when his secretary, Joseph Tumulty, urged it. Tumulty had learned from sources in Chicago that even conservatives thought that Redfield was mishandling the investigation. At Wilson's direction, Tumulty met with a few Cabinet members in Washington, and the group agreed that a presidential commission should be appointed but only after Redfield had requested it. Redfield refused to cooperate. The issue before Wilson was no longer on the merits of the case but on the authority of his Secretary of Commerce. On the one hand, Wilson agreed with his Secretary of the Navy who thought Redfield was misguided in championing subordinates who might yet face serious criminal charges. On the other hand, he told his Attorney General, he deplored the intensity and tone of the attacks on Redfield. On August 1, Wilson abandoned plans for a separate investigation, saying simply that Redfield had gone "too far to justify me in insisting upon a substitute course of action which might seem to discredit him."

Local officials had launched investigations into the accident without waiting to hear Wilson's response. The coroner's jury, the police, the Common Council, and state and federal grand juries, all sought to locate and fix responsibility for the accident. The state grand jury examined the ship's officers in order to master the technical information they would need, though Redfield doubted that lay people could "deal very intelligently with this accident, which is after all a problem in physics applied disastrously." They listened to angry people and examined immediate and long range causes. Victor Olander had no specific knowledge of the *Eastland* accident but he testified about his experience with shipping and safety inspection.

Redfield believed that all of this activity amounted to a partisan attack on Woodrow Wilson and that is how he reported events to the President. Factions within the Democratic party were trying to discredit him, Redfield wrote, and he advised Wilson to take more care in dispensing patronage in Chicago. In his last letter from Chicago, he summed up his experience with a heroic metaphor: "You are the object at which they aim. I am the anvil on which the blows are struck. I am glad to be pounded in so good a cause, and yet I confess the blows have hurt." One day later, Redfield closed his hearings because Federal District Judge Kenesaw Mountain Landis prohibited all witnesses scheduled to appear before the federal grand jury from testifying before any other body. Although Redfield interpreted the order as yet another hostile act, he was content with the results he had obtained so far. He reassured Wilson "that nothing that reflects discredit upon the service or any man in it has yet been discovered."

In the long run Redfield took advantage of the excuse to halt his inquiry. Though he promised to resume as soon as the grand jury issued its indictments, he never reopened the *Eastland* investigation and the board of inquiry's interim report of August 5 became, in effect, its final word. The report deferred a statement on the accident and a decision on responsibility because the inquiry was incomplete, but it did recommend reform in the Inspection Service. The board suggested that by immediate departmental order inspectors be required to visit ships before changing passenger load limits and be empowered to order inclining tests if they had any doubts about a ship's stability. The report addressed two of the most casual practices to have come to public notice after the accident, but its proposals perpetuated the agency's reliance on the discretion of inspectors.

The report also proposed more substantial changes for efficient administration of the Service to be effected by legislation, two of which won departmental support and lumbered through Congress to become laws in 1918 and 1919. First, local inspectors were required to submit to their supervising inspector any change in a ship's passenger load limit—a practice which might have prevented the erratic inspection of the *Eastland*. Second, a new procedure allowed "any person directly interested in or affected by" a decision of local inspectors to appeal it through the departmental chain of command. Both laws made inspectors more accountable to their superiors.

But when the board of inquiry's report crossed the line between bureaucratic efficiency and structural change, Redfield ignored its recommendations. The board concluded that naval architects in the Department of Commerce should oversee ship production and test vessels for seaworthiness. Even without an accompanying report to explain how they reasoned from the facts of the *Eastland* accident to this recommendation, the implication is clear that they thought that the ship's design contributed to the accident. Redfield believed that himself. He later told a congressional committee that in his opinion the ship's lack of stability explained the accident. Nonetheless, these recommendations vanished like smoke. Not a single reform accepted by Redfield spoke to the issues of safety in the shipping business. Instead the federal investigation resulted in making the Inspection Service less vulnerable to the embarrassment it suffered from the accident. No one need repeat the discomfort of defending a Robert Reid whose routine and unnoticed decision had put an entire federal agency on the line.

The state grand jury issued a report that explained what had happened on July 24. When the chief engineer tried to trim ship, he succeeded at first in correcting the list, but the system of cocks and valves and his lack of experience with the ship proved inadequate to the job. His tanks were then partially filled so that the "water could surge with every movement of the boat and produce a condition more dangerous than if the tanks had been empty." The grand jury also concluded that the *Eastland*'s past record of successful operation under similar or identical conditions of load and ballast did not excuse owners, operators, and inspectors for the risks they had taken. The state grand jury returned indictments for "criminal carelessness or incompetence" against the four top officers of the St. Joseph-Chicago Steamship Company and the ship's captain and chief engineer on August 10. On August 27 the jury added an indictment for manslaughter against the president of the Indiana Transportation Company which had chartered the boat to Western Electric. Federal indictments followed on September 22. In addition to those already indicted under state law, the federal jurors included the inspectors at Grand Haven, Michigan.

The indictments met a strange end in a Michigan courtroom early in 1916. Federal prosecutors had filed a petition for the defendants' removal from Michigan to stand trial in Illinois, and Federal District Judge Charles Sessions denied their motion. He argued in his opinion that the accident occurred outside federal waters since the ship "was securely tied to a dock in the Chicago River at least one-half mile from Lake Michigan," and therefore beyond the reach of the federal statute governing punishment for ship accidents. This bit of reasoning prompted one congressman to ask his colleagues why the federal government threw away money every year to keep the Chicago River navigable, but it also in effect denied the Inspection Service any jurisdiction over the accident, because the same statute authorized its investigation.

Judge Sessions inflicted more damage on the prosecution by declaring that the only actions which could be considered as contributing to the accident were those that occurred on July 24 in the Chicago River. Even Redfield had not made such a strong defense of inspectors. By the logic of the decision, no inspector could ever be accountable under the statute unless the accident occurred as an immediate consequence of his inspection. Finally Sessions dismissed the charge of a conspiracy to be "criminally negligent" because it was "unimaginable, unbelievable, and unthinkable." Without offering any explanation of what had occurred in the accident, Sessions thus cleared all the defendants. Without defendants the cases in Chicago fell apart.

The effort to locate responsibility for the accident had ended. Ambivalence crept into the minds of some reformers such as Graham Taylor, who wondered whether the *Eastland's* stockholders deserved to suffer after all. Redfield applauded the judge's decision and sent it on to Congress with a covering letter explaining that he had reinstated the *Eastland's* inspectors and restored their back pay because the decision "exonerated" them of any wrongdoing. The impetus to secure reform in response to the accident had withered without a forum to keep the issue alive. Wilson read the report of August 5 but he left it to Redfield to decide what action to take and never questioned his refusal to impose any new regulations on shippers. By the time Redfield had reinstated the inspectors, Wilson felt no political pressure to champion this particular reform. The dozens of identical telegrams from all of

The Eastland *hull was later raised, and the vessel was rebuilt into a naval training ship, the* USS Wilmette. *(CMS Collection)*

the labor organizations in Chicago were no longer arriving. Congressman A.J. Sabath of Chicago led a limited debate on the floor of the House of Representative in March 1916 on whether the Inspection Service should be cut from the federal budget, but no one took his motion more seriously than courtesy required. The American Federation of Labor sent strong resolutions to President Wilson about the need for significant controls on ship owners' greed in December 1915, but let the matter drop when the Federation reconvened one year later.

On the anniversary of the accident in 1916 hundreds of residents of Cicero filled the churches for memorial services. More than 700 damage suits were on file in state and federal courts, awaiting determination of responsibility. Edith Wyatt retold the story in the *Tribune*, a lone voice reviving the spirit of indignation and outrage. She compared the accident to the war in Europe which the United States had not yet joined. The accident had "destroyed more than seven times as many American lives as all the foreign sea attacks together have taken since August, 1914," she emphasized. Wilson had promised to pursue a just investigation, she recalled, and then became preoccupied with the war. In her mind he had made an indefensible choice. The investigation raised issues of "quality" in civil government, of whether government "connives in the betrayal" of victims of the accident. War addressed only the nation's "fortunes." It was not an argument likely to convert President Wilson as he prepared to enter the war.

PART VI

The Lakes at War

Completed LSTs were launched sideways into the Illinois River at Seneca. Sideways launchings were a common practice on the Great Lakes and inland rivers because of the limited space available. (Frank W. Bazzoni Collection/ Seneca Public Library)

Chapter Twenty-Nine

Aircraft Carriers on Lake Michigan

Except for the Fort Dearborn massacre in the War of 1812, Chicago has never been on or near any frontlines of combat. The World War II term arsenal of democracy better describes its roles in the various wars the nation fought over the years. Besides supplying and training men and manufacturing war materiel, it was sometimes the site of prisoner-of-war camps — the Civil War Camp Douglas being the best known.

Somewhat surprisingly in view of the fact that Chicago is located in the center of the continent more than a thousand steaming miles from the nearest ocean, the city's role in naval warfare has been relatively more important — at least more obvious — than has its contributions to warfare on land or in the air. And some strange vessels have plied Lake Michigan off Chicago's beaches. The long-forgotten USS Michigan, *the world's first iron warship, steamed there in the nineteenth century, as did, a century later, the only two paddle-wheel aircraft carriers ever built.*

This chapter on those carriers, the Wolverine *and the* Sable, *is reprinted from the winter 1988 issue of the U.S. Naval Institute's publication* Of Naval History.

by Duane Ernest Miller

By nightfall of 7 December 1941 most of the U.S. fleet in Pearl Harbor had either been sunk or reduced to smoldering ruin. Nearly 200 Army and Navy aircraft had been destroyed — mostly on the ground — or knocked out of action.

Amid all the chaos, however, there was one bright spot. The Pacific Fleet aircraft carriers were not in Pearl Harbor during the Japanese attack and had escaped the devastation inflicted on the once-proud Battleship Row. Historian John Winton noted later that "Unwittingly, the Imperial Japanese Navy had thrust the United States Navy into the aircraft carrier age."

When the United States suddenly found itself violently hurled into World War II, it had a fleet of eight aircraft carriers, and more in varying stages of construction.

The new emphasis on carriers demanded many qualified pilots—fliers who had acquired some carrier experience before joining the fleet. Nevertheless, all of the carriers in commission had been committed to combat zones. None could be spared for training.

There was a further complication. To be effective, carrier pilot training had to be conducted without interruption. But the submarine threat off both the East and West coasts precluded continuous use of these areas for flight training.

Captain R.F. Whitehead devised a novel solution to this vexing problem. He recommended that carrier pilot training be conducted in the protected waters of the Great Lakes. Captain DeWitt C. Ramsey, assistant chief of the Navy's Bureau of Aeronautics, quickly recognized the possibilities of such a plan, and the two worked together to develop an appropriate program.

In January 1942, the Navy began negotiations with the C. and B. Transit Company for the purchase of a large, coal-burning, side-wheel excursion steamer. The ship had been built in 1913 by the American Shipbuilding Company, Wyandotte, Michigan, and was placed in service as the *Seeandbee*.

The cruise ship was converted at the Erie Plant of the American Shipbuilding Company in Buffalo, New York. In August 1942, the ex-*Seeandbee* was commissioned as the USS *Wolverine*. She had a standard displacement of 7,200 tons and an overall length of 500 feet; a beam of 58 feet, 1 inch; and a draft of 15 feet, 6 inches. She was powered by inclined coal-fired com-

The colorful career of the Seeandbee, *a side-wheel excursion steamer on Lake Erie, culminated during World War II when she was requisitioned by the Navy and converted into an aircraft carrier (commissioned in 1942 as the USS* Wolverine*) operating out of Chicago—one of two such vessels used to train carrier pilots on the Great Lakes. (Great Lakes Historical Society, Vermillion, Ohio)*

pound engines, with 8,000 indicated horsepower (IHP), and boiler uptakes to four funnels. Maximum speed was 16 knots. She did not mount any armament. Her normal complement was 325.

The *Wolverine* was classed as a miscellaneous auxiliary (IX-64). She was named in commemoration of the Navy's first iron-hulled warship. [ed. The paddle frigate originally was christened *Michigan* upon its launching in 1843 but renamed *Wolverine* in 1905 to clear her original name for reassignment to a battleship then under construction.]

A small island was erected over the large paddlebox sponson on the ship's starboard side. This was constructed primarily to route up the four funnels and enhance the ship's appearance as an aircraft carrier—not to provide the command and control spaces found in real carriers.

No hangar space was provided below decks for aircraft storage nor were any catapults fitted. A basic eight-wire arrester system was installed to secure planes after landing. Radar was never a part of the carrier's equipment.

The *Wolverine* crossed Lake Erie from Buffalo and arrived in Chicago on 22 August 1942. Braving a ferocious summer storm, the official welcoming party included Chicago's mayor, Edward J. Kelly, Captain E.A. Lofquist, Chief of Staff, 9th Naval District, and members of the press. One of the journalists covering the event, Ward Walker of the *Chicago Sunday Tribune,* described his first impressions on sighting the uss *Wolverine.* "Thru the mist of Madison street, the *Wolverine* appeared as a fantastic sight to a landlubber more than two miles away. Her flight deck, more than 500 feet long, seemed to ride at water level. She looked like a floating book."

As if by a prearranged signal, the skies suddenly cleared and the sun began to shine brightly. A flight of Grumman f 4 f Wildcat fighters from nearby Glenview Naval Air Station swooped out of the now-cloudless sky. Pilot training got under way almost immediately as aircraft from nas [Naval Air Station] Glenview began to make landings and takeoffs from the flattop.

Not all takeoffs and landings aboard Chicago's two carriers went well, and into the twenty-first century divers in Lake Michigan still look for the wreckage of downed planes on the lake bottom. (CMS Collection)

In the sometimes heavy seas of Lake Michigan, takeoffs and landings could be hazardous. Since the carrier had no hangar deck, her flight deck was only 26 feet above the waterline. Pilots had to maintain altitude when taking off.

Fortunately, most of the training was completed without incident. During the first four months, more

Chicago's carrier fleet was docked at Navy (Municipal) Pier during World War II. The USS Wolverine *(ex-SS* Seeandbee*) is at the left, alongside the USS* Sable *(ex-Greater Buffalo). At the extreme left at the mouth of the Chicago River was docked the gunboat USS* Wilmette *(ex-SS* Eastland*). (CMS Collection)*

than 400 pilots qualified for carrier duty, making more than 3,000 takeoffs and landings.

Even though the *Wolverine* had more than lived up to all expectations, it proved impossible for her to keep up with the ever-increasing demand for carrier-qualified pilots. Consequently, the Navy acquired another large Great Lakes passenger steamer, the SS *Greater Buffalo*, for conversion to its second training carrier.

The latest acquisition joined the *Wolverine* in the Chicago area in mid-1943 as the uss *Sable*. The *Greater Buffalo* was constructed in 1923 by the American Shipbuilding Company at a cost of 3.5 million dollars. In the Great Lakes trade she could accommodate 2,120 passengers and carry 1,000 tons of freight. Her conversion was also carried out in Buffalo.

The *Sable* was only slightly larger than the *Wolverine*, displacing 8,000 tons, with an overall length of 535 feet. She, too, was powered by inclined compound engines that could develop 10,500 ihp and attain a maximum speed of 18 knots. Also a coal-burner, she had boiler uptakes leading to two funnels. No armament was installed. She was manned by a crew of 300.

Designated the IX-81, the *Sable* featured a more elaborate island structure with a covered bridge. A more durable mast was also installed. Like the *Wolverine*, she had no aircraft storage facilities and no catapults.

The *Sable*, also a side-wheel paddle-steamer, was the Navy's first aircraft carrier to have a steel flight deck.

Modifications to the newest training carrier included the installation of two outriggers to accommodate parked aircraft forward of the island, and the fitting of YE and YG aircraft homing beacons.

With two carriers now in service, the tempo of training increased. Work began at sunrise and ended either at sunset or when fog rolled in and made takeoffs and landings too risky. Pilots completed their prescribed landings and takeoffs and returned to Glenview. Only rarely would a plane remain parked on the flight deck overnight.

Steaming at full speed, each ship consumed an average of 150 tons of coal during a 14-hour training period.

Naval aviators who had earned their wings at Pensacola or Corpus Christi reported to NAS Glenview and received orientation training before commencing the required minimum of eight landings and takeoffs from the carriers. Before any shipboard landings were attempted, however, practice landings took place on runways that had been marked like carrier decks.

Every attempt was made to qualify pilots in the same types of aircraft they would be flying with the fleet. As a result of combat priorities, however, shortages of aircraft frequently precluded such a practice. Pilots destined for assignment to carrier fighter groups would qualify in Grumman F4F Wildcats, while scout and bomber pilots flew missions in the North American SNJ Texan.

During a normal day, 30 pilots would be qualified. But on 28 May 1944 the *Sable* broke her own record by qualifying 59 pilots in a normal operating day—with 498 landings made in 531 minutes.

Training on board the carriers was not limited to pilots.

Arresting gear crews were given experience on board before their assignment to escort carriers then under construction. At two-week intervals, classes of 15 men reported aboard to receive four weeks of intensive training in flight deck procedures before assignment to carrier duty at sea.

Instructors and technicians from the radar school at Chicago's Navy Pier also received practical shipboard training, along with thousands of other aircrew members.

Both the *Wolverine* and *Sable* conducted operations year-round, even during inclement weather. In 1945, for example, the Chicago area suffered its worst winter in 39 years, but carrier training continued without interruption. A Navy journalist, reporting on the severity of that winter and its impact on the carriers' operations, learned that " . . . Even though the temperature continually hovered near the zero mark, crew members stayed on their posts from

The aircraft carrier Wolverine *was photographed with some of its crewmen at the bow. (CMS Collection)*

before sunrise until sunset . . . the ships' doctors reported an incredible drop in the number of reported illnesses. It was a fine tribute to Navy scientists who had designed special foul weather gear for the men."

The two carriers remained actively employed until the end of the war. The *Wolverine* recorded an impressive 65,000 landings while the *Sable* had more than 51,000. By the time the war ended, more than 12,000 pilots had been qualified by the Lake Michigan carrier task force.

The *Wolverine* was decommissioned on 7 November 1945 and transferred to the War Shipping Administration on 26 November 1947. She was sold for scrap a short time later.

The *Sable* was decommissioned on the same date as her partner and was taken over by the Maritime Administration. She was sold on 7 July 1948, and scrapped soon afterward.

Though not intended as combatants, the *Wolverine* and the *Sable* made incalculable contributions to winning the war at sea. They, too, were gallant ladies.

Chapter Thirty

The Navy's Secret Hooligan Fleet: Stealth Yachts Against the U-Boats

Things were so desperate for America in early World War II that the Navy had to impress into its fleet privately owned yachts to patrol for U-boats in the Atlantic Ocean. Yachts could sail quietly, for they had no engine noise to give away their position, and they could stay at sea continuously for a month without having to refuel. This is the story of one such vessel, a big yacht—actually, a schooner—built to entertain corporate clients on Lake Michigan. A Milwaukee beer baron donated use of the ship to the Navy, and during the war it stealthily plied coastal waters and the Caribbean Sea looking for U-boats.

Chicagoan Glenn Ruhge commanded the patrol yacht Atlantic *during the war, and his son, Justin, put together this account based on their conversations, as well as interviews with the yacht's later owner and assorted letters, documents in federal archives, and newspaper clippings. The author is a retired California aerospace project manager with degrees in physics and engineering. His avocation is history, and he has written ten books, including one on maritime history and one on shipwrecks.*

by Justin M. Ruhge

This is the story of a ship called the *Moby Dick*, or the *Atlantic*, or the *Blanco*, or any of a half dozen other names. The history of this ship ran the gamut from a pleasure yacht of the rich and famous to a fighting ship in two wars. A large part of the history of this ship took place during World War II. After that war the *Atlantic* reverted to its pleasure craft status, became an oceanic research vessel, and then took part in rescue missions in Vietnam at the end of that unfortunate war.

When America declared war on Japan and Germany in December 1941, the German Navy lost no time in attacking vital shipping all along the eastern coast with its U-boat fleet. The United States was ill prepared for this well-planned onslaught by the German Navy. In its rush to defend itself, the U.S. Navy commandeered hundreds of sailing and power craft of all sizes from the private sector and used them as pickets along the East Coast to warn of the presence of submarines. Some of the larger ships were converted to stealthy antisubmarine sailing vessels and used in the Atlantic, Caribbean, and Gulf of Mexico shipping lanes. The *Atlantic* was one of those sailing ships.

In the first year of World War II, the United States lost 385 ships of a thousand gross tons or greater, totaling about 2,448,000

America's war needs were so severe that it even impressed big yachts for use on U-boat patrol in the Atlantic Ocean. This vessel, which began its career in 1923 as a yacht called the Moby Dick, *was renamed* Atlantic *after a Milwaukee beer baron acquired it, was renamed* Blanco *after the U.S. Coast Guard acquired it, armed it, and sent it to look for U-boats. (Postcard from collection of Justin M. Ruhge)*

tons. A frantic effort by the Navy and the Coast Guard was initiated to employ every possible means of sea power to stop this loss due to the German submarines lurking off the Atlantic Coast. One of the organizations that emerged was the Coastal Picket Patrol, or the Hooligan Navy (its colloquial name). The official Coast Guard title, Corsair Fleet, was little used. The prime mover in organizing this branch of naval defense was Alfred Stanford of New York, commodore of the Cruising Club of America. On May 23, 1942, Admiral King, commander of the Eastern Sea Frontier, ordered all sea frontier commanders to expedite rigorous selection of craft for transfer from local defense forces to sea frontier forces. By this time the Cruising Club had lined up 70 seagoing yachts and 100 smaller ships. A mad scramble ensued in which all ships in the country, including in the Great Lakes, were sought, along with their owners and crew. All were inducted for the duration to support the national defense of the homeland. Eventually, some 4,000 craft were pressed into service. Most craft were assigned to the Charleston (6th), New Orleans (7th), and Florida (8th) Naval Districts. These were in place by mid-1942.

Partly because of the presence of the pickets and because of the formation of escorted convoys, the German submarine fleet left the area of the East Coast in late 1943 and moved its focus of operation to the Caribbean and the Gulf of Mexico. As a result, a cutback of the Hooligan Navy was begun in January 1943 and completed by November 15, 1943. Only the largest of the ships that could stay at sea for a month at a time were retained for convoy flanking duty in the Gulf of Mexico.

One other aspect of this decision was to free up fuel for the fighting forces. All those pickets required gasoline, which was rationed. One of the major reasons that sailing yachts were commandeered was that they could operate without the need for fuel most of the time. The other major advantage to the use of sailing yachts to search for and track submarines was their silent mode of operation. It was difficult to hear them coming when under sail—

they were quite stealthy. And when armed with sound gear, radar, depth charges, and a deck gun, they were quite dangerous.

One of the ships located by the Coast Guard on the Great Lakes was a 145-foot, three-masted schooner with a long history of lake and river travels. At the time this ship was entered into the Coast Guard flotilla of coastal pickets, it was named the *Atlantic* and was owned by Erwin C. Uihlein, president of the Joseph Schlitz Brewing Company of Milwaukee.

The ship's prior name was the *Moby Dick*. Its first owner was Seniham Fish of South Bend, Indiana, president of the Colgate-Palmolive Company. This ship was built of steel in 1923 at the Bethlehem Steel Holland Plant in Wilmington, Delaware. It was 138 feet long and had a 24-foot, 10-inch beam; a 7-foot, 10-inch draft; and a gross weight of 198 tons. Its maximum speed was 10 miles per hour with a cruising range of 2,400 miles. The ship had one main engine of 180 horsepower made by Krupp Diesel in Germany. This engine drove the ship's 40-inch diameter bronze propeller. A generator and compressor were also attached to the engine. The voltage source was 120 volts DC. Fuel for the engine was stored in three steel tanks with a total capacity of 4,500 gallons. Fresh water was stored in one steel tank, with a capacity of 5,000 gallons, located amidships. There were two Hershey anchors and one Kedge anchor. Two 17-foot lifeboats were located on either side of the ship. The ship was rigged as a schooner with three masts of 90 feet, 83 feet, and 75 feet, spaced 23 feet, 6 inches apart. Navigation equipment consisted of two uncovered compasses and deck binnacles, one forward and one aft. There were five toilets and mess facilities for 26 men. The galley was located forward below deck with a kerosene stove and icebox. The ship had nine inches of concrete inside its bottom plates and 18 tons of old iron for ballast. A centerboard 12 feet deep could be lowered to prevent excessive rolling in heavy seas. It contained 900 pounds of lead. The approximate cost of construction was $56,000. The ship's home port was New York City.

In 1937 Mr. Uihlein acquired the *Moby Dick* and renamed it the *Atlantic*. Uihlein operated the *Atlantic* as a pleasure craft on the Great Lakes. The vessel came with an engineer, Peter Delfs, who maintained the ship's Krupp diesel engine, machines, and rigging.

In 1942 the word went out that the Navy needed oceangoing sailing vessels. Mr. Uihlein made a gift of his ship to the war effort. As a result, the ship, then based in Milwaukee, was requisitioned by the War Shipping Administration for Coast Guard use on August 20, 1942. The *Atlantic* was renamed the *Blanco* on September 14, 1942, and assigned a permanent station at Miami on April 6, 1943.

But before it could assume its new role in the Atlantic, the Coast Guard had to get it out of the Great Lakes. It needed a crew to move it to New Orleans. Fortunately, the Coast Guard had contact with many yachtsmen around the Great Lakes. One of these was Glenn A. Ruhge, who had a reputation as a seaman and was a member of the Chicago's Columbia Yacht Club. A graduate of Lane Technical High School and an electrician by trade, Mr. Ruhge spent most of his free time at the harbor. It was here that the Coast Guard sent a cab to find him and bring him back to headquarters, where he was inducted into the Navy on September 12, 1942. With only half a uniform, Lieutenant J.G. Ruhge was assigned as commander of the *Blanco* and sent to Milwaukee to take command

The conversion of the pleasure craft Atlantic *into a sub chaser was done at* New Orleans. *(Collection of Justin M.*

and move it down to the Mississippi River via the Chicago River. To do this, the three masts had to be unstepped and stowed on deck so the vessel could pass under the numerous bridges on the rivers. The *Blanco* and its new crew were en route to Joliet on September 16, 1942, and arrived in New Orleans on September 29.

Upon arrival in New Orleans, the *Blanco* was given a complete going-over to determine if it was seaworthy and what detail work needed to be done before going to sea. This review was held at the 8th Naval District Coast Guard Depot in October 1942. The ship was thoroughly inspected, and although the *Blanco* was deemed seaworthy, an initial estimate of work needed before sailing was $13,000. Additional dry-dock work was also recommended.

The initial repair work took place during October and November 1942. At this time, binnacle wheelhouses were constructed forward and at the stern so that the ship could operate in foul weather on the high seas with added safety for the crew. During December 1942 the *Blanco* was moved to the Todd-Johnson Yards at Algiers, Louisiana, located across the Mississippi River from New Orleans, for exterior overhaul of the hull and the centerboard in the dry docks. The added costs of these repairs raised the original estimated costs to about $26,000. All rigging was replaced, a new rudder was installed, new thrust bearings for the engine coupling were fabricated and installed, and cleaning, chipping, and painting occurred on every square inch of the vessel. When completed the ship was painted gray—the *Blanco* was in the Navy now! It had to be converted to a fighting lady.

The ship was informally called the "Admiral's Baby" and was numbered W P Y 343, but the number was not placed on the hull. It only flew the U.S. Coast Guard flag and the commissioning pennant. The ship was a secret. It carried a towing device called P H L V, Doppler radar, two scopes, Doppler sound gear, and two K-guns with 350-pound depth charges. Three transmitters, five receivers, and seven radiomen were assigned to the ship. A three-inch gun called Marmaduke by the crew was installed amidships. Two 50-caliber machine guns were also a part of the armament installed. The ship's radio call letters were N O B I - N - L - K - T.

During this three-month period of preparation, a crew of 25 was gathered and assigned to the new fighting ship. Glenn A. Ruhge was the captain, Robert J. deFraga was executive, and Peter Delfs was ship's engineer (remember, he came with the ship). The ship also acquired a mascot, a small female dog named Scoogie (the Coast Guard's slang for cleaning and polishing all white surfaces on a ship).

The *Blanco* was assigned to the Gulf Sea Frontier, which was organized on February 6, 1942, with headquarters at Key West, Florida. The Gulf Sea Frontier was responsible for the protection of the Florida Coast and Straits, most of the Bahamas, the entire Gulf of Mexico, the Yucatan Channel, and most of Cuba. The commander of the Gulf Sea Frontier was always the same person as the commandant of the 7th Naval District, and the same was true for the 8th Naval District at New Orleans. The Gulf Sea Frontier moved to Miami on June 17, 1942, with Captain Russell S. Crenshaw as commandant. On June 3, 1942, Admiral James L. Kauffman was transferred from the Icelandic command to head up the Gulf Sea Frontier. The *Blanco* was assigned to the 8th Naval District with staff located at Bucksport, South Carolina, under the command of Captain A. D. Ayrault.

The *Blanco* set sail on its maiden voyage as a fighting ship of the Navy on February 22, 1943, just four months after being acquired by the Coast Guard. The initial task was to precede convoys passing through the Florida Straits and to locate any submarines in the South Atlantic area around the straits. This often meant negotiating the minefield that surrounded the convoy assembly anchorage on the Gulf side of Key West. The *Blanco* was at sea in an assigned patrol area for 30 days at a time, with ten days off to return to base and resupply. While at sea, training was conducted in the uses of the three-inch gun, K-gun depth charges, and 50-

A major part of the Blanco's *new armament was a three-inch gun nicknamed Marmaduke. The vessel also carried two K-guns and a couple of 50-caliber machine guns. (Collection of Justin M. Ruhge)*

caliber machine guns. Depth charges raised 50-foot plumes of water when exploding under water. The depth charges had to be removed from the ship whenever it returned to the coast and started up the river to New Orleans or Key West. Except for river trips, almost all sea operations were made under sail.

The scene changed when the U-boat fleet found the South Atlantic convoy scene too hot for them. Sensing better hunting in the southern Caribbean and Gulf of Mexico, the U-boat fleet moved farther south to those locations and made their presence felt with numerous sinkings. To counter this action, the Navy moved its antisubmarine fleet farther south, and in the process the *Blanco* was reassigned to a tour that took it regularly from New Orleans south to Trinidad, where many convoys were assembled for South Africa and Europe. This tour continued through the remainder of 1943 and into early 1945.

A description of everyday life on the *Blanco* was located on the Internet in the biography of the ship's cook, George Mullins Jr., written by Philip Mullins in 1999. An Internet search on "Ruhge" included this biography among the results. The document provides a short diary with details about the ship's kitchen, daily life, and where the beer was stored (in the bilge). Everyone not on duty, including Lieutenant Commander Ruhge and all the others, ate together. Following are some of Mullins's observations:

> Water was rationed on the *Blanco*. The crew was allowed one shower a week. A yeoman stood at the valve with a clock in his hand. When a man's time was expired, the yeoman closed the valve and there was no more water. The two cooks on board were allowed to bathe every second day. The ship had a small ice maker and the cook saved the ice all week so that on Sundays he would have just enough to make three gallons of ice cream. The ice cream was made in a hand-cranked machine. The man who volunteered to crank the handle was given an extra helping of the ice cream, and there were always volunteers weeks in advance.

While the *Blanco* was on station in the Gulf, it would often encounter hurricanes. When the weather got very rough, the portholes would be sealed with metal plates, a couple of topsails would be hoisted, and the engine turned on. This gave the helmsman control of the ship to prevent it from turning sideways to the wind. Some of the crew would crowd into the wheelhouse, where they would watch the ship climb waves 75 feet high and then see it fall off the crest and down the other side.

Besides its role as a stealthy antisubmarine vessel, the *Blanco* was a training ship for the Navy. Ten officers and 64 enlisted men trained on the *Blanco*, and most were reassigned to other ships. Three officers went to the Naval Academy. Peter Delfs, the ship's engineer, was assigned to a large transport as chief engineer in 1944. He was wounded in action off Manila. Lieutenant Henry Rolling was assigned as navigator on the transport *Admiral Capps*. The captain of the *Blanco* was asked to go along with Captain

Ferguson, head of Navy Operations in the Gulf, assigned to command the transport *Hampton Roads*—a biggie—but Ruhge declined. However, as recognition for his good work, Lieutenant Commander Ruhge was assigned as commodore of a flotilla of the *Woodbury*, *Active*, and four cutters, as well as the *Blanco*.

In May 1945 the war in Europe ended, and so did the need for anti-submarine patrols. However, the war with Japan was still under way, so the Gulf duty continued, but the primary effort was weather patrol—chasing hurricanes. In September the war in Asia finally came to an end. The *Blanco* was ordered to Charleston, South Carolina, for decommissioning. Fifteen men and Lieutenant Commander Ruhge took the *Blanco* from New Orleans to Miami for some R&R, then up to Charleston for a little more, and finally (on October 30) to Bucksport, South Carolina, where the ship's naval equipment was removed. The *Blanco* was decommissioned in November 1945 and declared surplus on July 30, 1946. In the meantime the *Blanco* was moored at Sullivan Island, Moultrieville, South Carolina. The *Blanco* was said to have been credited with two U-boat sinkings. In all it traveled some 66,000 sea miles during its World War II service.

Upon turning in his papers at Bucksport, Lieutenant Commander Ruhge was assigned to a new ship, named the *Tallapooson*, located at Bath, Maine, but declined and headed home ASAP, as did many others who served in the Navy for those four long years. Lieutenant Commander Ruhge returned to private life but kept in touch with his "hooligan" crew. He sailed Lake Michigan during the yachting season for all his life until retiring; he died in 1988.

In *U.S. Coast Guard Cutter and Craft of World War II*, published in 1982, the *Blanco* is listed, as are the *Woodbury* and the *Active*, among many others that served the country with the Hooligan Navy. The *Blanco* won three chevrons for her war contributions.

In May 1945 Erwin C. Uihlein (remember him, the owner of the *Atlantic* in 1942?) sent a letter to the Coast Guard headquarters, Washington D.C., requesting the return of the *Atlantic* to him when it was decommissioned. Well, as we all know, the wheels of government turn slowly. In May 1946 the War Shipping Administration agreed to return the ship to Mr. Uihlein for a price of one dollar. In November 1946 Mr. Uihlein sent another letter, to the U.S. Maritime Commission in Charleston, South Carolina, in which arrangements were made to reacquire the *Blanco* for one dollar, provided the ship was in full working order. Plans were to return the ship to the Great Lakes via the St. Lawrence Seaway. Further delays resulted in a return to its owner on January 7, 1947.

The next reference to the *Atlantic* is in the *Milwaukee Journal* dated Saturday, August 23, 1947, which stated that a Captain Charles Reilly returned the schooner to Milwaukee. For the next six years the owner of the *Atlantic*, which is the name restored to the ship, used it for his pleasure and for the pleasure of the Joseph Schlitz Brewing Company.

In 1952 the *Atlantic* was offered to the Texas A & M Research Foundation for oceanographic expeditions. For outfitting, the ship was to be moved 1,800 miles to Galveston, Texas.

Again the *Atlantic* had to be moved from Milwaukee down the Chicago River to the Mississippi, this time to its new home in Texas. The captain for this move was Homer L. Hadley. Also on board were Henry von der Hofer, the mate; Paul Butler, the cook; Daniel A. Wray, the operations manager; and Walter Lang, a marine technician. Seeing the crew off was Peter Delfs, the ship's engineer. The date was March 19, 1952. The news media covered the story and the transition at both ends of the trip. It would be 18 years before the *Atlantic* would reappear on the Great Lakes.

Erwin Uihlein died in 1968. The history of the *Atlantic* gets murky after it became a research ship, but it seems that the following happened, though no exact dates are known. Texas A & M abandoned the *Atlantic* after several years of research work. The ship was then acquired by another owner, who rebuilt her for about $160,000 and changed her name to *Louise*. Where this owner used the ship is unknown.

The Blanco's *skipper was Chicago electrician and yachtsman Glenn A. Ruhge (right, with binoculars), who was commissioned a lieutenant, junior grade. (Collection of Justin M. Ruhge)*

The next owner, Art Hammond with the Bower Dredging Company, renamed the ship *My Lin* and took a world cruise that ended up in Hawaii. Hammond put in twin 550 aluminum diesel engines and enlarged the fuel tanks from 4,500 to 6,500 gallons. With the new engines the ship could run at 14.2 miles per hour. Hammond also removed the center board and welded the well closed. Somewhere along the route the hull of the ship had been painted black, and later yet a white stripe was added.

Another world cruise was completed by a new owner named Zucker. This cruise ended in Puerto Rico, where this owner died.

In 1970 enter the last owner of the *Atlantic*, Conrad Mikulec of West Falls, New York. Mr. Mikulec, a 35-year-old millionaire and owner of Power-Pak Products (a manufacturer of fire extinguishers), had acquired the *Atlantic*, renaming it the *Star of the Pacific*, in San Juan, Puerto Rico, and had it sailed up the St. Lawrence Seaway to Chicago to attend a convention, where he and the vessel received a lot of media attention. Glenn Ruhge lived in Chicago and was very surprised to see the old *Blanco* after 25 years. A meeting was arranged, and some of the ship's history for the past 18 years was filled in, as just reported.

About $59,000 in improvements had been made in the *Star of the Pacific* to date, and another $100,000 was planned before the ship was to begin a world cruise. Its main salon now contained soft leather sofas, wall-to-wall carpeting, fine wood paneling, a library, and a color TV. Scattered through the yacht were several double-bunked staterooms, a forecastle that slept eight, and several bathrooms, including one with a full tub. The kitchen had an eight-burner electric stove and walk-in freezers. The ship slept 33, including a volunteer crew of two women cooks and eight experienced seamen. The twin diesels installed by Mr. Hammond had burned up, so Mr. Mikulec replaced them with twin GE 328-horsepower diesels. Three new generators for electrical power were also installed.

Unknown to anyone, the plan for the *Star of the Pacific* was to sail to Vietnam and take part in the war effort to support the American withdrawal. This gallant ship had gone to war for the second time in its life in another stealthy role. In 1970 the *Star of the Pacific* left for its announced around-the-world trip with this mission as its purpose. After three years stationed off Vietnam, the ship continued around the world and returned from Asia in 1974 to Fort Lauderdale, Florida, logging about 60,000 miles.

President Nixon's chief of staff, General Haig, wanted the *Star* to lead the tall ships in New York Harbor in the July 4, 1976, parade. However, disaster intervened. On January 30, 1975, the *Star* was in the South Atlantic off the Bahamas. The crew was filling scuba tanks below deck when one of them blew up and blasted

The Coast Guard's big advantage in using sailing yachts to chase subs, besides their being readily available, was that they were silent runners. U-boat crews couldn't pick up the sound of their engines on hydrophones. (Collection of Justin M. Ruhge)

a hole through the side at the waterline. The ship flooded and sank within five minutes. The crew made it to life rafts, but they could hear the diesels running as the ship went under. At that time the *Star* was located 40 miles east of Eleuthera Island and in line with San Salvador Island. She went down in about 12,000 feet of water at 75 degrees 30 minutes west and 25.5 degrees north.

So ended the life of a very unusual ship. In its 53 years, it saw the world at least six times over and provided a safe passage for its owners and crew. It went to war twice for the U.S. and improved our knowledge of oceanography. A berth at a maritime museum would have been a happier ending for such an outstanding record. The only remains of this ship is some of its bow's wooden gingerbread that was blown loose in a gale during World War II, and inherited by the author from Glenn Ruhge.

Chapter Thirty-One

The Grebe Shipyard of Chicago

Henry C. Grebe was a yacht builder who owned a shipyard on the north branch of the Chicago River within sight of the once-famous Riverview amusement park. He was best known for his fine wooden vessels. As progress would have it, they were eventually displaced by boats with aluminum and fiberglass hulls, and the Grebe yard, like Riverview, faded into memory.

CMS member John Heinz in his youth worked for a year at the Grebe yard, and this is his recollection of what happened there.

by John Heinz

Henry C. Grebe was a private person. We know that he was born in 1890. He was a naval architect, but his education was not advertised. He first appeared in Milwaukee and seems to have had a reading knowledge of German. We know what he did in World War II, but we don't know if he was in the service in World War I. He gave no interviews. Like many prominent and eminent men, he avoided Who's Who in America. There are no Henry Grebe jokes.

The Great Lakes Boat Building Corporation (GLBB) was founded in Milwaukee, not Chicago, in 1911, when Grebe was 21 years old. In World War I it turned out small wooden patrol boats for the Navy. These were 110-foot craft armed with machine guns and depth charges. One was built just for the Inland Steel Company, maybe for company security or maybe for some kind of

One of Chicago's best-known shipyards was Henry C. Grebe's facility on the north branch of the Chicago River. It specialized in building yachts and pleasure craft until World War II came along, when it began building minesweepers for the Navy. (Collection of John Heinz)

naval militia training. Another of the erstwhile patrol boats, sc-419, or maybe 420, now rests on the lake bottom and is known to sport divers. sc 419 was sold to Alfred J.L. Lowengrand of Kodiak, Alaska. sc 420 was never taken by the Navy and was sold to Edward P. Farley & Co. of Chicago.

Meanwhile, Philip K. Wrigley, the chewing gum heir who eventually would go into partnership with Grebe on their common love—yachts—spent World War I as an aircraft engine instructor for the Navy. After the war one of their first maritime collaborations was to rebuild a 54-foot Great Lakes cruiser, an early Grebe design, which Wrigley renamed *Wasp*—the first of a series of Grebe-Wrigley boats with that name. These were used in the upper Great Lakes and for the Wrigley family's Catalina Island estate.

A newspaper observed that the *Wasp* had all the conveniences of a modern hotel, but Mrs. Wrigley had a different view of life on board. She said that she never saw a harbor because she was cooking dinner when the boat put in and was cooking breakfast when it left.

In 1919 the GLBB team built the long-lived cruiser *Sonja*. According to a writer of the time:

If you have cruised on Lake Michigan perhaps you came upon the beautiful *Sonja* of yesteryear and today. Her long range cruising ability is a delight to distant port power boaters. The *Sonja* is a 42' power yacht of vintage character. In respect to her long cruising range . . . can you imagine her easy go of 500 miles on 400 gallons of 1919 gasoline? *Sonja* was originally built for Mr. August Von Block who sailed her about Lake Superior and eastern Georgian Bay. With her cabins aft, amidship and fore, and total engine room, tan canvas shelters, inlaid magnificent wheel, total varnish, this beautiful yacht of 1919 is today used, and always wet stored in her original boathouse on Round Lake, Charlevoix.

In 1926 GLBB moved to Chicago to a site up the Chicago River near the Belmont Avenue cantilever bridge. GLBB eventually built about 68 boats, many of which were Henry Grebe designs. The *Lake Michigan Yachting News* once noted:

Today, Hank is THE yacht designer, builder and broker on the Lakes. He has a suite of offices in the Wrigley tower. He has a Cadillac car. He lives in the fashionable yacht harbor district (tiled bath, fireplace, concession to October 1st) and has a six tube radio, two suits, a straw hat with a fancy band and a list of satisfied customers as long as your boat hook that reads like a page from the Blue Book.

Henry married Marguerite Luckett in 1921, and they became liveaboards on a schooner in Chicago's Belmont Harbor. Although they joined the Chicago Yacht Club and kept an apartment in the Belmont Harbor area, they were modest people, and, unlike friend Phil Wrigley, they kept out of the news. The *Lake Michigan Yachting News* went on to say:

He started as a sailor, and deciding that the ordinary Atlantic Coast power yachts were unsuitable for the Great Lakes, started to produce his own hulls. The characteristics of Grebe's boats are a prominent flare that is well suited for the short weighty seas that can rumple these mill ponds—and a graceful sheer.

Grebe powerboats show a strong flare and sheer, in contrast to the wall-sided, steamboat look of other great yachts of the time. Grebe yachts were mostly large but did not imitate steam yachts. They were comfortable and private. Hank would never build a 20-foot boat to sleep six people. The functional raised fore deck was a Grebe trademark in the 1920s and 1930s. This step-up fo'c'sle deck helped the vessel navigate Lake Michigan's wave—and it has a naval look that foretells the salty style of later Grebe minesweepers.

The first Grebe yacht built in Chicago (in 1927) was *R. Dream*, 109 feet long, for R.C. Vilas of Chicago. The largest Grebe sailboat built in Chicago was the schooner *Freedom*, an 88-footer built in 1931 for Sterling Morton and later given to the U.S. Naval Academy for racing. *Freedom* is still afloat, though in deteriorated condition, in Brooklyn, New York.

The largest Grebe sailing design was the *Northern Light*, a 140-foot wooden schooner built for John Borden's successful Field Museum expedition of 1927—the subject of a well-illustrated book by Mrs. John Borden, *The Cruise of the Northern Light*.

The Borden book was a good testimonial for Grebe's design talents. The vessel had coal heating, bathtubs, and 3,600 gallons of freshwater—all comfortable and private in the Grebe style. The dining table was a replica of an early American trestle table in the Metropolitan Museum in New York.

In 1932 William Wrigley—"Anybody can make chewing gum, the trick is selling it"—died and gave his son, Philip K. Wrigley, his gum company, much of Catalina Island, and also a baseball team known as the Chicago Cubs. It was probably at this time that GLBB became Henry C. Grebe & Co. (HCGCO).

Philip Wrigley in 1938 sold his share of the company to Grebe, apparently for a dollar, after a lawsuit over a workman's death in the explosion of a yacht's stove at the yard dock. However, the for-

*A 68-foot standard cruiser (as shown here) was one of Grebe's prewar special-
ties. (Collection of John Heinz)*

mer partners remained friends, and Wrigley over the years ordered
at least three power cruisers from Grebe.

At about this time Grebe began putting his logo on the bow of
his creations. *Vagabond Lady's* model shows the monogram
H C G C O. These mirror-image signatures also are visible in many
Grebe yacht photos.

Although Grebe in 1928 had started building steel boats—the
first was a welded tug for Great Lakes Dredge and Dock—in
1940 he built the steel towboat *Sohio*, the yard's biggest metal vessel to date. Metalworking skills would come in handy as the war
loomed, although the company ultimately built mostly wooden
minesweepers, called Y M S S (yard minesweepers). They were just
136 feet in length and might be built in as little as four months.
The YMS had a raised fore deck, like the Grebe yacht designs of
the roaring twenties. The yard also produced welded-steel tugboats and finished the work on 221-foot minesweepers from
Lorain, Ohio.

Grebe's yard was a lost world hidden between the bungalows of
Washtenaw and Racine avenues. Most Chicagoans were unaware
of the shipyard and its activities, despite its proximity to
Riverview Park, just across the north branch of the Chicago River.
The yard was known to high society, however. The list of women

who were invited to launch boats read like a who's who of Chicago—Mrs. Helen Wrigley, Dorothy Wrigley, and Mrs. Loyal Davis, mother of the future first lady Nancy Reagan and sister of Mrs. Grebe. The wives and daughters of many Grebe employees were also pressed into service with the champagne bottles. "Some gals, and kids, were so small they couldn't break the bottle and needed help with a second swing," remembers Art Kosar, a draftsman in the yard who arranged the launching ceremonies.

Henry Grebe was empowered to halt the annoying music from nearby Riverview, but only during the launchings. The little ships then chugged off to the Pacific and the Mediterranean. Many never returned, having splashed to the bottom of the sea off of the Caroline Islands, southern France, Balikpapan, Borneo, Okinawa, Normandy, or Tarakan.

In 1944 Grebe & Co. had its largest number of employees, 1,000—some 4-F (unfit for service) and a lot of older guys. Subcontracting for these ship fittings employed many more people in other Chicago companies. The Grebe yard was a miniature naval base, administered by Commander Edward Titus and guarded by sailors and marines in sentry towers. Then there were the Coast Guard police in their black uniforms—scary from a distance. But up close, in their group photo, you could see that they were all what we would now consider senior citizens.

Kosar recalled that the Grebe yard was furious with activity during the war and how tempers sometimes flared. He also recalled his boss, Hans Mauerhof:

> When I started in there they told me to refuse to work for the quick-tempered Mauerhof, and I soon found out why. Finally I had to flat out tell him to stop swearing at me: "You can tell me anything you want, but I can't take anymore of your swearing." After that Hans and I got on so well that when I left to go into the service he became good friends with my father and they even went fishing together. I remember once Hans wanted to throw some guy out of his office, and called for the Marines for help. I can still hear him yelling, in his thick accent: "Marines! Marines!"

About 1950 there was a big fire in the yard. There are vivid photos of Chicago firemen fighting the blazing wooden boats, and the exact date is not recorded, but one photo has '50 written on the back. No former Grebe hands known to this writer can remember such a blaze

In 1952 Henry Grebe died at age 62. His wife, Marguerite, succeeded him as president of the company (1952–54). The couple was childless, so there had been no one else in the family to succeed him. She began the program of building four AMSs (auxilary mine sweepers) for the Korean War, but the company began to encounter problems.

In the 1950s things seemed to go against the company. Orders began to decline. Even the cats were evicted. In its glory days the Grebe yard had cats. They had a good life there, keeping away rats and mice, until one day they scampered over a freshly varnished deck, after which it had to be sanded down to bare wood and refinished. That was the end of the Grebe cats. They were relocated to another neighborhood. But the Grebe cats took the Grebe good luck with them.

Because of the limited space available in the north branch, minesweepers were launched sideways (in typical Great Lakes fashion). This minesweeper was photographed in 1943, just after launching. (Collection of John Heinz)

In 1955 Mrs. Grebe sold out to a Michigan accountant and sailor for payment of the yard's small mortgage. She died in 1972.

In 1959 the yard got into the business of building sightseeing boats, including the steel *Congress Queen*, now called the *Skyline Queen*. This boat still cruises the river and lakefront with loads of tourists. As the number of orders for new vessels declined, the yard also took on the task of refurbishing older boats. In 1965 Dan O'Conner refurbished a classic Seabird yawl in the yard and renamed her *Rugger* after his interest in rugby.

The revolution from wood to fiberglass began in the 1950s and 1960s. Fiberglass is glass fiber held together with polyester resin. Hulls made from it can be produced in series by small boatyards or mass-produced in large ones. Fiberglass won't rot, but it becomes unsightly as it ages. In the marine trades the increasing use of fiberglass in boat construction resulted in fewer jobs for wooden ship carpenters, and proved to be a challenge to Grebe's traditional yacht building techniques.

Aluminum was also becoming a more popular material for boat construction, and in 1969 the yard built a prototype frogman reconnaissance vessel of aluminum with jet turbine engines. The last boat built in the Grebe yard (in 1970) was of aluminum: the *Karen J*, a 65-footer. But it was a money loser for the yard. After the *Karen J*'s launching, the yard was used strictly for service and storage.

The Grebe yard subsisted on repairing vessels into the 1980s but finally was shut down in 1994. I heard that in the last days, a delegation of the owners of larger yachts came and begged that the yard be kept going. These were people of considerable skills at persuasion, but the last owner's compass was fixed upon redevelopment of the yard as a residential project. And development was not easy, because it needed a zoning change, and the Grebe yard, despite all its history and social connections, never had any political clout. The city put a nail in the coffin when it locked the Belmont Avenue bridge and thus limited the size of ships that could reach Grebe.

Chapter Thirty-Two

The ABCs of Life in a Storm

Chicago shipbuilder Henry Grebe may have specialized in building wooden yachts for the wealthy, but during World War II his north branch shipyard was pressed into service grinding out minesweepers for the Navy. This was true of all Great Lakes shipyards. Their outlet to the ocean was not the St. Lawrence Seaway, which didn't exist at the time, but the Illinois Waterway—a term that applies to the continuous shipping channel between the Great Lakes and the Mississippi River formed by the Chicago River, Sanitary and Ship Canal, Des Plaines River, and Illinois River. The YMS 421 (YMS for "yard minesweeper"), just one of the vessels built for the Navy by Grebe, sailed that route to the war.

This is the story of that minesweeper, from its birth in the shadow of Chicago's Riverview Park till its death in a typhoon off Okinawa. Ensign Richard Brady was assigned to the YMS 421 as part of her precommissioning crew and spent several weeks at the Grebe yard, where he met Henry Grebe. Ensign Brady sailed with the YMS 421 down the Chicago River for a few miles to Navy Pier, where the crew unstepped the mast to clear the bridges on the Sanitary and Ship Canal to Lockport and the Illinois River at Grafton. At New Orleans the mast was restepped and the vessels fitted with radar and other gear to begin the long voyage across the Pacific Ocean to Guam.

This is an edited version of an article that originally appeared in the winter 2002 issue of the Chicago Maritime Society's newsletter. Its author, CMS member Richard Brady, who survived the typhoon that sank his ship, died in 2002.

by Richard Brady

The sea outside Apra Harbor [ed. a naval base on Guam] was smooth with long lazy swells. Carmine streaks tinged the cerulean eastern sky. Feathery clouds stretched across the horizon, lighted on the bottom in gold and pink with a tinge of silver. The sun had not yet reached the horizon, but its glow, like a sunflower, promised a sunny day. Gulls circled overhead as if to see us safely off on our voyage, and dolphins played in our frothy bow wake. It was a beautiful morning with no hint of the gathering storm; we had no reason to believe the cruise over the next several days would be anything but pleasant.

The other ships in our company standing out astern formed up in line as we departed the sea buoy marking the end of the harbor channel; we were en route to Okinawa. We must have appeared to be a rather insignificant group—just six small specks on the vast Pacific. The other ships in our company were three minesweepers, a subchaser, and, the largest, a seagoing tug. We were under way on a cruise to Okinawa about a thousand miles and five days away.

It was September 9, 1945. The Japanese had surrendered just one week earlier. Our orders were to join a sweep squadron being formed to clear mines from the Sea of Japan to make the waters safe for all ships in the area. Some of our crew had participated in invasions during combat in the Mediterranean and the Pacific—from Italy to Okinawa.

Probably my own most horrifying experience to that time was duty on the picket line north of Okinawa during the desperate kamikaze attacks at the very end of the war. Then we were assigned positions north of Okinawa, where we were expendable decoys sailing back and forth to lure the inexperienced Japanese suicide pilots to attack us and thus spare the larger ships of the fleet closer to Buckner Bay. When relieved of that assignment a few weeks earlier, we were moved back to Guam. But now the hostilities were over, and there was a lot of housekeeping to be done.

So these were our first sailing orders since the surrender, and we were looking forward with great anticipation to a peaceful and uneventful cruise. Our orders were to depart Guam at 0530 and sail to Buckner Bay, Okinawa, where we would be assigned to a sweep squadron to clear the minefields that both we and the Japanese had laid in the Japan Sea.

As we departed the sea buoy at the entrance of the harbor and crossed the bar, we could make out the island of Rota on the horizon to starboard. It was an unusually clear day and presented an exceptional view of this tiny island not often visible from Guam. With the soft breezes and the gently rolling seas, we expected the cruise to Okinawa to be pleasant and free of concern for any threat from the enemy. We anticipated the good weather would hold, but as in life, the sea and weather are unpredictable except for one thing—when things are so very good, change is inevitable.

Change was not long in coming. The next day we received a report on Guam weather radio that a large tropical disturbance had formed about 200 miles southeast of the island. On our chart we plotted its position hourly. The storm's forward speed was about ten knots, and we were only making a little more than seven knots, our most economical speed. Considering the distance, according to the area commander, at that speed we should be able to make it to Buckner Bay without refueling. There was no provision for refueling in our orders, so we were concerned with conserving fuel. There was no margin for delays from weather or other emergencies. We weren't comfortable with the situation, but orders are orders.

Obviously, with each hour the storm was gaining on us, about three miles per hour, or 70 miles a day. The hourly weather plots of the center of the storm were consistently only a mile or two on either side of our plotted course. The outlook was not good. We calculated the storm would overtake us about the time of our arrival in the vicinity of Buckner. The race was on.

Twenty-four hours later the storm was upgraded to a typhoon about 250 miles in diameter with sustained winds of 95 knots [ed.

A knot, or nautical mile, equals 1.15 statute miles, so winds of 95 knots would be 109 miles an hour on land.] and gusts reaching well over a hundred knots [ed. 115 miles per hour]. But at the same time the storm intensified, its forward motion slowed, reducing the closing speed on us. Good news.

Nevertheless, with due diligence my captain, who was also acting group commander of this small covey of ships, none ever intended for duty in typhoons on the open sea, called the area commander in Okinawa for permission to change course away from the path of the storm. The response: "Maintain course and speed. Proceed to Buckner Bay, Okinawa, as ordered."

Early on our scheduled day of arrival, the wind was picking up, swells were getting higher, and the skies were scuddy. Rain was blowing harder, the visibility was poor. Again the skipper radioed our weather conditions and requested permission to change course to move us to the safer left quadrant to the west and out of the threatening situation. The response was the same, repeating curtly, "Maintain course and speed. Proceed to Buckner."

Things didn't get better. One of the ships with us had a mechanical breakdown, and we circled her for almost three precious hours until her engineers were able to make repairs. The delay made our situation worse. Our concern on the bridge was that this three hours may be the difference between making it safely or not. The latest storm position showed it gaining again and moving exactly on our track. Its forward speed had increased to 14 knots—twice our speed. It was now certain we were going to be overtaken. Our condition was critical. Winds near the center were reported to be gusts of 180 and sustained at 145. The only question now was whether we would be able to maneuver into the relative shelter of Buckner Bay before the full fury hit. We knew from previous experience at Okinawa that the channel of Buckner was narrow, and in high seas and winds of typhoon magnitude, it would be a dangerous—if not impossible—passage. It would be only luck if we were not blown onto the shallow coral reefs on either side.

We reached the area of Buckner Bay. The seas were mountainous by now, running about 80 feet high and often curling and crashing like breakers on a beach. We recorded a gust of 207 knots [238 mph] just before our mast splintered and then parted, only to end up flopping in the sea. Sustained winds were 185 knots [213 mph]. With the loss of our mast, we lost our radio and radar antennae. We were now cut off from the world. Occasionally, a wave would cause us to roll so severely on our side that it was questionable whether we could recover. Several times the ship laid over until another waved crashed completely over us and incredibly turned us back—up on our keel again. I felt terror stricken, of course, but I don't remember having even one thought of giving up. Every moment required all I could muster to survive. I wanted desperately to live.

A lookout shouted to the bridge that he saw a flashing light dead ahead. It was determined through the heavy rain and mist that somehow we had made contact with our destination, the net tender at the entrance to Buckner Bay. They challenged us by signal light, and when we identified ourselves they replied, "Denied entrance . . . heavy traffic . . . stand by . . . BB 55 is standing out the channel."

BB 55 was the battleship *North Carolina*, a 45,000-ton dreadnought with a complement of about 4,500 men aboard. We got brief ghostly glimpses of her struggling in the storm. When she came to the top of a wave, her bow would pop up so that a third of her keel was bared, and then she would dive, burrowing into the next wave, and her huge screws could be seen churning in the air. Despite her size and powerful turbines, she was struggling, nearly out of control in the gigantic seas. She almost ran us down. From the time we were ordered by the net gate tender to stand by, in order to avoid being blown on the beach and to keep away from the *North Carolina*, we had been struggling to make a turn back out to sea. Any maneuver was just about impossible.

Our condition was grave. All hope of turning back to the harbor was gone. We continued to power up the watery mountains in a quartering fashion so as not to snap over the crest. This was working quite well. We were light enough that we didn't burrow in and out of waves like the *North Carolina*; instead, we sort of bobbed on top like a cork. There were times, however, when we took green water [ed. from giant waves] over the top of us, smashing the sides of the deck house and the bridge—each time losing a little more of our ship to the sea. The sound of the wind was ear-splitting, and the accompanying low barometric pressure caused ears to pop and ache.

We observed from the bridge that several of our depth charges had been torn loose from their racks and were rolling around on the fantail. Two men volunteered to crawl back to secure them and be sure they had not become armed. Each contained 50 pounds of high explosive, and if they became armed and were washed overboard by the violent motion and crashing of the waves or if they went down with the ship, certainly any men in the water would be killed if they exploded. Just one of them had the capability of sinking the ship if it were detonated on deck or in the water nearby. After 30 hair-raising minutes the men crawled back to the bridge and reported the charges were not armed and had been secured in their racks. We felt a little better.

Suddenly, as we reached the top of the biggest wave yet, it broke out from under us and the ship dove through the air nearly 80 feet in a free fall. When she hit solid water again, we broke up forward and were rapidly taking on water. In diving through the air, we lost the seawater suction required to cool our twin 500 H.P. diesel engines. They instantly overheated, froze up, and stopped. We had no power.

We were out of control and floundered to a position broadside to the oncoming swells. For a time we were in a deep trough like a vast smooth valley. We were so far below the tops of the waves that we were sheltered from the wind; it was eerie but almost peaceful. Could this be what death is like? There was little time to ponder. Another huge swell was fast approaching and from a different perspective than all before. We had been running with them. Now we were dead in the water, and this one was racing to devour us broadside. Everyone grabbed something, the strongest thing at hand — a machine gun mount, a stanchion, a signal light, whatever was handy — to brace against the force of the wave towering 100 feet above us.

It was a horrendous crash. Untold tons of solid green water rushed all around us. After the monstrous wave passed us, we saw that the ship had capsized and was on her port side.

There was no panic — again we were in a quiet trough. But we soon realized it was another valley of death. Some of the men had disappeared in the sea. The executive officer was floating face down near me. The water turned him over, and I could see a massive gaping wound to his head. Obviously, he had been hit or violently thrown against something when we capsized. The water's surface was unbelievably smooth, though around us it was littered with floating debris from our broken ship. Compared to the violence of the last wave, it was rather quiet and actually a peaceful respite. The men nearest to the ship, and who were able, had scrambled up the side of the hull and were standing or lying down.

The lull was short-lived. Another wave was roaring down on us, and it certainly would crush us all. The captain shouted, "Let's go now! Hit the water, now! Abandon ship!" At that instant we jumped in. We were pushed down under at least 80 feet of violently turbulent water filled with all kinds of debris — clothing, file drawers, chairs, huge timbers from our broken wooden hull.

The ship's log, floating by covered with diesel oil, caught my eye. I had made many of the entries in it while standing watch. There would be no final entry closing the life of this doomed ship. For a moment I reached out, attempting to retrieve the log book, but a wave washed it away. "Who needs it now," I mused. "Moments ago it was important, but things are different now."

Until that moment life was so structured and ordered in the Navy. But now priorities had changed, switched as they often are in our daily lives by unforeseen chaos and trauma. We were still floating on the stormy surface, but our ship, the *YMS421*, was plunging to her final resting place on the bottom of the Pacific, more than a mile beneath us. We were all bruised and cut, some perhaps with serious internal injuries. Things that once seemed so important were no longer. Death and survival were now the only alternatives.

I remember that my thoughts became singular and very selfish, focused solely on my own survival. I no longer had control of my own life let alone the lives of others. I was scared and suspended somewhere below the surface of the Pacific Ocean.

Time and again I was pushed under by tons of crashing waves. My lungs were bursting from trying to keep from inhaling more seawater. I was retching. Having taken in so much seawater, I was literally half drowned. Could I hold out till I reached the surface? I had no control over when that would be, but I could sense my kapok jacket slowly tugging me up to the surface. When I reached the top, the water was so broken up from the wind, my first breath included more of the repulsive seawater—more water than air. I was sick. I looked around and maybe 30 feet away, the last 10 feet of the stern of my ship was sticking up out of the water; seconds later the transom disappeared in the sea as she dove bow first into the deep. There was a large plume of spray as she exhaled her last breath. She had served us well through many hard situations of past storms and battles, but she had succumbed to this violent storm. Now we were abandoned, helpless, and alone at sea.

Initially, there were several shipmates nearby holding on to debris. We had nothing to keep us afloat but our kapoks, and in seas like these they did not keep you on top though they did help you get back up. So we continued to be dunked by 50- to 100-foot waves. I quickly learned that floating debris is not a viable choice for survival, no matter how inviting it might have seemed. The debris was little more than floating missiles moving violently through the water and was to be avoided. Each time a wave passed, there were fewer of us. At one time three of us came

Minesweepers were intended for coastal duty, but the YMS 421, *built on the north branch of the Chicago River at the Grebe shipyard, made it across the Pacific Ocean, with Ensign Richard Brady aboard, only to be lost in a typhoon on September 16, 1945, after the war had ended. (Collection of Richard Brady)*

together and grabbed a minesweeper float from desperation and hung on a few minutes, but we were soon torn loose from it and again we floated apart in the coming darkness. Just as well—it was beating us to death.

Though it was midafternoon, it was very dark and the visibility on the surface was nearly zero. At one point while under water, I could hear the throbbing of a ship's screws close by—so close that I envisioned being chewed up by the giant propellers. Although there was a ship very close, there was little chance anyone could see us in the water, and if they did it was unlikely they could rescue us.

As long as there was light enough to read my watch dial, I kept checking the time, but it was passing so slowly. Finally it occurred to me that time was no longer important. It has to do with sunrise, sunset, tides, navigation, departures, arrivals, and appointments. I was going nowhere. I had nothing planned except to last however long I could. So I loosened my watchband and let my watch sink into the sea. How does one measure eternity anyway? Certainly not by a watch.

There would be no visible sunset. All day it had been nearly as dark as night. I knew the sun must be setting because the last I checked my watch before giving it the deep six, it said 1800 [6 P.M.], three hours since we lost the ship. By now she would be resting on the bottom, a mile down. The coming long hours of total darkness and the continuing storm didn't offer much hope. It seemed no one could find us. Deep inside was the reality that we were very possibly waiting for the end.

When a mate appeared nearby, there wasn't much said between us. There was nothing to say. After all we fully knew the gravity of the situation we were in and we were doing all we could to survive. We were too busy trying to breathe to talk. When we weren't taking a breath or vomiting, we had to keep our mouths closed or drown.

Suddenly, one of the men nearby began to scream. Every time he reached the surface after a wave, he screamed so ferociously that finally, even though his mouth was open, no sound came out. After a few more waves we didn't see him again. Later another mate grabbed me, trembling, and muttered, "I'm scared." I answered, "So am I, but hold on . . . we can make it." He took me literally and grabbed me, clutching with all his remaining strength and holding on to me as we tumbled and twisted through several more crashing waves. Then his grip loosened, and moments later I saw him a few feet away, face down, limp in his jacket and floating off in the mist.

In the face of the only other man near me, I saw horrible fear and futility. All of a sudden, wide-eyed, looking at me face-to-face, he unfastened his jacket and slipped under the surface. Now I was alone.

From then on it was all the same. Submerge, reach the surface, get a breath, submerge, reach the surface, and so on. Occasionally I interspersed the routine with prayers. Then out of the blowing mist I could faintly see the red and green running lights of a ship. I must be losing my mind, I thought. But then I heard the sound of screws in the water again. Very close. One time when I came to the surface I was near the top of a high wave and looking nearly straight down on the ship a hundred or so feet below. There were bright lights on deck and I could see men there. I thought, "Fools, you'll be in here with me." The scene was as if I were rising above this ordeal and maybe this was some mystical vision of the end. The wave broke and the next time I surfaced, I was looking up at the ship. High above me was the crest of its own wave. In a moment things shifted again, and I could see men on a landing net over the side.

The ship was now broadside to me. She took solid green water completely over the top of her mast. Then she rolled back toward me, and I was thrown into the steel sides. I thought, "There is no way they can get me out of here. Just leave before you crush me to death; I'd rather just drown."

Momentarily, the ship rolled toward me again, and one of the sailors clinging to the cargo net grabbed me. He held me while another wave passed over the ship, but he was torn loose from the net and now we were both in the water. I was sure neither of us would make it.

The ship lurched again, and the sailor, holding me with one hand, grabbed the net with his other. Finally, with the help of another sailor on the net above him, he was able to get me up on deck. I vaguely remember an officer saying, "Get him below."

That's all I remember until the middle of the next morning. By then the storm had passed, and the ship was moving gently. I was resting in a bunk in sick bay.

I am convinced that that ship, that captain, and the crew members of that ship were all instruments of a miracle of God. There is no other way to explain an otherwise incredible event that snatched me from the violent seas in that killer typhoon. Over the years, I still ask myself, "How did they see me in the vast Pacific in the height of a raging storm?" And even more often, "Why me, Lord?" I have often thought about the captain of that landing craft, having its own struggle to stay afloat, who somehow had the skill to maneuver into a position to make a rescue possible.

I heard while recuperating in the hospital on Brown Beach that the captain of the LSM [landing ship mechanized] had also rescued several others in the area. I never knew his name, but from this experience, I learned that help can come from unknown sources—that there are truly angels in our midst. I always strongly believed that if I had not prudently used every bit of the strength left in me and if I had not maintained a positive and prayerful attitude toward life, I would have lost my will. I would not then have been around for the miracle. I saw men around me give up, lose their will. I no longer question why—I just thank God for his miracle.

Chapter Thirty-Three

The Prairie Shipyard

When the United States was finally dragged into World War II, the government found itself so short of saltwater shipyards that it had to press into service the freshwater ones as well—some as much as a thousand miles from the nearest ocean. The Great Lakes shipyards were readily available, and so were the towboat and barge yards on the Western Rivers, as the Ohio-Mississippi-Missouri river network is known. When even those facilities proved inadequate for the task, the government had a contractor build an entirely new yard on a muddy prairie alongside the Illinois River to build vessels too large to for the Sanitary and Ship Canal—the Great Lakes' connection to the ocean. The San had some low bridges.

This is the story of that prairie shipyard, adapted by CMS member David M. Young from his article in the Chicago Tribune *of November 6, 2004.*

by David M. Young

Of all the lore of the Great Lakes and its connecting waterways—the disasters, the colorful characters that manned the vessels, and the motley assortment of boats and ships—none is stranger than the Prairie Shipyard. It erupted in a matter of months from a weed-infested river bottom more than a thousand miles from the nearest salt water for the purpose of building oceangoing warships. Then three years later it was disassembled, leaving no trace.

Even the type of ship it built—the LST—is fading from the collective memory. The generations that lived during World War II know that LST stands for "landing ship tank"—an ungainly, low-profile, shallow-draft vessel designed and mass-produced in a hurry for large-scale amphibious warfare. The LSTs were built in such quantity that the U.S. Navy for the most part didn't even bother to give them names. They were known simply by number.

The LSTs were equipped with large doors in their bows to disgorge, on the beaches of North Africa, Italy, Normandy, and countless Pacific islands from Guadalcanal to Okinawa, the men and materiel necessary to liberate those places from the Axis powers. They did the job for which they were designed, delivering tanks, vehicles, supplies, and men to the battles.

The largest warships built in the general Chicago area were LSTs assembled at a new shipyard in Seneca. LSTs were too large to clear bridges on the Sanitary and Ship Canal, so the Chicago Bridge & Iron Company built this shipyard from scratch, on a prairie alongside the Illinois River (explaining how the yard came to be known as the Prairie Shipyard). Completed LSTs then steamed under their own power down the Illinois and Mississippi rivers to the Gulf of Mexico. (Frank W. Bazzoni Collection/Seneca Public Library)

Because the United States did not have enough saltwater shipyards necessary to build more than a thousand LSTs in a hurry when the war began, it pressed into service assorted shipyards on the Western Rivers that theretofore had specialized in building barges and towboats. When that proved inadequate it built from scratch an entirely new shipyard in the sleepy Illinois river town of

Seneca, about 75 miles southwest of Chicago. That place became known as the Prairie Shipyard.

The ability of the United States to build large warships and auxiliaries on the Great Lakes and the prairies that surround it was due almost entirely to the Depression-era decision by the federal government to improve the nation's major inland rivers to permit large-scale shipping. By the time the nation got into World War I, competition from the railroads had driven the river steamboats out of business. But the railroads proved inadequate to handle the big volume of wartime traffic, forcing Washington to take control of them for the first and only time in history. The government also realized that for purposes of national defense, it had to rebuild the inland waterways that had fallen into disuse. That meant creating from scratch a federal barge line as well as building locks and dams on the Ohio, Mississippi, and Illinois rivers, among others, to allow the big new barges and towboats to use them.

Although it is not widely known, the Illinois River since Chicago's inception was crucial to the city's development as an inland port. The river—which originates at the confluence of the Fox and Kankakee rivers near Channahon in Will County, about 45 miles southwest of Chicago, and flows for 273 miles across the state until it empties into the Mississippi at Grafton—has been the Windy City's maritime link to the interior. Long before the city was founded, American Indians used the Chicago portage to get between the Great Lakes and Illinois River and later told the French voyageurs about it.

Soon after Illinois came into existence in 1818, the new state began to investigate the possibility of improving the sometimes difficult portage route by digging a canal between the Chicago and Illinois rivers. Such a canal would permit a much larger scale of commerce than was possible by dragging canoes between the two waterways. When the Illinois and Michigan Canal was finally finished in 1848, it ran for 97 miles from Chicago to La Salle—

the head of navigation of the Illinois, or the northernmost point at which steamboats could travel before the river became too shallow.

The canal was an instant success. Lake ships off-loaded their cargoes onto canal boats in the Chicago River, and the boats plodded down the canal to La Salle, where they transferred their shipments to steamboats or were towed down the Illinois to their destinations. The process was reversed for cargo bound east. The state's namesake river was a busy place in those days: between 1849 and 1852, before the newly built railroads began to make a dent in traffic, an annual average of 741 steamboats arrived in St. Louis from the Illinois River. This meant that including local traffic, the river handled something in excess of 2,000 steamboat passages annually.

Rivers like the Illinois were vulnerable to seasonal disruptions of traffic due to low water in dry summers and ice in the winter. So the state late in the nineteenth century began a program to upgrade the waterway to improve its navigability. Dams were built at Henry and Copperas Creek, and locks were installed in 1889 at downstate LaGrange and in 1892 at Kampsville. However, the improvements could not prevent the railroads from driving the steamboats and canal boats out of business. By 1900 when the Sanitary and Ship Canal was completed from Chicago to Lockport, both the I & M Canal and the Illinois River had very little traffic left.

The Army Corps of Engineers since 1867 had repeatedly recommended improving the Illinois and Des Plaines rivers to replace the I & M Canal. The southern 80 percent of the river was not much of a problem, given that it dropped only 21 feet in elevation in the miles between La Salle and Grafton, but the northern section of the two rivers fell 99 feet in just 60 miles. Because the federal government was preoccupied with improving the Ohio River, the state in 1908 committed a $20 million bond issue to improving the Illinois River with a series of seven locks and dams.

The dams were intended to create pools of water deep enough (nine feet) for barge traffic, and the locks would enable the barges to get around the dams. The locks were designed to be 600 feet long and 110 feet wide— sufficient to handle a towboat pushing as many as eight barges carrying 12,000 tons of cargo.

Illinois didn't get started on the improvements until 1921, however, and ran out of money in 1930 during the Great Depression with the project only three-fourths completed.

Work on the LSTs continued around the clock, winter and summer, at Seneca. (Frank W. Bazzoni Collection/Seneca Public Library)

The federal government, which had completed its Ohio River improvement program, agreed to take over and finish the Illinois Waterway. That took three years, and the first commercial transit, the towboat *Turnbull* pushing two barges with 250 tons of cargo consigned to 25 different shippers, arrived in Chicago via the waterway on March 13, 1933. By 1975, barge loadings on the river exceeded 31 million tons.

The decision to upgrade the Western Rivers for commercial navigation turned out to be prescient when the United States suddenly found itself involved in World War II. Shipyards that had built barges, towboats, pleasure craft, and lakers were for the first time available for wartime construction because their vessels could be sailed through Chicago, down the Sanitary and Ship Canal, and the Illinois and Mississippi rivers to the ocean. The St. Lawrence Seaway would not be built for another 15 years, and the locks on Welland Canal between Lakes Erie and Ontario and the St. Lawrence River when the war began were not large enough to handle anything but the smallest vessels. Those seaway locks were only 270 feet long, less than half the length (600 feet) of those on the Illinois Waterway.

Within weeks of the surprise Japanese attack on Pearl Harbor, the Navy began to parcel out contracts for Great Lakes and Ohio River shipyards to build warships. In the case of Seneca, an entirely new shipyard was carved out of the prairie on the banks of the Illinois River.

Some of the planning even predated the war. In 1940 the Electric Boat Company, the sole builder of submarines in the United States, approached Charles West, president of the Manitowoc Shipbuilding Company in Manitowoc, Wisconsin, about taking a subcontract to build submarines. West at first demurred, but as the war in Europe and China intensified, he decided to take a second look at the proposal.

Lake Michigan was a large enough body of water to fully test the submarines, but how could West get them to the ocean? The 311-foot length of the class of submarine the Navy wanted meant the St. Lawrence route was out of the question. The Illinois River's locks were long enough, but with a channel only 9 feet deep, the river was too shallow for submarines with a 13-foot draft (distance between the waterline and bottom of the keel). West solved the problem by employing a floating dry dock on which the submarines would be towed downriver. Ultimately, he built 28 submarines and shipped them through Chicago to the war.

Various small patrol and auxiliary craft were no problem for shipyards on the lakes and in Chicago, but the big problem for the Navy was how and where to build the estimated 1,000 landing ships it was going to need to get troops and their equipment onto enemy-held beaches in the Pacific and Europe. The solution was the LST, which was already on the drawing boards when the United States entered the war.

It was a flat-bottomed ship more than 328 feet in length with an extremely shallow minimum draft (of 3½ feet) to enable it to snuggle onto enemy beaches to discharge its 2,100-ton cargo of tanks, men, and vehicles. Using a technique developed on the Great Lakes years before (the ill-fated *Eastland*, among others, had a similar system) to enable ships to get into shallow river harbors, like Chicago's, the LSTs were equipped with pumps to control the water level in their bilges and raise or lower their drafts depending upon conditions. Water could be pumped onto the ship to lower it for ocean steaming and pumped out to lighten the vessel to get close to shore.

The British had discovered a need for LSTs during the evacuation of Dunkirk in 1940 and, after unsuccessfully modifying some tankers, approached the United States in August 1941—four months before Pearl Harbor—about a joint solution. John Neidermair of the U.S. Navy's Bureau of Ships had a preliminary design within days. Congress approved the production of LSTs

Seneca-built LSTs ranged far and wide across the oceans. Number 202 landed tanks to fight the Japanese on New Britain in the South Pacific in 1943. Other Seneca ships landed men and matériel at North Africa and Normandy in the Atlantic. (Frank W. Bazzoni Collection/Seneca Public Library)

two months after Pearl Harbor, and the first one (*LST 1*) slid off the ways and into the Ohio River at the Dravo Corporation yard in Pittsburgh on September 7, 1942.

Meanwhile, the contractor hired by the Navy to oversee the program had approached the Chicago Bridge & Iron Company about building LSTs at one of its facilities. The low clearance under some bridges in the Chicago area precluded any Chicago Bridge facilities there, but the company owned a barge-building operation and 200 acres of adjacent vacant land in downstate Seneca. The site had a rail spur for transportation and a nearby electric line for power. Additionally, the vacant land sat atop a shallow sandstone formation suitable for bearing the weight of ships without having to drill pilings into bedrock. (Each ship's hull contained 1,340 tons of steel.)

The finished vessels could be launched sideways into the river and steamed under their own power on the rivers to New Orleans' port. Sections of the vessels could be fabricated at other Chicago Bridge plants and shipped by train or truck to the Seneca site for final assembly.

Construction on the yard started in early 1942, and by June the keel for the first LST (*LST 197*) was laid. Inexperienced crews, a high turnover in workers because of men being drafted into the military, and the lack of even a rudimentary telephone system in the new yard resulted in delays that prevented the launch of *LST197* for six months. But by the middle of 1943 the time of construction from keel to launch had been reduced to four months. The next year the yard on average was grinding out a new ship every four and a half days. Before the war ended, Seneca had built 157 such vessels—28 of them converted to repair ships.

The Navy discovered early in the war that it was critically short of repair ships, especially vessels that could get close to shore to do their work, and began to ponder the conversion of some LSTs. The first such conversion, the *Atlas*, was launched in October 1943. The design was so versatile that the Navy also converted one

LST into a "junior carrier" for reconnaissance planes and several other LSTs into floating rocket launchers to soften up the beaches before invasions.

LSTs were typically identified only by number, although some were named after counties. But the repair ships bowing to Navy tradition received fanciful names based on mythology. There was the *Zeus*, the *Edymion*, and the *Krishna*. There was also the *Midas*, named after the mythical king of Phrygia whose touch turned things into gold.

The experience of the *Midas* was typical of what happened to Seneca's vessels after they left the Prairie Shipyard. The hull of *LST 514* was laid down on August 31, 1943, but before her launch on Christmas Eve, the Navy decided to convert her to a repair ship, rename her, and renumber her *ARB 5*. Unlike most LSTs, which got their crews in Seneca and sailed immediately for their assigned war zones, the *Midas* was sent to Baltimore to be fitted with the specialized equipment she would need for her new role. ARBs were armed, floating machine shops that could fabricate damaged machinery on other ships and that carried a complement of divers to repair underwater shell holes.

In early 1944 the *Midas*'s crew was assembled in Philadelphia and Norfolk for training, and within two months the ship began her long journey to join the 7th Fleet in the Pacific. The outbound trip sounded like an itinerary for a cruise ship, with stops in Cuba, Panama, Bora-Bora, Nouméa, and the Admiralty Islands, but en route the *Midas* had to make assorted repairs on other vessels, including an LST with a hole in its hull caused by an errant starboard anchor. One crewman quipped that the assorted resort stops had the effect of relieving the complement of their paychecks, and because there was no mail received along the way, there was no way to write home for money. Somewhere on the voyage the *Midas* acquired as a mascot a wirehaired terrier named Hammerhead, after the man-eating shark. The dog eventually went AWOL.

Some of the LST hulls built in Seneca were converted to repair ships. The Seneca-built Midas *(right) was photographed repairing a hole in the hull of an Australian cruiser damaged in a Japanese attack off New Guinea in 1944. (David M. Young)*

The action began on August 27, 1944, when the *Midas* arrived at Sak Island, New Guinea, and began fixing other ships. She was then sent to Leyte Gulf in the Philippines to repair the damage resulting from the great sea battle fought there. In those six months the *Midas* repaired 251 ships, went to general quarters 79 times, and filed six reports after being involved in battles, according to the official report of the captain. Despite the *Midas* being an auxiliary ship, her gunners claimed three Japanese planes shot down and several near misses from enemy fire. The vessel also acquired another mascot, a monkey named Jocko, which some crewman described as the foulest primate to grace the planet. Jocko developed a fondness for the taste of human ears. Its fate was not recorded.

The *Midas* steamed home to San Francisco after the war, discharged its crew, and was mothballed and placed in the Navy's reserve fleet. She was sold for scrap in 1980.

Meanwhile, back in Seneca, the end of the war meant the end to the local boom—an event almost everyone in town expected.

Scholars Robert J. Havighurst, of the University of Chicago, and H. Gerthon Morgan, who together did a study that turned into a 1951 book on Seneca's wartime boom, noted that most merchants in town expected that the end of hostilities would return the community to its former size and pace.

The boom was the second in the community's history. After being settled in 1849 by I & M Canal contractor Jeremiah Crotty, the town boomed because of the canal and also the Chicago & Rock Island Railroad, which arrived in 1852. Then as the canal declined in importance in the late 1800s, Seneca slipped into somnolence.

Antebellum Seneca, population 1,235, was "a small agricultural-industrial town," Havighurst and Morgan wrote. "Life was slow. There was little in the way of formal recreation—not even a movie theater. Much of the social life in town centered on the (four) churches.

The scholars quoted an anonymous local resident as describing Seneca thusly: "It was a ghost town before the boom. Half the stores were empty." The statement was something of an exaggeration—only 8 of the 40 stores in town were vacant.

Within a year after the commencement of hostilities, the town had a daytime population in excess of 10,000. Chicago Bridge & Iron and assorted federal agencies scrambled to find housing for everyone, although many shipyard workers received subsidies in the form of extra gasoline and tire rations to commute from other nearby towns. Single-family homes were subdivided into apartments, trailers appeared overnight in backyards and vacant lots, and the Federal Public Housing Authority built 1,497 apartment units and a 300-bed dormitory for men. Another federal agency hauled in 225 trailers for shipyard housing.

The population explosion caused some grumbling. According to Havighurst and Morgan, the older residents of Seneca often referred to the newcomers as "damn shipyard trash," and one newcomer was quoted as saying, "But Seneca people needn't be too snooty; there were only four bathtubs in town before the shipyard came."

The four local taverns did a booming business during the war. With little else available in the way of entertainment, drinking and gambling became the principal forms of entertainment. Those pastimes accompanied the Seneca-built ships throughout the war. The repair ships' crews, which had the necessary equipment for the task, even built on-board stills: the moonshine they produced was used as a trade commodity with other vessels for such things as movies and wartime luxuries.

Pay for workers at the Prairie Shipyard ranged from 83¢ an hour for unskilled workers to $1.20 for craftsmen (contrasted to 2004 local wage rates ranging from $6.16 an hour for unskilled workers and $18.13 for craftsmen), but the big money was made in overtime. Crews were expected to work 54 hours each six-day week and were paid time and a half after 40 hours. Much of the money was spent locally. Ten new grocery stores opened in Seneca during the war, and the number of restaurants increased from two before the war to eight during the hostilities.

The end of the war in August 1945 brought an abrupt end to all of that. Within months the shipyard was abandoned, the trailers were hauled away, and apartments were vacant. People simply moved away. Seneca returned to its 1940 environment.

Today the town has a population of slightly more than 2,000 and a number of vacant storefronts. No remnants remain of the old shipyard. An industrial park now sits on the site. Perhaps the only vestiges left are a collection of literature and photographs in the local library and the signs announcing its corporate limits that state the place once built LSTs.

Epilogue

It is possible as the third millennium progresses that Chicago's waterways will regain some of the commercial utility they enjoyed during the nineteenth and twentieth centuries, although the trend seems to be toward recreational uses.

With the continued decline of Great Lakes shipping, Lake Michigan's primary role is that of supplying fresh water to the growing Chicago metropolitan area, and the Sanitary and Ship Canal's main task is to carry away the city's effluent. Boating on the Chicago River is predominantly recreational, and the river itself is in the process of being transformed into an aquatic urban park with walkways lining its banks. Out in the lake, Navy Pier has experienced a renaissance as a recreational facility; its concrete side walls are lined with tour boats.

The last vestige of the once great Port of Chicago is the Calumet River and lake on the South Side, where ocean-going ships still call, and the two canals which link it to the western rivers still carry barge traffic. Even there, change is noticeable. The old Illinois and Michigan Canal corridor is being transformed into a linear park on the banks of the Sanitary and Ship Canal. The ill-fated Iroquois Landing container port is now a park, and United States Steel's abandoned South Works at the mouth of the Calumet River is being redeveloped, in part, as a park.

So the nature of Chicago's maritime lore is likely to change in the future. Reenactments like Ralph Frese's re-creation of the Jolliet-Marquette voyage in Chapter 3 may become more frequent than the events they portray. Disasters on the scale of the *Eastland* and *Lady Elgin* are less likely to occur than are archaeological expeditions that find and record old wrecks. The development of sonar has taken the mystery out of ship (and aircraft) disappearances that provided such wonderful tales of Flying Dutchmen and Great Lakes triangles. Folk singers Chris and Tom Kastle (Chapter 18) by necessity have become philologists discovering and preserving the musical heritage of the lakes because no one has yet written a rock opera about those inland seas. There was a play written about the *Christmas Tree* ship, however.

The lakes at least in the foreseeable future belong to the yachtsmen, as the rivers were appropriated by the canoeists and pleasure boaters. The tales they tell at the clubs up and down the lakefront will supplant the yarns told in years past by the mariners in the dives along the Chicago River. Though Cap'n Streeter is long gone, there are still a few characters left in Chicago's maritime community: the owner of a line of tugboats who was preoccupied with finding a cache of gold hidden in a cave comes to mind, as does the local businessman who tried to sell shares of a salvage operation off Guam of an as of yet undiscovered Spanish galleon laden with Ming Dynasty ceramics.

Perhaps in another hundred years our successors at the Chicago Maritime Society will assemble a second volume of stories that reflect the city's maritime lore in the twenty-first century.

—David M. Young

Index

About the Chicago Maritime Society

The Chicago Maritime Society, established in 1982 by a group of historians, educators, and civic-minded individuals, is committed to creating a world-class maritime museum for Chicago. CMS seeks to increase public awareness of Chicago's uniquely important maritime past through public exhibits and programs. The organization's rich variety of educational presentations include seminars for historians and educators, lectures for the general public, publications, and exhibits of maritime artifacts and images at various locations throughout the Chicago area. Society membership is open to anyone, and particularly those with an interest in the history and continuing maritime concerns of Chicago, the Great Lakes, and the region's inland waterways.

To date, the Chicago Maritime Society has amassed a very large collection of vessels, maritime artifacts, manuscripts, movies, and photographs pertinent to its mission. They are currently reviewing and planning a suitable location and configuration for a museum. Learn more at their website: www.chicagomaritimesociety.org.

Lake Claremont Press

Founded in 1994, Lake Claremont Press specializes in books on the Chicago area and its history, focusing on preserving the city's past, exploring its present environment, and cultivating a strong sense of place for the future.

Visit us on the Web at www.lakeclaremont.com.

Selected Booklist

Rule 53: Capturing Hippies, Spies, Politicians, and Muderers in an American Courtroom
For Members Only: A History and Guide to Chicago's Oldest Private Clubs
The Politics of Place: A History of Zoning in Chicago
Wrigley Field's Last World Series: The Wartime Chicago Cubs and the Pennant of 1945
On the Job: Behind the Stars of the Chicago Police Department
Great Chicago Fires: Historic Blazes That Shaped a City
Chicago's TV Horror Movie Shows: From Shock Theatre to Svengoolie
The Golden Age of Chicago Children's Television
A Chicago Tavern: A Goat, a curse, and the American Dream
Today's Chicago Blues
A Cook's Guide to Chicago
Graveyards of Chicago
Finding Your Chicago Irish

Award-winners

The Chicago River: A Natural and Unnatural History
Finding Your Chicago Ancestors: A Beginner's Guide to Family History in the City and Cook County
The Streets & San Man's Guide to Chicago Eats
Near West Side Stories: Struggles for Community in Chicago's Maxwell Street Neighborhood
Hollywood on Lake Michigan: 100 Years of Chicago and the Movies
The Politics of Place: A History of Zoning in Chicago
A Cook's Guide to Chicago